SLEEPY HOLLOW
Birth of the Legend

by
Gary Denis

SLEEPY HOLLOW – BIRTH OF THE LEGEND

Copyright © 2015 Gary C. Denis

All Rights Reserved

No part of this book may be reproduced in any manner whatsoever, including Internet usage, without written permission from the author, except in the case of brief quotations embedded in critical articles and reviews.

ISBN 978-1-5116-4546-1

Front cover illustration of the Headless Horseman by Leonard Everett Fisher, reprinted by permission of Franklin Watts, an imprint of Scholastic Library Publishing, Inc.

Back cover illustration by Sarah Bailey, licensed for use.

Gary Denis
P.O. Box 766
Patuxent River, MD 20670

garycdenis@comcast.net

www.GaryDenis.com

"The following writings are published on experiment; should they please, they may be followed by others."

Acknowledgements

I would like to express my sincere thanks to the following individuals and organizations (listed here in no particular order) whose contributions and support made this book possible:

David Trafton; Dr. Michael L. Black; Roger L. Jewell;
Prof. Susan Manning, University of Edinburgh;
Sara Mascia and The Historical Society Serving Sleepy Hollow and Tarrytown <WWW.THEHISTORICALSOCIETY.NET>;
John Merwin, Lee Merwin and the Miles Merwin Association <HTTP://MERWINASSOCIATION.COM>; Terry Holmes;
Suzanne Carroll and the Columbia County Historical Society, Kinderhook, NY <WWW.CCHSNY.ORG>;
Sandy Schlosser <HTTP://AMERICANFOLKLORE.NET/>;
Jim Logan and Friends of the Old Dutch Burying Ground <WWW.ODCFRIENDS.ORG>; Leonard Everett Fisher;
Ruth Piwonka, Village Historian, Kinderhook, NY;
Catalina Hannan, Jessa Krick and Historic Hudson Valley <WWW.HUDSONVALLEY.ORG>; Dr. Elisabeth Paling Funk;
Glenn Fisher and Random Acts of Genealogical Kindness;
Brian Jay Jones <HTTP://BRIANJAYJONES.COM/>;
Lynn Rogers and Friends of Abandoned Cemeteries of Staten Island; Kit Gentry <WWW.KITGENTRY.COM>;
Don Troiani <WWW.HISTORICALIMAGEBANK.COM>;
Lucas Buresch <HTTP://ARCHIVESLEUTH.WORD-PRESS.COM/CATEGORY/LEGEND-OF-SLEEPY-HOLLOW/>;
Patrick Raftery and the Westchester County Historical Society <WWW.WESTCHESTERHISTORY.COM>;
Dennis Simpson and the Daughters of the American Revolution <WWW.DAR.ORG>; Nicola Beech and the British Library, London, England <WWW.BL.UK>.

...and a few Disclaimers

This work quotes extensively from Washington Irving's correspondence and journals. Although Irving's punctuation and spellings sometimes conflict with modern convention and style, his writings are reproduced here as closely as possible to the originals, and are not cluttered with multiple (and distracting) uses of "sic" or other notations to indicate spelling or other errors.

All Internet references contained in this work were current at the time of publication; however, I cannot guarantee that they will continue to be maintained or accessible.

The genealogical information contained in this work was obtained from a variety of sources, including modern websites as well as 19th century genealogies and family histories, many of which contained conflicting data. Therefore, some minor discrepancies may exist between the information published herein and "your" sources, such as number of children, birthdates, etc.

A bit of legalese: "Although the author/publisher has made every effort to ensure that the information in this book was correct at press time, the author/publisher does not assume and hereby disclaims any liability to any party for any loss, damage, or disruption caused, or alleged to have been caused, directly or indirectly, by the information contained herein."

And finally – Some people are not happy unless they are able to find mistakes, so in an effort to please everyone, I have deliberately includeed a few...

Contents

Introduction.......i

1. America's First Storyteller.......1

2. A Little Valley Among High Hills.......21

3. A Knickerbocker Story.......81

4. The Headless Horseman.......93

5. A Worthy Pedagogue.......123

6. A Blooming Lass of Fresh Eighteen.......165

7. A Burly, Roaring, Roystering Blade.......191

8. Conclusions.......231

Epilogue.......247

Endnotes.......251

Bibliography.......283

Index.......299

About the Author.......313

Introduction

"I am always at a loss to know how much to believe of my own stories."
— Washington Irving, 1824

Who doesn't know the story of Ichabod Crane and the Headless Horseman??

Washington Irving's "The Legend of Sleepy Hollow" tells the story of gangly schoolmaster Ichabod Crane's efforts to win the heart of the beautiful Katrina Van Tassel (although it is whispered that what he is *really* trying to win is the deed to her father's bountiful farm, which she will someday inherit). But first, Ichabod must outwit Katrina's jealous boyfriend, the half-bully, half-hero Brom Bones. The tale culminates with a midnight encounter with the legendary Headless Horseman, and Ichabod is carried off by the spectre... *or is he?*

Considered a classic of American literature, "The Legend" was originally published in 1820 as part of a collection of 34 essays and short stories titled *The Sketch Book of Geoffrey Crayon, Gent*. Translated into almost every language, it has been republished countless times, both in *The Sketch Book* and as a stand-alone volume... not to mention graphic novels and comic books geared toward kids (and those of us who are still kids at heart!).

In addition to the untold number of print versions, "The Legend of Sleepy Hollow" has been the subject of more than a dozen movie or cartoon adaptations. The earliest was probably a silent film produced in 1908 by the Kalem Company. Another silent version from 1922 starred Will Rogers as Ichabod Crane.

One of the most beloved is the one many of us remember from our childhood, the 1949 Walt Disney cartoon narrated by Bing Crosby. "Sleepy Hollow" made up the second half of an animated double-feature titled *The Adventures of Ichabod and Mr. Toad*.

Shirley Temple starred as Katrina Van Tassel in a 1958 episode of her *Shirley Temple's Storybook* TV series.

A made-for-TV movie of *The Legend of Sleepy Hollow* premiered October 31, 1980, starring Jeff Goldblum as Ichabod Crane, pro linebacker-turned-actor Dick Butkus as Brom Bones, and the stunning Meg Foster as Katrina Van Tassel.

In 1985, "The Legend of Sleepy Hollow" became the first of nine installments in the series *Shelley Duvall's Tall Tales and Legends*, which starred Ed Begley, Jr. as Ichabod and the stunning Beverly D'Angelo as Katrina.

The Headless Horseman has also made guest appearances on a number of children's shows, including *Scooby-Doo, The Real Ghostbusters, Alf Tales, Wishbone,* and *The Smurfs*.

INTRODUCTION

One especially noteworthy animated version of "The Legend" was released in 1988 by Rabbit Ears Productions. Narrated by Glenn Close, this multiple award-winning adaptation featured rustic artwork by Robert Van Nutt and a spooky soundtrack by Tim Story.

Director Tim Burton's gothic reworking of the story, titled simply *Sleepy Hollow,* was released in 1999, starring Johnny Depp as Ichabod Crane and the stunning Christina Ricci as Katrina Van Tassel. Although the opening credits state that it was "based upon" Irving's story, it would be far more accurate to say that Burton's interpretation was merely *inspired by* Irving's tale – in this somewhat darker version, Ichabod is a constable from New York City, sent upstate to the village of Sleepy Hollow to investigate a series of decapitation murders committed by a mysterious headless rider.

A much more faithful rendition of *The Legend of Sleepy Hollow* was produced by Hallmark for Canadian television that same year, starring Brent Carver as Ichabod and the stunning Rachelle Lefevre as Katrina.

The most recent incarnation of Irving's enduring tale is the *Sleepy Hollow* TV series which debuted in September 2013 on the Fox network, starring Tom Mison as Ichabod Crane. In this latest treatment, Crane is a Revolutionary War soldier who is resurrected in modern-day Sleepy Hollow to once again do battle with his old nemesis, the Headless Horseman, revealed to be one of the Biblical Four Horsemen of the Apocalypse. The series features Nicole Beharie as Crane's investigative partner, police detective Abbie Mills, as well as recurring appearances by the stunning Katia Winter as Katrina *Crane.*

"The Legend" has also been adapted for the live stage numerous times, beginning with a 1948 Broadway musical at the St. James Theater, which lasted only 12 performances. A 2004 musical titled *Ichabod!* starred the stunning Charisse Stewart as Katrina. More recently, the musical *The*

Real Legend of Sleepy Hollow premiered in Sewell, New Jersey in November 2013.

And we mustn't overlook "the other" visual medium which has contributed to the longevity of "The Legend": the video game! Promotional material for *Mystery Legends – Sleepy Hollow*, released in 2009 by Play Pond, invites players to "discover the secrets of Sleepy Hollow... investigate the freakish residents and witness their fate at the hands of the Headless Horseman." Taking this concept one step further, *Headless Havoc*, an online game from Kongregate, proclaims "You are the headless horseman! Decapitate as many villagers as you can!"

Of course, the influence of "The Legend" has not been limited to visual media, but has extended to popular music as well. The Headless Horseman has been featured in the songs of a wide variety of recording artists – some well-known, some not-so-well-known – including Gargoyle Sox, Brando, Pegazus, Marcel Bontempi, and most recently, Kanye West!

1974 Legend of Sleepy Hollow and
1940 Washington Irving postage stamps

"The Legend of Sleepy Hollow" has even appeared on a postage stamp picturing the Headless Horseman in pursuit of Ichabod Crane, both of them silhouetted against a bright orange harvest moon. The stamp was issued October

10, 1974 – just in time to mail Halloween cards. (Washington Irving had previously been honored with a postage stamp of his own, issued January 29, 1940.)

Headless Horsemen have also become integral characters in various fantasy role-playing games, with their own game pieces and power cards. And let's not forget the recent Headless Horseman mini-figure from Lego!

My little girl Lucy wearing her "Headless Horseman" Halloween costume

The availability of Headless Horseman costumes (not just for people, but for pets as well!) ensures his presence at scores of Halloween parties every October 31st.

The very name "Sleepy Hollow," with its implications of solitude and tranquility, has become part of the American vocabulary. The American landscape is peppered with Sleepy Hollow campgrounds, motels, country clubs, bed &

breakfasts, and at least one state park; and Sleepy Hollow subdivisions have sprouted up in the suburbs of many large cities.

But is "The Legend of Sleepy Hollow" a true story?

Almost from the first appearance of "The Legend of Sleepy Hollow" in March of 1820, there have been those who have maintained that much, if not all, of the story was based on actual events, and the characters based on real people. Numerous theories sprang up regarding the "true identities" of the principal characters of the story.

Many of these theories have been passed down as "oral traditions" over the years. However, the problem with oral traditions is that after being repeated over and over again, many facts, although often rooted in truth, can become distorted as they are embellished with each new retelling; individuals with the same (or similar) names become confused; dates become blurred, and generations overlap.

The purpose of this book is to attempt to gather *all* of these various theories and traditions in one place, and weigh each of them against historical "evidence" obtained through more than seven years of studying Irving's stories, letters, journals and notebooks; contemporary newspaper and magazine articles; genealogical records; and 19th century local histories. The ultimate goal was to definitively prove which theories were correct (and which were nonsense), and to finally, *conclusively,* identify Washington Irving's sources of inspiration.

However, I quickly found that after almost 200 years, most of the trails have long gone cold, as primary sources have been lost to time. In many cases, the best that can be done is to try to reach the *most likely,* although not always definitive, "conclusion."

INTRODUCTION

By uncovering previously unknown (or ignored) information, it can be much easier to debunk a theory than to prove it. Even then, when challenging "local traditions" that have been repeated as fact over many generations, there will always be those for whom no amount of evidence will ever be sufficient. It isn't easy to rewrite "history" – even spurious history!

I have tried to consistently "stick to the facts" and not let personal opinion cloud any possible conclusions; however, being human, I may have inadvertently allowed personal opinion to creep in from time to time. Where I sometimes found it necessary to deliberately inject opinion, I tried to clearly state that it was only my *opinion* or *theory*, although based on extensive research and observations... but you, the reader, are always free to disagree and form your own conclusions.

So – Is "The Legend of Sleepy Hollow" a true story? Were Ichabod, Katrina and Brom modeled after real people? Let's find out...

Chapter 1

America's First Storyteller

"I have attempted no lofty theme, nor sought to look wise and learned... I seek only to blow a flute accompaniment in the national concert, and leave others to play the fiddle and French horn."
— Washington Irving, 1819

A study of "The Legend of Sleepy Hollow" would not be complete without a brief biography of its author, Washington Irving. It should be noted, however, that the biography that follows is only intended as an overview, primarily focusing on events that relate to the creation of "The Legend." Many significant events of Irving's life are more or less glossed over; some are omitted altogether.

For the reader wishing to learn more about Washington Irving, much more comprehensive biographies exist, such as the classic works by Charles Dudley Warner (1881) and Stanley T. Williams (1935). More recently, two excellent biographies have appeared: *The Original Knickerbocker* by

Andrew Burstein and *Washington Irving, An American Original* by Brian Jay Jones, published in 2007 and 2008 respectively.

The Early Years

Washington Irving was born in New York City on April 3, 1783, to William and Sarah Irving. Washington was the youngest of 11 children, three of whom died in infancy. Irving's father, a Scottish immigrant, owned a successful hardware import business in Manhattan, not far from the family's home.

Growing up, Washington Irving was a mediocre student, having little interest in formal study. He did, however, love to read and was fascinated with books of travel and adventure, such as *Robinson Crusoe* and *Sinbad the Sailor*. In "The Author's Account of Himself" in *The Sketch Book*, he would later write, "Books of voyages and travels became my passion, and in devouring their contents I neglected the regular exercises of the school."[1]

Irving Discovers Sleepy Hollow

At age 10, Washington Irving befriended future novelist James Kirke Paulding. James was the younger brother of Julia Paulding, who married Washington's brother William in 1793. James Paulding is credited with being "the one who introduced Washington Irving to Sleepy Hollow." Paulding's family was from Tarrytown, NY, where Paulding had lived with his uncle prior to moving to New York City.[2]

In 1798, New York City was struck by the worst yellow fever epidemic since 1702, resulting in the deaths of more than 2,000 people. To avoid the epidemic, Irving's family sent him upstate to Tarrytown with James Kirke Paulding, where they stayed with Paulding's relatives. It was at this time that the 15-year-old Washington Irving first explored the Sleepy Hollow region that he would later make famous in his story.

Irving would later reminisce about his "holiday rovings of boyhood" in an essay titled, appropriately, "Sleepy Hollow." He described venturing "far in the foldings of the hills, where the Pocantico 'winds its wizard stream'..." This was where he first tried his "unskillful hand at angling," which eventually gave way to simply sitting on the rocks "beneath towering oaks and clambering grape-vines," and indulging in his "incipient habit of daydreaming."[3]

It is not known if Irving made any additional visits to the region "when a stripling" – most biographers say "no" – but regardless, his 1798 Sleepy Hollow adventure clearly made a lasting impression on him and, luckily for the rest of us, had a major influence on his future writings.

A Career in Law?

Irving left school at age 16 and began an apprenticeship studying law at the office of Henry Masterson, more out of a necessity to learn some sort of trade than an actual interest in a career as a lawyer.

In 1800, Washington made his first sailing voyage up the Hudson River to visit his married sisters Ann and Catherine in Johnstown, NY, near Albany. He described seeing the Catskill Mountains for the first time: "Of all the scenery of the Hudson, the Kaatskill Mountains had the most witching effect on my boyish imagination... As we slowly floated along, I lay on the deck and watched them through a long summer's day; undergoing a thousand mutations under the magical effects of atmosphere."[4]

Washington Irving became a clerk at the law office of Josiah Ogden Hoffman in 1802. Irving would grow very close to the Hoffman family and they remained life-long friends.

In November of that same year, the 19-year-old Irving began his literary career, writing a series of satirical letters under the pen name "Jonathan Oldstyle" for the *New York Morning Chronicle*, a political newspaper founded by Aaron Burr and edited by Irving's brother, Peter.

Summer of 1803 found Irving accompanying the Hoffman family on a longer voyage up the Hudson River, westward across the then frontier of New York State to Ogdensburg, and then on to Montreal, Canada. In later years, Irving would reminisce, "All the country was then a wilderness; we floated down the Black River in a scow; we toiled through forests in waggons drawn by oxen; we slept in hunters' cabins, and were once four and twenty hours without food; but all was romance to me."[5]

Battling health issues from an early age, Washington was sent by his brothers William and Ebenezer to tour Europe in May 1804. It was hoped that exposure to the sea air during the trans-Atlantic voyage would improve his breathing difficulties. Irving visited France, Italy, Switzerland, the Netherlands and England. He returned to the United States in February 1806 and returned to Hoffman's law firm.

Matilda Hoffman

Having been away for almost two years, Irving found himself suddenly taking notice of the Hoffman's youngest daughter, Matilda, who had blossomed during his absence. Irving recalled in an 1823 letter, "what a difference the interval had made... there was a softness and delicacy in her form and look... I thought I had never beheld any thing so lovely."[6]

The marriage-minded Irving began working harder at his law studies, with Judge Hoffman having offered him a partnership, as well as his daughter's hand, when he became "capable of undertaking legal concerns."[7]

In 1807, Irving, his brother William and his friend James Paulding started a magazine together, called *Salmagundi*. Full of humor and satire about life in New York City, the magazine's stated mission was "to instruct the young, inform the old, correct the town, and castigate the age."[8] *Salmagundi* was Irving's first taste of literary success.

Washington Irving and Matilda Hoffman became officially engaged during the winter of 1808 and began making wedding plans. However, the marriage was not to be, as Matilda succumbed to a sudden illness on April 26, 1809. Irving was devastated.

Washington Irving as he appeared in 1809 at age 26, painted by John Wesley Jarvis; currently in the Drawing Room at Sunnyside (Courtesy of Historic Hudson Valley)

Kinderhook

Following the death of his beloved Matilda, Irving felt the need to escape the "scene of gloom and heart-aching distress" of New York City. He spent the next two months in Kinderhook, NY, as the guest of his friend Judge William P. Van Ness at his family's estate, known as "Kleinrood" (Dutch for "small red").

Lindenwald in Kinderhook, NY, former home of President Martin Van Buren, and before that, the home of William P. Van Ness, where in 1809 Irving first met Jesse Merwin, a schoolteacher from Connecticut...
(Photo courtesy of Glenn Fisher)

Irving eased his sorrow "by constantly exercising [his] mind... in useful and agreeable occupation." He turned to his writing, and completed a manuscript that he had begun with his brother Peter, titled *A History of New York from the Beginning of the World to the End of the Dutch Dynasty*, under the pseudonym Diedrich Knickerbocker.[9]

While staying with the Van Nesses, Irving befriended the local schoolmaster, Jesse Merwin, whom he described as having "much native, unimproved shrewdness and considerable humor."[10] Merwin, who was originally from Connecticut, "boarded and lodged a week at a time" with various Kinderhook families whose children he taught...

Washington Irving returned to Manhattan in June 1809.

Knickerbocker's History of New York was published in December 1809 to widespread acclaim. Despite the success of *Knickerbocker's History*, Irving opted to "not meddle with [his] pen" and did not write any new material for several years. Instead, he focused on editing and rewriting previously published articles and essays for publication in England and France.

In 1813, "for the sake of pastime and employment of idle hours,"[11] he accepted the position of editor of the Philadelphia-based magazine *Select Reviews*. Renamed *Analectic Magazine*, Irving referred to it as a "motley collection" of articles, poems and political essays.[12]

Irving's Military Career

During the War of 1812 between the U.S. and England, Irving remained relatively passive, other than penning the occasional nationalistic-themed essay. However, when the British army invaded and burned Washington, DC in August 1814, Irving became enraged, declaring, "The pride and honor of the nation are wounded; the country is insulted and disgraced by this barbarous success..."[13]

Washington Irving joined the New York State Militia, was commissioned a colonel, and accepted an assignment as aide-de-camp to New York's Governor Daniel D. Tompkins. Irving accompanied Gov. Tompkins to Brooklyn, Hellgate and Ellis Island to inspect fortifications there, and then went on to Sackets Harbor on Lake Ontario.[14]

It was at Sackets Harbor that Col. Irving is believed to have made the acquaintance of a young artillery captain with the unusual name Ichabod Crane. The odd-sounding moniker was one that Irving would, quite understandably, remember in years to come...

When the War of 1812 ended in February 1815, so did Washington Irving's military career.

In England

In May 1815, Washington Irving left New York to visit his brother Peter in England. Peter was then running the Liverpool-based offices of the family's import company, established by Peter and Ebenezer, doing business under the (somewhat unimaginative) name "P. and E. Irving."

Irving arrived in Liverpool to find his brother ill and the family business failing. Washington began working in the Liverpool offices in an attempt to put the business back on its feet; he soon discovered that he hated numbers and accounting as much as he hated studying law.

Having immersed himself in the family business, Irving found he had no time for writing. He did, however, make time for frequent visits to his sister Sarah and her husband Henry Van Wart in Birmingham, about 50 miles away. Irving also made time to tour London and Wales.

Summer and fall of 1817 found Washington Irving exploring his father's native Scotland. On the morning of August 30, 1817, Irving arrived unannounced at Abbotsford, the home of the well-known Scottish poet Walter Scott. Unbeknownst to Irving, Scott was a great admirer of his work. Scott had once described reading passages from *Knickerbocker's History* to his wife and some houseguests until their sides became "absolutely sore with laughing."[15]

Scott welcomed Irving warmly; where Irving had only hoped for a few hours' visit, he found himself being persuaded to stay for several days with the Scott family. Irving was given a tour of the neighboring countryside, and the two men spent hour upon hour discussing literature.

In a letter to Walter Scott, Irving wrote, "I shall ever recollect the few days I passed with you and your amiable family as among the choicest of my life."[16]

The Sketch Book

Sir Walter Scott is credited by many with inspiring Washington Irving to resume his own literary pursuits. Not long after his return to England, Irving began to develop a collection of essays and short stories that would become *The Sketch Book of Geoffrey Crayon, Gent.*

P. and E. Irving finally went bankrupt in the spring of 1818, and Washington Irving found himself broke. He turned to writing as a source of income. Irving became determined to support himself as a full-time author, and refused to accept any other employment that would occupy his time and interfere with his ability to write.

On March 3, 1819, Washington Irving mailed the manuscript of the first volume of *The Sketch Book* to his brother Ebenezer in America, with a request that he find a suitable publisher and make the arrangements on his behalf. This first installment consisted of "The Author's Account of Himself," "The Voyage," "Roscoe," "The Wife" and "Rip Van Winkle."

Irving's intent was to publish *The Sketch Book* in several volumes, depending on the success of the preceding group of stories. In the "Prospectus" contained in the first volume, Irving wrote, "The following writings are published on experiment; should they please, they may be followed by others."[17]

Published in June 1819 by Cornelius S. Van Winkle of New York, the first volume was, of course, extremely well received. Additional manuscripts were mailed at irregular intervals throughout the remainder of 1819 and up until June 1820, for a total of seven volumes.

"The Legend of Sleepy Hollow" was included in the sixth installment, mailed to Ebenezer on December 29, 1819. Volume 6 of *The Sketch Book* was released in March 1820.

Gilbert Stuart Newton portrait of 37-year-old Washington Irving as he looked in 1820, about the time The Sketch Book of Geoffrey Crayon *was published (Courtesy of Historic Hudson Valley)*

Irving's *Sketch Book* was republished in England in two volumes in February and July of 1820. The British public's enthusiasm for *The Sketch Book* rivaled that of Irving's audience in his native America.

Irving the Celebrity

The enormous success of *The Sketch Book* earned Irving the respect of his fellow authors on both sides of the Atlantic. One contemporary reviewer wrote of Irving, "It would appear that America now has its first literary lion."[18] The first commercially successful American author, Irving earned the unofficial title "Father of American Literature."

But perhaps a more noteworthy accomplishment is that Irving is considered by many to have invented, or at least perfected, a new genre – the Short Story.

In a December 1824 letter to his friend Henry Brevoort, Irving explained, "I have preferred adopting the mode of sketches and short tales rather than long works, because I chose to take a line of writing peculiar to myself, rather than fall into the manner or school of any other writer… I believe the works I have written will be oftener re read than any novel of the size that I could have written."[19]

That same year, in his *Tales of a Traveler*, Irving would offer a more typical, light-hearted explanation: "If the tales I have furnished should prove to be bad, they will at least be found short."[20]

Walter Reichart, writing in 1957, summed up Irving's new-found international popularity: "Whereas *Salmagundi* amused only a small coterie of kindred spirits in New York and *A History of New York* gave Irving prestige at home as a distinguished American writer, *The Sketch Book* made Irving famous in England as well as America."[21]

Now a celebrity, Irving found himself warmly welcomed into London's literary circles. In an 1822 letter to Henry Brevoort, he wrote, "The success of my writings has given me ready access to all kinds of society... where you find the most distinguished people of the day in various departments of literature, art & science brought into familiar communion with leading statesmen and ancient nobility."[22]

Irving spent the next several years traveling through Europe, with extended stays in France and Germany. Writing once again under the pseudonym Geoffrey Crayon, Irving followed *The Sketch Book* with *Bracebridge Hall* in 1822 and *Tales of a Traveler* in 1824.

In 1826, Irving relocated to Spain, having accepted a position from the newly-appointed U.S. Minister in Madrid. Irving was to translate Spanish manuscripts and historical documents about Christopher Columbus; however, this simple translation project expanded into a full biography titled *The Life and Voyages of Columbus*. Published in January 1828, *Columbus* was the first book to display Washington Irving's name on the title page, rather than a Crayon or Knickerbocker pen name.

The Life and Voyages of Columbus was followed by the *Chronicle of the Conquest of Granada* in 1829, and *Voyages and Discoveries of the Companions of Columbus* in 1831.

Irving left Spain in July 1829, returning to London to assume the position of Secretary to the American Legation. Irving served in this position until September 1831, when he resigned so that he would have more time for writing. The result was *Tales of the Alhambra* in 1832.

Irving Returns Home

In May of 1832, after 17 years in Europe, Washington Irving returned to the United States. Now a celebrated author, he was honored with a dinner at the City Hotel in New

York, attended by the city's literary elite and most distinguished citizens. In a speech to his dinner guests, Irving addressed speculation that he had only returned for a visit, saying he intended to remain in America "as long as I live."[23]

Many changes had taken place in his absence. The population of his home town of Manhattan had grown to 200,000, while the state of New York as a whole now contained more than a half a million people. The nation itself had greatly expanded westward beyond the Mississippi.

Irving once again indulged his love of travel, and set out to explore the country that had grown so much in the time he had been away. His journey began in New England, crossing New York State to Niagara Falls, to Ohio, Kentucky, and then west to Arkansas, Oklahoma and Kansas as far as "the borders of the Pawnee country."[24] Irving also traveled by steamboat on the Ohio and Mississippi Rivers, and ventured as far south as New Orleans. Irving's travels eventually yielded *A Tour on the Prairies*, published in 1835.

In September 1833, Irving spent time "visiting old scenes about the Hudson" with Vice President Martin Van Buren, whom he had befriended in England in 1831 while serving as Secretary of the U.S. Legation. He accompanied Van Buren to his hometown of Kinderhook, NY, where he also visited with his old friend, Jesse Merwin.[25]

Sunnyside

In "The Legend of Sleepy Hollow," Irving had written, "If ever I should wish for a retreat, whither I might steal from the world and its distractions, and dream quietly away the remnant of a troubled life, I know of none more promising than this little valley."[26] Having led a semi-nomadic life for some 17 years in Europe – always someone else's guest or tenant – Washington Irving found himself wanting to settle down in a home of his own. In June of 1835, he purchased a small stone cottage on 10 acres of land situated on the banks of the Hudson River, adjacent to his nephew Oscar's farm, just a few miles south of Sleepy Hollow.

Sunnyside, the home of Washington Irving (Author's photo)

Irving hired artist George Harvey to oversee the renovation of what was to become known as "Sunnyside." In a letter to his brother Peter, Washington described his plans "to make a little nookery somewhat in the Dutch style, quaint but unpretending."[27] A reflection of the author's eclectic tastes, the small cottage was transformed into "a little old-fashioned stone mansion, all made up of gable-ends, and as full of angles and corners as an old cocked hat."[28]

To pay for the renovations, Irving consented to regularly supply essays and short stories to *The Knickerbocker* magazine, for which he would receive an annual salary of $2,000.[29]

A life-long bachelor, Washington Irving ensured that he would never be lonely by making his home a "complete little family hive." Sharing his cottage with him were Ebenezer and his five daughters, his sister Catherine and her daughter, along with "casual visits from all the rest of [their] family."[30]

Self-portrait of Washington Irving with the Hudson River in the background, sketched at Sunnyside (Courtesy of the New York Public Library, Astor, Lenox, and Tilden Foundations, Berg Collection of English and American Literature)

In 1842, Irving was approached once more to accept the position of U.S. Minister to Spain. He felt morally obligated to accept the assignment, and entrusted his beloved

Sunnyside to the care of his brother Ebenezer and his nieces.

While in Europe, Irving revisited many of his previous haunts; this time, however, Europe didn't hold the same charm that it once did, and he found himself homesick for Sunnyside. In a letter to his sister Catherine, Irving wrote, "amidst all the splendors of London and Paris, I find my imagination refuses to take fire, and my heart still yearns for dear little Sunnyside."[31]

The Final Years

In September of 1846, Washington Irving returned home to Sunnyside for good.

However, the author was not yet ready for retirement. In 1848, Irving began editing all of his previous writings, which were to be published by George Putnam as a fifteen volume "complete works" collection. The first volume, *Knickerbocker's History of New York*, appeared in September of 1848.

Two new books were completed, *Mahomet* (1849) and *Mahomet's Successors* (1850). These were followed by *Wolfert's Roost* (1855), a collection of stories that had previously appeared in *The Knickerbocker* magazine.

Around this same time, Washington Irving began focusing his efforts on his *Life of George Washington*, which he had first conceived in 1829, but worked on only sporadically in the ensuing years. Irving's long-anticipated biography of his namesake was his most ambitious effort, and would eventually consist of five volumes.

In the fall of 1855, Washington Irving returned to Kinderhook one last time to visit his old friend, former President Martin Van Buren. Van Buren was by then the owner of the former Van Ness estate, which he renamed Lindenwald – the same mansion where Irving had been a guest some 45 years earlier.

Daguerreotype portrait of Washington Irving taken "about 1849" by John Plumbe, Jr. (Library of Congress)

By then in his seventies and in failing health, Irving enlisted his nephew Pierre Munroe Irving to assist with the completion of his *George Washington* effort. The fifth and final volume of *The Life of George Washington* was published in April 1859.

Washington Irving died of heart failure on November 28, 1859, at Sunnyside.

It is interesting to note that Irving's funeral procession, which consisted of more than 150 carriages plus an estimated 500 mourners on foot, followed the approximate route taken by Ichabod Crane during his flight from the Headless Horseman – past the site of Major Andre's capture, continuing north along the Albany Post Road, and finally crossing the "church bridge," which had been draped in mourning black.

Washington Irving's funeral, December 1, 1859, at Christ Episcopal Church, Tarrytown (From an engraving in Harper's Weekly, *December 17, 1859)*

Washington Irving was buried in the Sleepy Hollow cemetery, on a hill overlooking the Old Dutch Church and graveyard that he had made so famous in "The Legend of Sleepy Hollow."

Washington Irving's grave in Sleepy Hollow Cemetery (Author's photo)

Chapter 2

A Little Valley Among High Hills

> *"I find the very existence of the place has been held in question by many; who, judging from its odd name and from the odd stories... have rashly deemed the whole to be a fanciful creation."*
> - from "Sleepy Hollow" essay, 1839

Sleepy Hollow was, and is, a very real place... as are most of the locations and landmarks mentioned in Irving's story. Let's take a walk in Ichabod Crane's footsteps...

The Village of Sleepy Hollow

"From the listless repose of the place, and the peculiar character of its inhabitants, who are descendants from the original Dutch settlers, this sequestered glen has long been known by the name of SLEEPY HOLLOW."

Entering Sleepy Hollow
(Photo courtesy of Kit Gentry)

The modern village of Sleepy Hollow is located in Westchester County, New York, about 30 miles north of Manhattan, near the wide expanse of the Hudson River known as the Tappan Zee.

The name Sleepy Hollow, which originally referred to the area where the Pocantico River flows into the Hudson, is believed to have been derived from the Dutch term "Slapershaven," which was coined by Dutch colonist Adriaen Van der Donck (1618-1655). The earliest known use of the term is in Van der Donck's *Beschryvinge van Nieuw-Nederlant* ("Description of New Netherland"), which was first published in 1655; specifically, it may be found on page 8, in his discussion of the "North River" (The Hudson) and the various streams which flow into it.¹

Earliest known use of the term "Slapershaven," precursor of "Sleepy Hollow," from Adriaen Van der Dock's 1655 book
Beschryvinge van Nieuw-Nederlant ("Description of New Netherland")

According to Sleepy Hollow Village Historian Henry Steiner, other variations of Slapershaven have included Slaeperingh Haven and Slaeperigh Hol.²

Washington Irving used the name Sleepy Hollow to refer to the Pocantico River Valley between the Old Dutch Church and Carl Brook, roughly the area that is now bordered by the Sleepy Hollow Cemetery and modern-day Sleepy Hollow Road. He described it as "a little valley, or rather lap of land, among high hills, which is one of the quietest places in the whole world. A small brook glides through it..."³

The Sleepy Hollow that Irving wrote about was not yet a true village per se, but was still mostly forest, with a handful of farms and a few dirt roads, which had once been Indian trails, criss-crossing the landscape.

The region was already inhabited by the Weckquaesgeek Indians when Henry Hudson, who had been hired by the Dutch East India Company, first explored the Hudson River in 1609. Soon afterwards, the Dutch began to colonize the area, which became known as New Netherland. The Dutch settlers were soon followed by the English.

The Dutch immigrants also included a smaller number of French-speaking Protestants, the Huguenots and Walloons, who were fleeing religious persecution in their home countries of France and Belgium. Many had taken refuge in the Netherlands before continuing to North America.

The colonists and the Weckquaesgeek were able to cohabitate peacefully for a time, but the Weckquaesgeek were eventually edged out by the influx of settlers in the 1640s and '50s.

In 1664, the British seized New Netherland from the Dutch and renamed it New York. In the 1680s, Dutchman Frederick Philipse swore an oath of loyalty to England, and was able to amass approximately 90,000 acres of land in the Hudson Valley. Philipse's holdings encompassed much of modern day Westchester County, including what was to become Tarrytown and Sleepy Hollow. He was granted a Royal Charter in 1693 which established the Manor of Philipsburg.

Philipse constructed a grist mill on the Pocantico River, and the immediate area, including the valley of Sleepy Hollow, became known as the Upper Mills.

By the time of the Revolutionary War, Philipse's grandson, Frederick Philipse III had inherited the Philipsburg properties. He remained loyal to the King of England, which resulted in the Philipsburg properties being seized by the State of New York after the war. The lands were divided and resold by the Commission of Forfeitures to the various tenant farmers who had been leasing them from Philipse.

Gerard G. Beekman became the owner of the Upper Mills in 1785. In the 1820s, the Beekman farmlands were divided into smaller lots and streets were laid out, at which time the growing village became known as Beekmantown.

In December 1874, the village, then boasting a population of approximately 2,500, was incorporated as the Village of North Tarrytown. It retained this name until 1996 when, in an effort to reconnect with its heritage, it was officially renamed Sleepy Hollow.

Now a modern-day suburb of New York City, the village of Sleepy Hollow has somehow maintained much of its small-town charm.

(Note: For *much* more about the history of the Sleepy Hollow region, readers are referred to Edgar Mayhew Bacon's fascinating *Chronicles of Tarrytown and Sleepy Hollow*, originally published in 1897, and Henry Steiner's excellent and thoroughly researched *The Place Names of Historic Sleepy Hollow and Tarrytown*, published in 1998. More recently, Steiner has published *The Historically Annotated Legend of Sleepy Hollow*, marrying Irving's original text with numerous footnotes which provide brief histories of many of the landmarks referred to in the story.)

Tarrytown

"In the bosom of one of those spacious coves which indent the eastern shore of the Hudson... there lies a small market-town or rural port, which by some is called Greensburgh, but which is more generally and properly known by the name of Tarry Town."

Washington Irving went on to explain that the village of Tarrytown had been so named "by the good housewives of the adjacent country, from the inveterate propensity of their husbands to linger about the village tavern on market days."[4]

This explanation is, of course, highly tongue-in-cheek, and is classic Knickerbocker – the same Diedrich Knickerbocker who once wrote that the Van Ness family name was derived from their being "valiant robbers of birds' nests"![5]

The name Tarrytown is actually a corruption of the Dutch name Tarwe Dorp, or Tarwe Town (sometimes spelled Terve Town), which means "Wheat Town."

The village of Tarrytown, NY, located just south of Sleepy Hollow, was first settled in the mid-1600s by Dutch farmers. Eighteenth-century maps show the earliest homes clustered close to the Hudson River, along what are now West Franklin and Main Streets.

The soil in the region was ideal for growing grain, especially wheat. The local wheat was ground at the mill built by Frederick Philipse. It was then distributed by the Dutch market-sloops which docked at Martling's and Van Wart's Landing, located near the foot of the Continental Road (modern-day Beekman Avenue), or at (another) Martling's Landing, later called Requa's Dock, near the west end of what is now White Street.

Primarily a farming region throughout the 1700s, the village began to take shape as taverns and other small businesses began to spring up along the Albany Post Road, which is now Broadway.

With the arrival of the New York and Hudson railroad in 1849, the area saw a surge in population, and the economy began to shift from farming to industry. These included a wagon factory in 1868 and the Silver Shoe Factory in 1871. Other 19th century enterprises included a steam pump factory, a silk factory, and boat-building.[6]

The automotive industry appeared around the turn of the 20th century with the Mobile Company, Maxwell Briscoe, and Chevrolet, which later became General Motors. More recent companies to take up residence in Tarrytown include Hitachi (1984) and Kraft Foods (1989).[7]

The current population of Tarrytown is estimated at approximately 11,500.

Ichabod Crane's Log Schoolhouse

"His school-house was a low building of one large room, rudely constructed of logs... The school-house stood in a rather lonely but pleasant situation just at the foot of a woody hill, with a brook running close by, and a formidable birch tree growing at one end of it."

The exact location of the structure that may have given rise to Ichabod Crane's log schoolhouse is still a matter of some speculation. In an 1898 letter to the editor of *The New York Times*, Daniel Van Tassel – local historian and editor of the *Tarrytown Argus* newspaper – stated unequivocally that there had never been a log schoolhouse in Sleepy Hollow; he asserted that the older residents he interviewed had attended the Squash Hill School, located on Bedford Road in Pocantico Hills.[8]

However, Mrs. Eliza Ann See, who died in November 1883 at age 92, disputed Van Tassel's claim. She recalled having attended school in a one-room log schoolhouse, not unlike the one described in "The Legend," when she was a young girl, "around" the year 1800 – which was also "around" the time Irving visited the region, give or take a couple of years. Built into the side of a hill, the back wall of the school was formed of earth, with the front and remaining two sides constructed of logs.

Mrs. See located this school "on the east side of the Sleepy Hollow Road, just north of... the gate of entrance" to

Glen Loch, the estate of local attorney Stephen D. Law.[9] This site is a little less than a half mile north of where present day Webber Road meets Sleepy Hollow Road.

Ichabod Crane's one-room schoolhouse
(Engraved by Charles O. Murray, 1880)

Did Irving's boyhood friend James Kirke Paulding also attend this school? According to his biography, Paulding attended a school located about two miles from his Tarrytown residence. Every day he would walk to the school alone, "a solitary figure trudging along the wooded road" – presumably the Albany Post Road? To be closer to the schoolhouse, he eventually moved in with one of his uncles who lived near the Sawmill River.[10]

The two-mile distance from Tarrytown to the school, along with its implied closer proximity to the Sawmill River, seems consistent with the location of the log schoolhouse on Sleepy Hollow Road which was described by Mrs. See.

If Paulding did indeed attend this school, might he have pointed it out to his young friend Irving during one of their forays into Sleepy Hollow?

Other Sleepy Hollow Schools

Authors Jeff Canning and Wally Buxton placed the Sleepy Hollow school "between the present Sleepy Hollow Road and the Croton Aqueduct."[11] This may or may not have been the same school described by Mrs. See; their description seems to place this one on the opposite side of Sleepy Hollow Road, and further to the west.

Writing in 1974 in *The Centennial History of North Tarrytown*, authors Lucille and Theodore Hutchinson stated, "There are stories of a tiny primary school that existed between the Mill Road and Gory Brook."[12] This location would have been further north than that of the school attended by Mrs. See.

The Hutchinsons also mentioned a school "west of the old Post Road but east of the modern road." A 1795 map shows this school south of the Continental Road, which is now Bedford Road.[13]

The early Sleepy Hollow schools are largely undocumented; the earliest school for which records exist was the Sleepy Hollow Free School, built in 1836 at the corner of what is now Sleepy Hollow Road and Tower Hill Road. This school was razed in 1865 and replaced with a larger, more modern school on the same site. Plans to sell the building in the late 1890s were met with some resistance by local residents who believed, incorrectly, that this was the school that Washington Irving had frequented, probably subconsciously linking it to Ichabod Crane of local lore.

Or Was it in Tarrytown?

Another early school has been suggested as the "original" Ichabod Crane Schoolhouse, this one closer to Tarrytown than to "the Hollow" as located by Irving. An August 1882 *New York Times* article quoted Tarrytown resident William L. Carae as stating that his grandfather, William

Sharpney, "used to tell him when a boy that Ichabod Crane's school-house stood on a knoll across the stream from the spot where Andre was taken... A tall birch stood before the door, and from it Ichabod cut his rods." The unnamed *Times* reporter asserted that the site had apparently since been razed, and upon it stood (in 1882) the "handsome residence of D. C. Reynolds."[14]

This location appears to correspond to the Tarrytown Academy, sometimes called the Tarrytown Institute, a boarding school established in the early 1800s at the corner of what is now Broadway and College Avenue.[15] However, a drawing of the Academy which appeared in the April 1, 1854 issue of *Gleason's Pictorial* showed it to have been a large three-story structure, located just north of the Captors Monument in what is now Patriot's Park; prior to the Academy, might a tiny one-room log schoolhouse have once existed on this site?

Irvington's "Old Red School-House"

One other schoolhouse which Irving may have encountered as a youth was located in what is now Irvington, about three miles south of Tarrytown. This school was built around the turn of the 19th century, just about the time the 15-year-old Irving was exploring the region.

Writing in 1874 in *The Old Home by the River*, Reverend Jacob Conkling Dutcher described a one-room schoolhouse, "squatty in appearance," which had once been painted red, but had become faded from exposure to time and winter weather.[16] The school was located on the west side of the Albany Post Road (modern-day Route 9) on what was once the John Jewell farm, near the modern-day intersection of Route 9 and Station Road, less than a mile south of Sunnyside Lane.

The structure, located "on a knoll... alone, without a tree to shade it," doesn't especially fit Irving's description of

Ichabod Crane's stronghold. However, Rev. Dutcher's narrative does contain one sentence of interest: "During the winter months, one evening a week, it was used for singing-school."[17] Coincidence? Or could this have been where Washington Irving found the idea for Ichabod's weekly singing school, where he would "instruct the young folks in psalmody" – that is, until Brom Bones would smoke them out by stopping up the chimney?

Kinderhook's "Ichabod Crane Schoolhouse"

Nineteenth-century author Harold Van Santvoord (1854-1913) believed that the old schoolhouse described by Washington Irving did not exist in Sleepy Hollow at all, but rather was inspired by one located in Kinderhook, New York. The Kinderhook school was presided over by Jesse Merwin, whom Irving had befriended in 1809. (Jesse Merwin is believed by many to have been the inspiration for the character Ichabod Crane; this is discussed in much more detail in a later chapter.)

Van Santvoord penned a series of letters to the editor of *The New York Times* in early 1898 stating his belief that the school, Irving's literary characters, and probably the entire story, had its roots in Kinderhook, and not Sleepy Hollow. In a letter published March 19, 1898, Van Santvoord wrote, "the old log schoolhouse... exactly as described by Irving in his romance, was for many years a familiar landmark endeared by its associations with Irving, who often visited it."[18] (Van Santvoord's pro-Kinderhook stance ignited a debate which played out in the editorial pages of *The New York Times* from February through May of 1898, with rebuttals from Westchester historian Edgar Mayhew Bacon and several others who rallied to Tarrytown's defense as the rightful "owner" of Irving's story.)

Washington Irving himself mentioned the Kinderhook school in an 1851 letter to Jesse Merwin, writing, "You tell me the old schoolhouse is torn down, and a new one built in its place... I should have liked to see the old schoolhouse once more..."[19]

Ichabod Crane Schoolhouse in Kinderhook, New York, built about 1850. (From an old postcard, circa 1910)

Van Santvoord's assertion that the Kinderhook schoolhouse was "exactly as described by Irving" seems a bit of a stretch; there is indeed a "brook running close by" the original site of the schoolhouse, but the other implied similarities fall short. Other than Van Santvoord's own statements, there does not seem to be any evidence that the Kinderhook school was made of logs. Also, the original site of the schoolhouse, the corner of Route 9H (formerly the Albany Post Road) and Fischer Road, is not "at the foot of a woody hill," but is on a gentle slope about 1,000 feet from the nearest hill.[20]

An old one-roomed, white-painted schoolhouse still stands on Route 9H just south of the Village of Kinderhook. Now a historical site, it is often incorrectly referred to as *the original* Ichabod Crane Schoolhouse. This schoolhouse was actually built in approximately 1850 as a replacement for the original; Jesse Merwin probably never taught at this particular schoolhouse, as he is believed to have abandoned teaching around 1811 to become a full-time farmer.

The Ichabod Crane Schoolhouse remained in use until the 1940s. On October 16, 1952, the remodeled schoolhouse was dedicated as a civic center by Eleanor Roosevelt. The original location of the building was on the opposite side of Route 9H; in 1974, it was moved across the road by flatbed truck to its present location on the Luykas Van Alen House grounds.

From his writings, Van Santvoord was apparently determined to link the Kinderhook schoolhouse to "The Legend of Sleepy Hollow" through its association with Jesse Merwin. True, Merwin does seem to be the leading contender to have been the prototype of Ichabod Crane (again, *much* more about this in Chapter 5), but that does not necessarily mean that all of the other elements of the story are from Kinderhook, especially since the various landmarks Irving mentioned – Andre's Tree, Andre's Brook, the churchyard – are clearly located in the villages of Sleepy Hollow or Tarrytown.

Where, then, did Irving's description of the log schoolhouse come from?

A Rude Building of Logs

One of Irving's 1818 notebooks contains the following passage: "Country schoolhouse a rude building of (pine) logs – green field – house sheltered by trees – a wild brook running close by..."[21]

Compare this to Irving's description of Ichabod Crane's schoolhouse in "The Legend of Sleepy Hollow": "rudely constructed of logs... just at the foot of a woody hill, with a brook running close by..."[22]

This notebook entry is immediately followed by "Virginia Negro going to market with the pig." Irving had traveled to Richmond in the summer of 1807 to attend the trial of Aaron Burr – could he have been recalling a scene from Virginia?

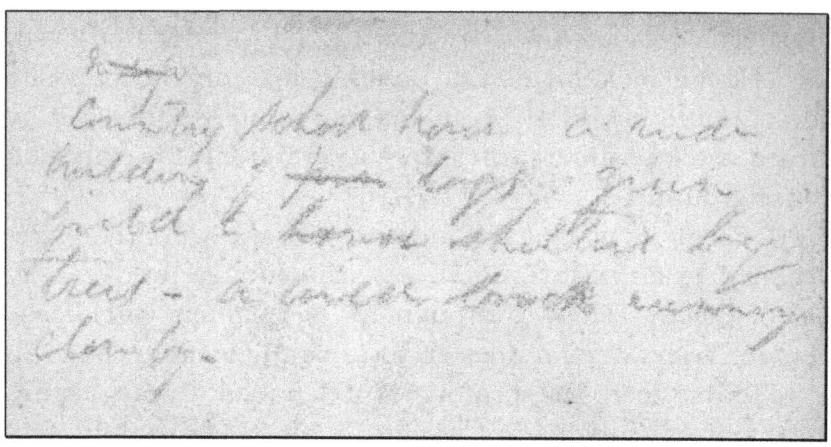

Washington Irving's hand-written notebook entry from 1818 describing a "country schoolhouse a rude building of logs..." (Photo courtesy of The New York Public Library, Manuscripts and Archives Division; Astor, Lenox, and Tilden Foundation; Washington Irving papers.)

Subsequent 1818 notebook entries describe scenes of New York State, many of them transcribed from *Travels into North America* by Peter Kalm, including mentions of Albany and the Hudson. Could Irving have merely been reminiscing about a schoolhouse he once saw in New York?

This notebook was kept while Irving was living in England; was he describing a schoolhouse he happened upon during one of his strolls through the English countryside?

It is unlikely that we will ever ascertain exactly which schoolhouse Irving was describing in 1818, but his brief description appears to have found its way into the text of "The Legend."

This is very typical of Irving's writing method; his notebook and journal entries were frequently repeated in his published writings. When once asked by author Donald G. Mitchell if he relied on his memory for his detailed descriptions of various scenes in his stories, Irving described how he always carried notebooks with him so that when he "saw a scene specially picturesque," he could "note down its distinguishing points, and hold it in reserve." Irving further explained that his notebooks were "equivalent to the little thumb-sketches from which a painter makes up his larger compositions."[23]

It is, of course, entirely possible that Irving did not base his schoolhouse on any one particular structure. His fictional schoolmaster needed a schoolhouse, so he provided one, its appearance drawn from his portfolio of literary thumb-sketches. His fictional school would have been built of logs (what else would one use to construct a rustic colonial-era school?), situated near a woody hill (no shortage of those in Sleepy Hollow!) and close by a brook (plenty of those as well)...

The Old Dutch Church

"It stands on a knoll, surrounded by locust-trees and lofty elms... a gentle slope descends from it to a silver sheet of water, bordered by high trees, between which, peeps may be caught at the blue hills of the Hudson... on one side of the church extends a wide woody dell, along which raves a large brook among broken rocks and trunks of fallen trees."

The church that Irving described so vividly is the Old Dutch Church, which still stands on Route 9 (Broadway) in Sleepy Hollow. Dating back to the 1680s, it is believed to be the oldest still existing church in New York State.

Local lore states that the mill pond created by Frederick Philipse was flooded several times, washing away the mill dam. One of Philipse's slaves reportedly had a dream that the dam would continue to be destroyed until a house of worship was built on the manor property. According to legend, Philipse immediately focused on the construction of the church, which was completed around 1685. The mill dam was never again washed away.[24]

The Old Dutch Church of Sleepy Hollow
(Photo courtesy of Kit Gentry)

The church has a very distinctive shape, rectangular with a three-sided "apse" projecting from the east end, behind the altar. It also features an unusual Dutch gambrel roof, topped with a belfry on the west end which contains the original circa 1685 bell imported from Holland, inscribed with the Bible verse "If God be for us, who can be against us?" in Latin. At the opposite end is a banner-shaped copper weathervane bearing Frederick Philipse's initials "VF," for the original Dutch spelling "Vredryk Flypse."

The Old Dutch Church was built of locally quarried granite and gneiss, as well as yellow brick imported from

Holland. The church door was originally on the south side of the building, but was moved in the 1830s to face the west. The yellow bricks which once outlined the original entrance may still be seen on the south exterior wall. Early maps of Sleepy Hollow indicate that there was a walk path from the Philipse manor house to the church.

The Old Dutch Church was designated a National Historic Landmark on November 5, 1961.

Now owned by the Reformed Church of the Tarrytowns, the Old Dutch Church, which seats about 200 worshippers, is still used for services during the summer months, on Christmas Eve, on Easter morning, and for the occasional wedding.

(For a much more extensive history of the Old Dutch Church, from its construction in 1685 through its recent 325th Anniversary celebration, readers are directed to the interesting *The Old Dutch Church of Sleepy Hollow* by Janie Couch Allen and Elinor Griffith, published in 2011 by the Friends of the Old Dutch Church and Burying Ground, <WWW.ODCFRIENDS.ORG>.)

The Churchyard

"Having been buried in the church-yard, the ghost rides forth to the scene of battle in nightly quest of his head..."

Now known as the Old Dutch Burying Ground, the 3-acre graveyard surrounding the Old Dutch Church of Sleepy Hollow is one of the country's oldest cemeteries. It is uncertain when the first burials took place at this site, but some may have been as early as 1645.[25]

The oldest still-existing gravestones are from the mid-18th century. It is believed that many of the earliest markers were made of wood and have long since succumbed to decay.[26]

Many of the tombstones from the 1700s are decorated with "soul effigies," which depict human faces flanked by a pair of angel wings. Some were also shown wearing a "crown of righteousness."[27]

The Old Dutch Burying Ground
(Author's photo)

The inscriptions include a number of names still recognizable in the Sleepy Hollow region: Van Tassel (or the old Dutch variation, Van Texel), Martling, Youngs, Hammond and Requa.

The Old Dutch Burying Ground, like the Old Dutch Church, is owned and maintained by the Reformed Church of the Tarrytowns. It is not part of the adjacent (and much larger) Sleepy Hollow Cemetery.

The Mill Pond

"How he would figure among them in the churchyard, between services on Sundays... or sauntering, with a whole bevy of them, along the banks of the adjacent mill-pond..."

The mill pond mentioned by Washington Irving is the one associated with Frederick Philipse's grist mill, which was built close by his manor house in the 1680s. (This is the same grist mill discussed in the "Village of Sleepy Hollow" section earlier in this chapter.)

The Mill Pond at Philipsburg Manor
(Photo courtesy of Historic Hudson Valley)

The large pond was created by a dam across the Pocantico, adjacent to the mill, built to direct the stream which supplied the mill's waterwheel.

As Irving implied, the mill pond was within walking distance of the Old Dutch Church. Ichabod and his "bevy" of female admirers probably would have strolled along the walk path that once led to the Philipse Manor house.

The pond may still be seen on the restored Philipsburg Manor property, across Route 9 from the Old Dutch Church. The grounds are maintained by Historic Hudson Valley (formerly known as Sleepy Hollow Restorations), <WWW.HUDSONVALLEY.ORG>. The mill pond is as picturesque today as it would have been in the days of Ichabod Crane.

Raven Rock

"Some mention was made also of the woman in white, that haunted the dark glen at Raven Rock, and was often heard to shriek on winter nights before a storm, having perished there in the snow."

Raven Rock (Photo courtesy of Lucas Buresch)

Raven Rock is "a detached portion of the steep, rocky, eastern side of Buttermilk Hill, which a deep fissure has long separated from the mass."[28] According to local tradition, the 45-foot rock formation was so named because of ravens gathering there. (It is *not* shaped like a raven, as depicted in some cartoon versions of "The Legend of Sleepy Hollow"!)

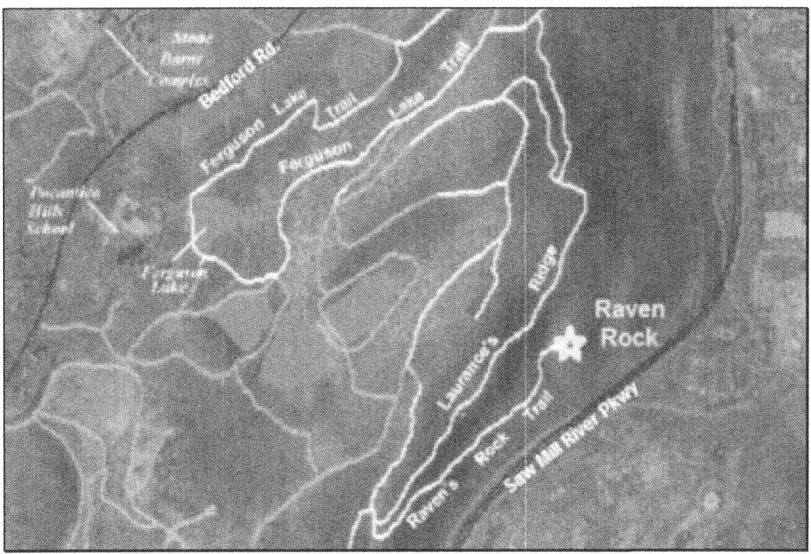

Detail from Rockefeller State Park Preserve Hiking Trail Map (with additional notations by the Author)

Raven Rock boasts not one, but at least three ghostly legends. In "The Legend of Sleepy Hollow," Washington Irving briefly touched upon the tale of the Lady in White as one of the stories heard by Ichabod Crane at the Van Tassel's party. This legend tells of a woman who became lost in a snowstorm and took shelter in a ravine behind Raven Rock, where she froze to death. Since then, her ghost has reportedly appeared to travelers, wailing and shrieking to warn them of impending storms.

A second Raven Rock legend, not mentioned by Irving, is an older tale of an Indian maiden who was thrown from the rock by her jealous boyfriend. Like the Lady in White, the Indian maiden's shrieks can still be heard late at night, especially when it is storming.[29]

The third legend of Raven Rock is the story of a woman who, during the Revolutionary War, "fled from the dreadful attentions of a too amorous Tory raider" to Raven Rock, where she leaped to her death.[30]

Raven Rock is located in Pocantico Hills, about two miles east of Sleepy Hollow, in the heart of the Rockefeller State Park Preserve. It is about a mile and a half north-east of the Tarrytown Reservoir, adjacent to the present-day Saw Mill River Parkway.

A series of hiking trails wind through Pocantico Hills, including one which terminates at Raven Rock. Brave readers wishing to explore the "dark glen" in hopes of meeting the Lady in White may download a free trail map from the Friends of Rockefeller State Park Preserve website: <HTTP://WWW.FRIENDSROCK.ORG/WP-CONTENT/UPLOADS/2014/06/2014-05-29-RSPP-TRAIL-MAP-BROCHURE.PDF>

Major Andre's Tree

"In the centre of the road stood an enormous tulip-tree, which towered like a giant above all the other trees of the neighborhood, and formed a kind of landmark. Its limbs were gnarled, and fantastic, large enough to form trunks for ordinary trees, twisting down almost to the earth, and rising again into the air. It was connected with the tragical story of the unfortunate André, who had been taken prisoner hard by; and was universally known by the name of Major André's tree."

Major Andre's Tree was a very large Tulip tree, sometimes called a Whitewood, which once existed in Tarrytown. Records of the exact measurements of the tree vary, but it appears to have stood approximately 111 to 112 feet in height, and 26 to 29 feet around the base of the trunk.[31]

Besides its immense size, one other notable feature is that the tree stood in the middle of the old Post Road, now Broadway, or Route 9; the road split to go around the tree on both sides. This imposing landmark must have made a lasting impression on 15-year-old Washington Irving when he visited the area in 1798!

The tree was named for British Major John Andre, an associate of the well-known traitor Benedict Arnold. On September 22, 1780, Major Andre was transporting plans of West Point, given to him by Arnold, to British forces in New York City when he was stopped a short distance from the tree by three local American militiamen, John Paulding, Isaac Van Wart and David Williams. Upon searching Andre, the three men discovered the papers concealed in his boot, and Benedict Arnold's plans to betray the American colonies began to unravel. Major Andre was hanged as spy on October 2, 1780.

Local lore sometimes claimed that Andre was captured directly beneath the tree. However, despite its name, the location of Major Andre's Tree was about 200 yards south of the actual capture site.[32]

Another erroneous local tradition was that the tree was the site of Andre's hanging; Major Andre was actually executed in Tappan, NY, about 4 miles southwest of Sleepy Hollow, on the opposite side of the Hudson River.

Andre's Tree was struck by lightning on July 21, 1801, at which time it was "rent almost exactly in two, from the top to the bottom."[33] Local legend claims that the destruction of the tree occurred on the same day that the news of Benedict Arnold's death in England reached Tarrytown.

Although there is no longer any trace of the tree, the site where it once stood is on modern-day Broadway in Tarrytown, approximately in front of the Warner Library, which is located at the northwest corner of Broadway and Wildey Street.[34]

Andre's Brook & Wiley Swamp

"About two hundred yards from the tree a small brook crossed the road, and ran into a marshy and thickly-wooded glen, known by the name of Wiley's swamp. A few rough logs, laid side by side, served for a bridge over this stream."

The brook Irving was referring to is Andre's Brook, which was located approximately one-tenth of a mile north of Andre's Tree. Once known as Clark's Kill, the name was changed to Andre's Brook shortly after the Revolutionary War due to the capture of Major Andre having occurred close by.

According to Village Historian Henry Steiner, the Post Road at the time of the American Revolution was located approximately 100 yards east of the current course of Broadway. Steiner locates the site of the log bridge described by Washington Irving as being close to the main entrance of the John Paulding Elementary School, directly across from Patriots Park on modern-day Broadway.[35]

Andre Brook in 1841; Note how the bridge is composed of several "rough logs, laid side by side" as described by Irving (From Historical Collections of the State of New York, *1841 Edition, by John W. Barber)*

Andre's Brook originates at Kykuit Hill, flowing below Broadway via a culvert and reemerging in the park a short distance beyond the Patriots Monument.[36] What is left of Andre's Brook is now a tiny rivulet within a stone and concrete border.

Andre Brook as it appears today in Patriots Park
(Photo courtesy of Kit Gentry)

Wiley's Swamp was a marshy wooded area, long since drained, which was once located along Andre's Brook where Patriots Park is today. Also known as Wildey's Swamp, it was named after Caleb Wildey (1765-1843), an early Tarrytown settler. ("Wiley" was a common corruption of the name Wildey.) Wildey owned the property adjacent to the swamp, bordered on the north by Andre's Brook and on the south by lands owned by the Storm family. He inhabited a "Dutch farmhouse on the future site of the Warner Library."[37]

The Church Bridge

"Over a deep black part of the stream, not far from the church, was formerly thrown a wooden bridge; the road that led to it, and the bridge itself, were thickly shaded by overhanging trees, which cast a gloom about it, even in the daytime; but occasioned a fearful darkness at night."

A blue historical marker posted adjacent to the modern-day Route 9 bridge, which crosses the Pocantico River just south of the Old Dutch Church, informs visitors that "The Headless Horseman Bridge described by Irving in The Legend of Sleepy Hollow formerly spanned this stream at this spot." Well... not quite. The original wooden colonial-era bridge featured in Irving's tale actually spanned the Pocantico quite some distance upstream (that is, to the east) of the current bridge.

The bridge did NOT span the stream "at this spot"... (Author's photo)

The 18th century Albany Post Road followed a much different route in the vicinity of the church than modern-day Broadway/Route 9. Coming from the north, the road made a sharp left turn just south of the church, and proceeded north-east, approximately along the route of the current dirt driveway leading to the maintenance garage. (This dirt road is known colloquially as "Horseman's Ride" due to its having been, according to local legend, the original route of the Headless Horseman...)

Past the garage site, the exact course of the road is not certain. Some maps of the period show the road continuing fairly straight to the river; however, at least two post-war maps depict the road as curving slightly to the left (north), following the river for a short distance, and then curving sharply back to the right before crossing the river. The road then continued roughly southeast, eventually curving back toward Tarrytown.

During the Revolutionary War, local militiamen built an earthen redoubt, or "lunette," on a hill just north of the church, its cannon overlooking the bridge across the Pocantico. Located in what is now the Sleepy Hollow Cemetery, Battle Hill is also the site of a Revolutionary Soldiers Monument dedicated in 1894, inscribed with the names of 76 patriots buried in the churchyard.

About 1806, the Post Road, including, of course, the river crossing, was relocated to follow more of a straight north-south route along the west side of the church, thereby eliminating the distinctive S-curve that it had formerly followed. This change was actually mentioned by Washington Irving in 1819 in "The Legend," when he suggested that the rerouting "so as to approach the church by the border of the mill-pond," the same course Broadway follows to this day, was at least in part to avoid sharing Ichabod Crane's fate.

(Irving probably would not have seen the rerouted Post Road, renamed the Highland Turnpike, prior to his departure for England; he most likely learned of it from his brother-in-law, Tarrytown native Henry Van Wart. Van Wart's possible contributions to "The Legend of Sleepy Hollow" are discussed in more detail in the next chapter.)

A Series of Wooden Bridges

The existing Washington Irving Memorial Bridge was built in 1912, funded by William Rockefeller (who refused to have his name engraved on the memorial plaque attached to the bridge). The 1912 bridge was preceded by a stone bridge, built in 1872 at Old Broadway, just slightly east of the current bridge location.

The 1872 stone bridge was itself preceded by a series of wooden bridges, several of which are pictured in 19th-century engravings or photographs. These wooden bridges, having been exposed to the elements, particularly the New York winters, were apparently replaced periodically with slightly improved designs, and each bridge located slightly to the west of its predecessor. (Henry Steiner identifies several different wooden bridges in his *Place Names of Historic Sleepy Hollow and Tarrytown*.)

A few of these wooden bridges may be found incorrectly identified by various sources – articles, websites, postcards, etc. – as "the original headless horseman bridge," apparently due to their relatively primitive appearances.

One of the earliest known bridge illustrations is an engraving by Benson Lossing for his *Pictorial Field Book of the Revolution*, first published in 1850. This Revolutionary War-era bridge (possibly the one remembered by Irving from his 1798 visit?) existed until the late 1830s. A rear view of the Old Dutch Church is visible in the background; does this view reflect the actual location of the bridge relative to the church, or is it a matter of artistic license?

*Early wooden bridge (Engraved by
Benson J. Lossing in 1850)*

*Another early bridge (Photographed by
George G. Rockwell in 1863)*

A slightly more modern-looking wooden bridge, photographed in 1863 by George G. Rockwell, was built around 1840. This bridge, featuring additional diagonal support beams, was also the subject of an engraving by P. A. Weber of Tarrytown, which appeared in 1866, and again in 1871, in *Harper's Weekly*. The Weber engraving shows a very similar view and was probably based on the Rockwell photo.

Another wooden bridge was pictured in 1866 in Benson Lossing's *The Hudson from the Wilderness to the Sea*. This may or may not be the same bridge as photographed by Rockwell in 1863; the subtle differences in the bridge's appearance may be attributed to artistic interpretation. While any landmarks included in the backgrounds of the previous engravings are difficult to discern, the 1866 Lossing engraving clearly pictures a side view of the church, which, *if accurate*, would place this bridge very close to the location of the 1872 stone bridge.

Yet another even more modern-looking wooden bridge appears in an undated Currier and Ives lithograph, likely published in the 1870s. However, the rear view of the church in the background suggests that this was meant to be an "artistic" rendering of the original colonial-era bridge, and not the then-current (circa 1870) bridge.

So... Where Was "The Original" Headless Horseman Bridge?

A number of Colonial-era maps and surveys of the Sleepy Hollow region are still extant, including works by Robert Erskine (1778 and 1779), William Adams (1788), and Christopher Colles (1789), as well as several "anonymous" maps in the collections of various historical societies. However, the focus of most of them appears to have been the routes of the various roads, and the locations of property lines. Most maps tended to depict the Pocantico River as a vague squiggle, rather than showing its actual shape, making it exceedingly difficult to discern exactly where the Post Road crossed the river.[38]

There are two maps, however, that do provide fairly accurate depictions of the river: an unsigned hand-drawn map titled "Manor of Philipsburgh, Tarwetown, 1725-1795," which is in the collection of the Historical Society serving Sleepy Hollow and Tarrytown, and a 1785 "Plan of the Manor of Philipsburg in the County of Westchester," prepared for the Commission of Forfeitures by surveyor John Hill. Both maps show the Post Road crossing the Pocantico at about the same location, northeast of the church, and in between two "arcs" in the river.[39]

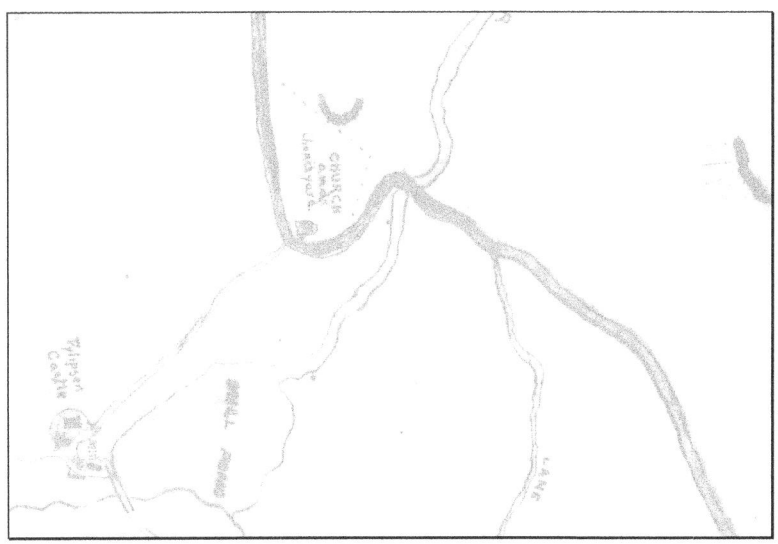

Detail from unsigned "Tarwetown 1725-1795" map (Collection of The Historical Society, Inc., Serving Sleepy Hollow and Tarrytown)

The Pocantico River has a very distinctive shape. Proceeding upstream (toward the east) from the modern-day Irving Memorial Bridge, the river is relatively straight for about 200 feet, then makes a sharp 90-degree turn to the southeast, just past the William Smith Memorials location. This is followed by a long, sweeping arc to the northeast.

Modern-day Dell Street generally parallels this 240-foot "arc," with a series of more than 30 side-by-side parking spaces lining the southern bank of the river.

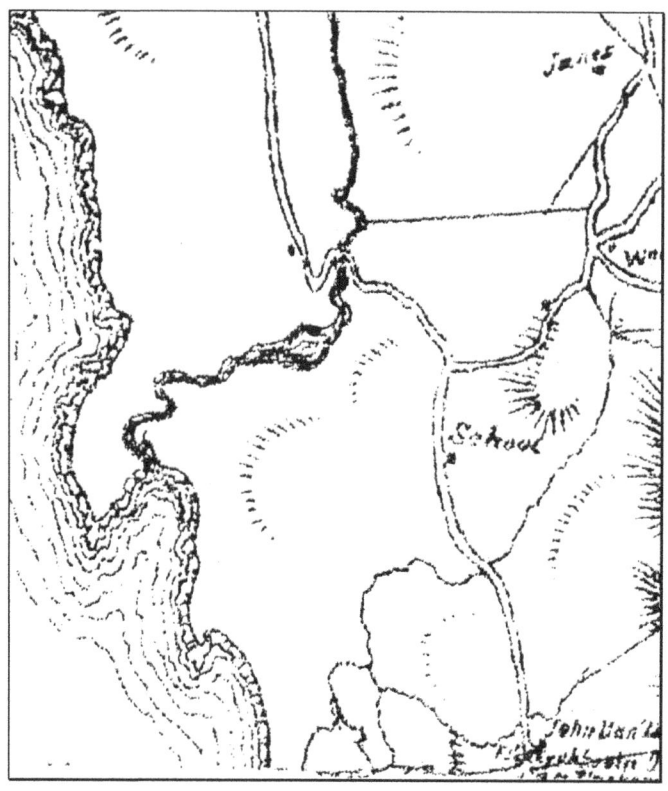

Detail from 1785 John Hill map created for the Commission of Forfeitures (From Scharf's History of Westchester County, New York, *1886)*

After the parking lot, the river then curves to the left, proceeding north for approximately 180 feet before curving back to the east; this is followed by a smaller arc, after which the river continues almost due north. (Note that we are still proceeding *upstream*; the river would actually be flowing toward us as we trace its shape from west to east...)

It is at the point where the Pocantico begins curving back to the east, before the final smaller arc, that both the John Hill and the "1725-1795" maps place the location of the post-Revolution bridge. *This corresponds to an area behind a private residence currently located at 47 Dell Street.*

Based on the unsigned 1725-1795 map and the John Hill 1785 map, could this be the (approximate) location of the post-Revolutionary War bridge and Post Road?

But of course, this, like so many others, is only a *theory*, based on two very old maps which may or may not be totally accurate. (The 1785 John Hill map in particular, despite its apparent attention to detail, contains at least one major inaccuracy – it places the church on the west/left side of the Post Road rather than the east/right side!)

However, with that said, this theory is corroborated by at least one noted 19th century historian, *Tarrytown Argus* editor and publisher Marcius D. Raymond. In his essay "Washington at Tarrytown," which he presented at the December 16, 1890 meeting of the Tarrytown Historical Society, he described how the route of the Revolutionary-era road, after passing below the church, "wound around" towards the east and then north, crossing the river at what was then the *Brombacher property*.⁴⁰

Raymond was referring to the residence, and just across the river, the Pocantico Tool and Machine Works factory, established in 1868 by Charles Brombacher at the end of what is now Dell Street (known in the late 1800s as Brombacher Lane). The former site of the Brombacher lot is currently occupied by a cul-de-sac with a small cluster of houses... including 47 Dell Street.⁴¹

Baltus Van Tassel's Farm

"It was one of those spacious farmhouses, with high-ridged, but lowly-sloping roofs, built in the style handed down from the first Dutch settlers; the low projecting eaves forming a piazza along the front, capable of being closed up in bad weather."

We know that Baltus Van Tassel was a fictional character, but was his "substantial Dutch" farm inspired by a similar large farm that Irving may have noticed in the Tarrytown vicinity in 1798?

Jacob Mott House

The predominant Tarrytown tradition regarding the home of Katrina Van Tassel is that it was modeled after the old Jacob Mott House. The Mott House once stood at the northeast corner of what is now North Broadway and Hamilton Place.

The house was built in approximately 1714 by the patriarch of the Martling family, Abraham Martlenghs (1693-1761). It was described by historian Edgar Mayhew Bacon (1855-1935) as a "solid sturdy stone structure, designed to withstand the ravages of time and weather and to repel the attacks of savage neighbors."⁴²

When the Albany Post Road (then called the King's Highway) was being laid out in 1723, this house was the first one listed in the record of the route of the highway south of the Old Dutch Church.[43]

Following Abraham Martlenghs' death in 1761, his farm was divided into smaller lots, which were subsequently leased out by Frederick Philipse III.

Situated on a 160-acre parcel, the building is known to have been operated as a tavern during the Revolutionary War, although there is some confusion as to the identity of the lessee. Several historians, including Robert Bolton and Edgar Mayhew Bacon, state that the tavern was run by an Elizabeth Van Tassel. Other sources, including Thomas Scharf and Daniel Van Tassel, omit the name Elizabeth, and indicate that the property was leased from Philipse by Johannes (John) Van Tassel.

John Van Tassel (1737-1807) was a veteran of the French and Indian War, and was a private in the Westchester County Militia during the American Revolution. Could Elizabeth have been a relative who operated the tavern on John's behalf when he found himself called away by his military duties?

Genealogical records do not show John to have had any close relatives – sisters, daughters, etc. – named Elizabeth. His wife, Rachel, did have a cousin Cornelius Van Tassel who was married to the former Elizabeth Storm; could she have been the Elizabeth who (possibly) ran the tavern in John's absence? The identity of Elizabeth Van Tassel remains a mystery...

The Van Tassel Tavern was used as the headquarters of the Continental Army whenever they found themselves "in this neighborhood." At some point, according to local tradition, a British cannon ball "found the tavern, but was considerate enough to enter by the window instead of making a breach in the walls."[44]

After the War, the property was purchased by John Van Tassel from the Commission of Forfeitures. Contemporary sales records indicate that the property was "now possessed" by John Van Tassel, which suggests that it had been John, and not Elizabeth, who had leased the property from Philipse.

John Van Tassel was the owner of the property when Washington Irving visited Sleepy Hollow as a youth in 1798. At this time, it is possible that Irving may have met John's then 24-year-old daughter, Catharine Van Tassel...

The structure was sold in March 1800 to Joseph Cutler. The property changed hands several more times in the early 1800s, first to Roelof (Ralph) Van Houter, Jr., followed by a Mr. Austin "about 1816," then Jonathan Odell in 1818, then Andrew Lamouroux, and then Jacob Lawrence Mott in 1826.[45]

Jacob Mott House (from 1900 New England Magazine *article)*

Jacob Mott (1813-1891), the son of Jacob Lawrence Mott, purchased the then 80-acre property from his father in 1834 for $3,800.[46] Washington Irving, who relocated to Sunnyside about the same time, became acquainted with Mott and his wife, the former Sarah Fowler (1817-1895). According to Bacon, Irving "was a frequent visitor at the old house."[47]

According to local lore, Mrs. Mott stated that Irving had confided to her that he "had in mind the post-Revolutionary Van Tassel Inn" as the residence of the fictional Katrina Van Tassel.[48] It was further asserted by Bacon that it was "due to his direct interposition that Mr. Jacob Mott refrained from making damaging alterations in the building after his purchase of it."[49]

A somewhat more romanticized view of the Mott House (Watercolor by Edgar Mayhew Bacon, 1897)

In "The Legend of Sleepy Hollow," Washington Irving provided a clue to the location of the Van Tassel farm, mentioning "the great tree where the unfortunate Major Andre was taken, *and which stood in the neighborhood.*"[50] The former site of Major Andre's Tree is indeed "in the neighborhood," only about a quarter mile north of the original location of the Jacob Mott House.

Old photographs of the Mott House show a "piazza" (porch) as described by Irving in "The Legend." Some have observed that the building seems smaller than the "spacious farmhouse" of the story, but this is easily attributed to "artistic license" on the part of Washington Irving.

The farmland surrounding the Jacob Mott House was gradually "sold off piece by piece" until only four acres remained.[51] The structure was torn down in 1896, and the Washington Irving High School constructed on the site. The school was renamed the Frank R. Pierson School in the 1920s. (The door from the razed Mott House was preserved and displayed for a time in the hall of the school as the "traditional" door of Katrina Van Tassel's house. It is currently in the collection of the Historical Society Serving Sleepy Hollow and Tarrytown.)

The school building was sold in 1983 and is now occupied by Landmark Condominiums.

Washington Irving's Sunnyside

There are others who believe that the original castle of Baltus Van Tassel was not the Mott House at all, but was actually Washington Irving's home, Sunnyside – located about two miles south of Tarrytown, and situated "on the banks of the Hudson," just as described in the story.

The house was already being associated with Baltus Van Tassel even before Irving took possession of it. A January 1835 *Westchester Herald* article (reprinted in both the January 30 *The Sun* and the February 7 *New York Mirror*) announced Irving's purchase, stating that a previous owner had been a Van Tassel, "one at least of whose descendants has been immortalized in story by the racy pen of its present gifted proprietor." The article continued, "We also understand that it is the identical house at which the memorable tea-party was assembled... in the inimitable Legend of Sleepy Hollow, on that disastrous night..."[52]

Irving, whether deliberately or not, also linked Sunnyside to his "Sleepy Hollow" story in his 1839 "Wolfert's Roost" essays in *The Knickerbocker* magazine. He wrote that at one time "it was in the possession of the gallant family of the Van Tassels, who have figured so conspicuously in [Knickerbocker's] writings"; Irving also later referred to it as "the mansion of the Van Tassels."[53]

The original structure which occupied the Sunnyside site was "a substantial log house" which, along with several outbuildings, was situated on 159 acres. Built around 1650, it is believed to have been one of the region's earliest homes, and some accounts state that it was second in size only to the manor house of Frederick Philipse himself. The house was leased by Philipse to Wolfert Acker (sometimes spelled Ecker) in 1685.[54]

Wolfert Acker (1668-1753) was at one time a counselor to New Netherland Governor Peter Stuyvesant, and was employed by the Dutch colonial government as tax collector of Philipsburg Manor.

In December 1692, Acker married Maretje Sibouts, with whom he fathered three sons, Steven (1693-??), Sybout (1698-1771) and Abraham (1703-1772), and one daughter, Mary (1696-??).

Acker purportedly favored the motto "lust in rust" (peace in quiet), and called his home "Wolfert's Roost," or Wolfert's Rest... although one might wonder how restful his existence there truly was, as his wife, according to legend, was said to have been exceedingly domineering. Irving himself later alleged that "the cock of the Roost was the most hen-pecked bird in the country."[55]

Wolfert Acker was a deacon and elder of the Old Dutch Church of Sleepy Hollow. When he died in 1753, he was interred in a crypt below the church, beside Philipse and his wife, and several other church elders.

Subsequent generations saw several marriages between the descendants of Wolfert Acker and members of the Van Tassel family. One of Wolfert's grandsons, Abraham Acker (1735-1811), married one Catherine Van Tassel (1733-1806). The lease to Wolfert's Roost was bought from Abraham Acker by Catherine's brother, Jacob Van Tassel.

Jacob Van Tassel (1744-1840) was the owner of the property during the Revolutionary War years, the period Irving dubbed "the Heroic Age of the Roost."[56]

Van Tassel was a well-known local patriot. He joined the Westchester County Militia in 1776, achieving the rank of Lieutenant in 1778. He also allowed "The Roost" to be used as one of the stations of the Water Guard, who used whaleboats to patrol the river and harass British vessels.

Van Tassel was also famed for his "goose gun," which was kept "on a row of hooks, above his fire-place... ready charged and primed for action." Whenever a British vessel ventured within range, he would take down the goose gun, and send "a shower of slugs and buckshot" – or the occasional load of nails – raining down on the startled enemy below.[57]

Following one of his "forays" with the militia in July 1779, Lt. Van Tassel was captured by the British and imprisoned in New York City for the remainder of the war. During his absence, Wolfert's Roost and the adjoining buildings were looted and burned by the British.[58]

Lt. Van Tassel was released in November 1781 as part of a prisoner exchange, and returned to Westchester County, where he first learned of the surrender of Cornwallis.[59]

Van Tassel purchased the Wolfert's Roost property for 500 pounds from the Commission of Forfeitures on December 6, 1785. He rebuilt his home, but on a much smaller scale, as a two-room stone cottage.

Captain Oliver Ferris (1753-1825) bought the property from Jacob Van Tassel in March 1802. Upon his death in 1825, the property passed to his son, Benson Ferris.[60]

Benson Ferris was the Roost's owner in August 1832 when Washington Irving made his first real visit to the region since his return from Europe. Irving was a houseguest of his nephew Oscar Irving when he apparently took notice of the stone cottage next door.

Many biographers have claimed that Irving had longed to own Wolfert's Roost ever since first seeing it as a boy in 1798. While a romantic notion, it does not at first seem a very realistic one – at age 15, wouldn't Irving have been more interested in hunting squirrels and hearing ghost stories than in perusing real estate? However, as with many "local traditions," this one just might have a kernel of truth to it...

According to historian Thomas Scharf, Irving told the wife of Benson Ferris that while boating on the Hudson as a youth, he had rowed from Tarrytown down to Wolfert's Roost, where he came ashore and spent some time "loitering along the slopes." He said that "the place so deeply impressed him that he then first conceived the idea... of [one day] buying it as a home for himself."[61]

These comments to Mrs. Ferris were purportedly made in the presence of her son, Benson Ferris, Jr. He later claimed to remember the conversation "distinctly," and it was he who related the story to Scharf.[62]

Regardless of when Irving first laid eyes on Wolfert's Roost, it was in the fall of 1832 that he initiated efforts to buy it. In a November 1832 letter to his sister Catherine, Irving wrote, "I am more & more in the notion of having that little cottage below [Oscar's] house and wish you to tell him to get it for me. I am willing to pay a little unreasonably for it..."[63]

Oscar's initial negotiations with Benson Ferris apparently fell through, and Irving "gave it up" for almost two years. However, in the fall of 1834, Ferris decided to build himself a new home on property he owned "above on the turnpike road," and he "was therefore more willing to sell." Irving's nephew "concluded the bargain" with Ferris in November 1834.[64]

Washington Irving finally succeeded in purchasing the house, along with 10 acres of land, in June 1835 for $1,800.[65] He did not immediately name his new home Sunnyside; in letters written in the months following the purchase, he typically referred to it as, simply, "the cottage."

Wolfert's Roost as Irving would have first seen it
(Watercolor by Irving's architect, George Harvey, 1835)

Irving hired artist George Harvey (1800-1878) to oversee the renovations. Irving and Harvey would collaborate on the artistic transformation of the stone structure into a pleasing blend of several architectural styles, including Dutch, Scottish and Spanish.[66]

While the "crow-stepped" gables are reminiscent of the colonial Dutch homes in early Manhattoes (Manhattan), Irving was obviously also influenced by his friend Sir Walter Scott's estate in Scotland, Abbotsford, which features similar gables. The resemblance is apparent when viewing pictures of Abbotsford – from some angles, Irving's home looks almost a miniature version of Scott's mansion.

(The tower, which contains four bedrooms, was added by Irving much later, in 1847, as a nod to the monastic towers of Spain, where he had just spent the previous four years as Ambassador.)[67]

Abbotsford, home of Sir Walter Scott; the towers, arches and stepped gables likely influenced Sunnyside's design. (From an 1890 photograph)

Irving wrote to his brother Peter in October 1835 that he planned to "write a legend or two" about his new purchase, "by way of making it pay for itself" – an apparent reference to the rapidly escalating renovation costs![68] These "legends" would eventually take the form of several mock Letters to the Editor of *The Knickerbocker* magazine, penned under the pseudonym Geoffrey Crayon, which were ultimately edited and repackaged as "The Chronicles of Wolfert's Roost."

Irving probably found it serendipitous that his new home had at one time been "inhabited by one of the Van Tassels," and undoubtedly enjoyed playing up the connection to his story.[69]

As the remodeling progressed, Irving appears to have still been in the process of learning the history of his new home. He first referred to it as "The Roost" in a September 28, 1836 letter to his friend Gouverneur Kemble, then again in a December 11, 1836 letter to his niece, Sarah Paris – had he only just heard the story of Wolfert Acker?[70]

Irving's fanciful "history" of his home, titled "A Chronicle of Wolfert's Roost," was first published in the April 1839 issue of *The Knickerbocker* magazine. In it, he blended a good deal of actual local history with more than a few Knickerbocker-isms, including a fictionalized account of how "he" (writing as Geoffrey Crayon) had first met the "venerable historian of the New-Netherlands," Diedrich Knickerbocker, when he was a houseguest of Jacob Van Tassel at the Roost. According to Crayon/Irving, Knickerbocker was then poring over ancient documents "pertaining to the Dutch dynasty" which had been "carried off" by Wolfert Acker when he left New Amsterdam; these would form the basis of Knickerbocker's *History of New York*.[71]

In contrast, the *true* details of the Revolutionary War exploits of Jacob Van Tassel contained in "Wolfert's Roost" were apparently obtained from Van Tassel himself when Irving interviewed him at his Greenwich Street home in Manhattan in 1839. Irving painted a vivid picture of the "gray-headed patriarch," who was then age 95, sitting by the fire "surrounded by his children, and grand-children, and great-grandchildren, all listening to his tales of the border wars."[72]

Irving delighted in keeping his home "full as a dove-coat." The inhabitants included his widowed brother Ebenezer's five daughters, Catherine Ann, Sarah, Julia, Mary Elizabeth, and Charlotte; occasionally Ebenezer himself, "whenever he [could] be spared from town"; and Irving's sister Catherine Paris with her daughter Sarah. Irving happily wrote in 1838, "I have generally some half dozen nieces with me to take care of my flower beds and to show their bright faces at every window." He continued, "It does not often fall to the lot of an old bachelor to be so well off for 'woman kind.' "[73]

Sunnyside after restorations
(Engraved by Benson J. Lossing, 1850)

A May 8, 1841 letter to his old friend Joseph C. Cabell bears the first reference to "Sunnyside Cottage, near Tarrytown" – soon shortened to just "Sunnyside."[74]

Except for a few years spent as Minister to Spain, Sunnyside would be Irving's beloved home for the remainder of his life.

After Irving's death in November 1859, Sunnyside passed to his nieces, Ebenezer's daughters Catherine and Sarah. They continued to live there until 1875, at which time they transferred the property to their nephew, Alexander Duer Irving, the son of Pierre Munroe Irving (and therefore Washington's great-nephew).

Alexander in turn willed the property in 1910 to his son, Louis, who lived there with his family during the summer months. Louis Irving was the last member of the Irving family to own Sunnyside, selling the property in 1945 to John D. Rockefeller, Jr., who had a strong interest in historic preservation.[75] Rockefeller opened Sunnyside to the public in 1947.

In the late 1950s, Sunnyside was carefully restored to its Washington Irving-era condition, which included the dismantling of a large wing added by Alexander Irving in 1896.[76] Most furnishings, including Irving's writing desk (a gift from his publisher, G. P. Putnam), are original. Sunnyside was declared a National Historic Landmark in 1962.

Sunnyside is now maintained and operated as a museum by Historic Hudson Valley, <WWW.HUDSONVALLEY.ORG>, which offers guided tours from May to November; Sunnyside is closed to visitors during the winter months.

Van Alen House, Kinderhook

As with Ichabod Crane's schoolhouse, many Kinderhook residents have long maintained that the residence of Katrina Van Tassel was located in Kinderhook, and not in Sleepy Hollow at all. "Local tradition" states that Washington Irving became acquainted with the prototype of Katrina in 1809 when she lived in the historic Luykas Van Alen House, located on the old Albany Post Road (now Route 9H), about a half mile from the Van Ness estate, now Lindenwald.

The house, which was built in 1737 by Luykas Van Alen (1682-1754?), is considered to be one of the finest examples of early Dutch architecture in the United States. Constructed of hand-made brick said to have been imported from Holland, the 69-foot structure features high sloping roofs and contains a large hall, or great room, not unlike Irving's description of the large hall "which formed the center of the mansion" of Baltus Van Tassel.[77]

Luykas Van Alen House, Kinderhook, New York
(Photo courtesy of Glenn Fisher)

However, even this description falls short – unlike the Van Tassel manor, the Van Alen House did not have a "piazza along the front." Although some early 20th century photographs show a small covered porch at the main entrance, this was evidently a more recent addition and not part of the original design, which featured a stoop at each Dutch door.

Following Luykas Van Alen's death "about" 1754, the property passed to one of his sons, Laurens (1727-1812), which is reflected in the 1790 Census. At some point in the early 1800s, although the exact date is uncertain, the property came into the possession of Laurens' son, David Van Alen (1752-1846), and his wife Maria (1762-1852), who lived there with their six children: Jane, Peter, Maria, Elizabeth, Cecelia and Helen.[78]

It was the youngest daughter, Helen, who was, *according to tradition*, regarded as "the belle of Kinderhook," and believed by many to have been Irving's inspiration for the character of Katrina Van Tassel. (Helen Van Alen is discussed at length in a later chapter...)

The house continued to be inhabited by members of the Van Alen family until the 1930s, when it was sold to a distant relative, also named Van Alen, but not directly descended from Luykas.

The then unoccupied structure fell into disrepair until 1964, when it was donated to the Columbia County Historical Society. The house was restored to its 18th century appearance and decorated with period furnishings made in the Hudson Valley.

The Luykas Van Alen House was designated a National Historic Landmark in December 1967. A historical marker in front of the property reads "Katrina Van Tassel Resided in this House According to Tradition." (Note: The marker was knocked over by a snowplow in February 2014; as of this writing, it has not yet been replaced...)

In addition to the Van Alen House having been the home of Helen Van Alen, Kinderhook proponents look to the existence of slavery as more evidence that Irving had this house in mind when he described the home of Baltus Van Tassel.[79]

Irving did not explicitly state, but rather implied that Baltus owned slaves (although we get the feeling that he was probably a kind slave owner). Ichabod's lessons were "suddenly interrupted by the appearance of a negro," sent by Baltus to deliver an invitation to his quilting frolic; and at the party itself, the music was provided by a "gray-headed negro." We were also told that "Ichabod's dancing was the admiration of all the negroes; who, having gathered of all ages and sizes, from the farm and from the neighborhood, stood forming a pyramid of shining black faces at every door and window..."[80]

Van Alen House advocates argue that Irving could not have been describing scenes he had observed as a youth visiting Tarrytown, as slavery was relatively non-existent in the region in 1798. They point out that while slavery was legal in New York State until 1827, only large landowners, including Frederick Philipse III, had owned slaves; the other Tarrytown area farmers were Philipse's tenants, not property owners. After the war, when the confiscated Philipse properties were parceled and sold, the new owners of these farms simply continued working them without slaves. The Philipse family's slaves were freed in 1786, 12 years before Irving first arrived in Sleepy Hollow.[81]

On the other hand, the Van Alens *were* slave owners. Since it was customary among the Dutch for slaves to live under the same roof with their owners, they would have been allowed to attend, at least as spectators, the various "frolics" that took place at the house. It has been suggested that Irving's vivid description of "shining black faces at every door and window" may have been something he had actually witnessed at the Van Alen House.[82]

It should be noted, however, that Irving did not need to venture to the Van Alen House to encounter slaves – his host, William P. Van Ness, was also a slave owner. The 1810 Census for Kinderhook counted four slaves among the 13 members of the Van Ness household.

Also, Irving's observations of slavery were not limited to Kinderhook. Having visited Virginia in the summer of 1807, his journals and notebooks from that period contain a number of references to slavery. In reality, the well-traveled Irving could have been describing something he had seen anywhere, not necessarily at a party at the Van Alen House.

The Luykas Van Alen House is currently maintained and operated as a museum, open to the public during the summer months, by the Columbia County Historical Society, <WWW.CCHSNY.ORG>.

So... Which house was it??

This is not an easy question to answer, as *none* of the structures that are claimed to have been the model for the Van Tassel farm completely match the description Irving provided in his story.

Nineteenth-century photographs and sketches of the Mott House depict it as a quaint cottage – possibly too small to have been the model for the "substantial" home of the Van Tassels. Some renderings show a covered porch, or piazza, as described in the story, but this may have been a later addition, as the original structure is believed by many to have possessed the traditional "stoop" found at the front entrance of most early Dutch dwellings.

Like the fictional Van Tassel residence, the original location of the Mott House *was* "in the neighborhood" of Andre's Tree, which was just a short distance up the Post Road. However, the house was not "situated *on the banks* of the Hudson," although it could be argued that the site does *overlook* it... a matter of semantics? Artistic license?

Sunnyside, on the other hand, *is* on the banks of the Hudson, but its appearance does not match Irving's description of Baltus Van Tassel's farmhouse: "one of those spacious farmhouses, with high-ridged, but lowly-sloping roofs" and "a piazza along the front, capable of being closed up in bad weather."

This is quite different from Irving's Sunnyside, which he quite accurately described in 1839 as "a little old-fashioned stone mansion, all made up of gable-ends, and as full of angles and corners as an old cocked hat."[83]

The previous incarnation of Sunnyside, when it had been known as Wolfert's Roost prior to Irving's renovations in the 1830s, was a small stone cottage, nothing like the opulent Van Tassel manor of the story. This was the version that Irving would have seen as a youth in 1798.

Some have suggested some of the other regional manor houses as having been the original setting of the Van Tassel farm, including the Philipse Manor House, or possibly even Van Cortland Manor.

While it is possible that Irving may have been impressed by the grandeur of these buildings, the geography is completely wrong for both of them. Irving clearly placed his fictional Van Tassel farm *south* of the church, some distance down the Albany Post Road; Van Cortland Manor, however, is located in Croton-On-Hudson, about 8 miles *north* of Sleepy Hollow. (Could young Irving have ventured that far from Tarrytown?) Philipsburg Manor, also known as Castle Philipse, is even closer, just across the Post Road on the opposite side of the Mill Pond.

And we cannot ignore Kinderhook – the Van Alen House does have the high-ridged roof and the requisite great room in the center – but it is also missing the covered piazza, and is, of course, located in a different village altogether.

Could it be that like many of Irving's living and breathing characters, the Van Tassel mansion was a composite of several structures? While he possibly "had in mind" the Mott House, he could have also incorporated features found in other period homes. It would be easy for a writer of fiction to add a piazza or fancy parlor to an existing structure, or to expand the size of an otherwise modest dwelling... or for that matter, to move it, at least on paper, nearer to the banks of the Hudson.

Another possible clue was provided by *Knickerbocker* magazine editor Lewis Gaylord Clark in "Reminiscences of the late Washington Irving," a two-part tribute published in the months following Irving's death. Clark recounted "a memorable excursion which the writer hereof once made with Geoffrey Crayon through the wizard region of Sleepy Hollow." Clark recalled how, after hosting dinner at Sunnyside, "Mr. Crayon, in a light open wagon" drove them "over the high eastern hills that inclose the sheltered valley *where in their day lived and flourished old Baltus Van Tassel, and his blooming daughter Katrina.*"[84]

Clark was clearly under the impression that the Van Tassel manor was located someplace other than Sunnyside; had his tour guide, none other than "Mr. Crayon" himself, disclosed the location of Baltus' castle? It could also be argued that "high eastern hills" paints a fairly accurate picture of the original Mott House location, although the writer did not explicitly identify it as the structure.

With that said, the most likely candidate still seems to be the Mott House – simply because it is the only one that makes the claim (whether accurate or not) that the owners had been *told by Washington Irving* that he "had this house in mind" as the home of Katrina Van Tassel when he wrote the story. All of the other theories are complete speculation based on the structures possessing a few similarities to the fictional Van Tassel manor, and/or they happened to have been inhabited at one time or another by someone with the surname Van Tassel.

Irving enjoyed pointing out that Wolfert's Roost had formerly belonged to "one of the Van Tassels" – well, yes, it did... to JACOB Van Tassel, not Baltus! As prolific as the Van Tassels were in the region, surely many homes could be said to have belonged to someone with that name. As

Edgar Mayhew Bacon wrote in 1898, "you could not throw a stone in Tarrytown without hitting a Van Tassel."[85]

And we mustn't forget that the Mott House, when Irving would have known it in 1798, had also been inhabited by one of the Van Tassels – JOHN Van Tassel – who also happened to have a daughter named Catharine...

Tracing Ichabod's Flight

"It was the very witching time of night that Ichabod, heavy-hearted and crest-fallen, pursued his travel homewards, along the sides of the lofty hills which rise above Tarry Town..."

The quickest and easiest way to reenact Ichabod Crane's flight from the Headless Horseman would be to simply start at Landmark Condominiums, located at the corner of Broadway and Hamilton Place, then follow Broadway north for a little less than a mile to the Washington Irving Memorial Bridge, just south of the Old Dutch Church. The modern bridge even displays a sign declaring it (incorrectly) to be located at the site of the original bridge from Irving's story, thus marking the end of our journey.

BUT, knowing all the changes that have taken place since the 1790s – roads rerouted, swamps drained, bridges relocated, buildings razed, to name but a few – can't we find a more historically accurate way to trace the route of Ichabod Crane's final flight?

Ichabod's journey probably would have indeed begun at the corner of Broadway and Hamilton Place, at one time the site of the old Mott House (although there are some who would still argue that we should begin several miles further south, at Sunnyside). Turning north from the Van Tassels' onto the Albany Post Road (the only real thoroughfare at the time), the three mile wide expanse of the Hudson known as the Tappan Zee would have been below him, to his left, with "lofty hills" rising above him to his right – just as described in the story.

"In the center of the road stood an enormous tulip-tree…"

Continuing north for about a quarter mile, Ichabod would have encountered Major Andre's Tree, towering "like a giant" in the middle of the Post Road, which split to go around it on the right and the left. This would have been approximately in front of the current Warner Library site, where Wildey Street meets North Broadway.

Historians generally agree that south of the Warner Library, modern-day Broadway/Route 9 closely follows the route of the original Post Road. North of the library, however, as it approaches Patriots Park, modern Broadway begins curving to the northwest, where the original Post Road continued on a more north-northeast route.

The course of the original Post Road (also known at various times as the King's Highway and/or the Queen's Highway) was changed about 1806 when the responsibility for road maintenance was transferred to the Highland Turnpike Company. The road was widened, straightened, had toll booths added, and was renamed the Highland Turnpike. (It did not become known as Broadway until sometime in the 1850s.)

The exact route of the original road north of the library is uncertain; or rather, as Edgar Mayhew Bacon observed in his 1897 *Chronicles of Tarrytown and Sleepy Hollow*, the route "has been determined differently by every man who has written on the subject."[86]

"As he approached the stream his heart began to thump… In the dark shadow of the grove, on the margin of the brook, he beheld something huge, misshapen, black and towering…"

Approximately 200 yards further up the road, Ichabod would have reached the crude log bridge spanning

Andre's Brook where it flowed into Wiley's Swamp. Village Historian Henry Steiner, citing a 1778 map by surveyor Robert Erskine, believes this bridge to have been located near the entrance of the John Paulding School, about 100 yards east of modern-day Broadway.[87]

"Away then they dashed, through thick and thin; stones flying, and sparks flashing at every bound…"

We know that the original Post Road was east of modern-day Broadway, but how far east? John Romer, writing in 1917, provided a possible clue in his statement that the original road was "officially closed by legislative enactment about the year 1838" due to the construction of the Old Croton Aqueduct.[88]

The Old Croton Aqueduct was essentially a tunnel system constructed between 1837 and 1842 to transport fresh water from the reservoir in Croton-On-Hudson (about 10 miles north of Tarrytown) south to New York City. When one traces the course of the Old Croton Aqueduct (which is now a popular hiking trail) on a modern topographic map, it becomes apparent that the builders, wherever possible, circumvented the steepest slopes and followed the course of existing ravines and valleys. These were often the same routes followed by the old trails and dirt roads of older times, which also tended to follow natural landscape features.

The avoidance of hills was actually a necessity, as the aqueduct, modeled after an ancient Roman design, was gravity-fed – no electric pumping stations in the 1840s! – designed with a downward slope of 13 inches per mile.

Following the creation of the new Post Road, also known as the Highland Turnpike, the old road would have remained, although it probably did not see as much use, and was probably not as well-maintained as when it had been the main thoroughfare. So what better place to construct the aqueduct, than to reclaim a mostly unused dirt road, already graded and cleared of timber?

Did the original Post Road, or some portions of it, follow the same course as that followed by the Old Croton Aqueduct? (And if not, why would the aqueduct construction necessitate the closing of the old Post Road?)

For anyone wishing to recreate Ichabod's flight from the Headless Horseman, it could be at least *approximated* by picking up the Old Croton Aqueduct hiking trail south of Sleepy Hollow High School, following it around the back of the building, and continuing northeast to Bedford Road. (The aqueduct actually passes *under* the school, but the hiking trail circumvents the building and links up again with the actual aqueduct route just north of the school; it then continues along the western edge of a large parking lot next to a baseball field.)[89]

"They had now reached the road which turns off to Sleepy Hollow; but Gunpowder, who seemed possessed with a demon, instead of keeping up it, made an opposite turn, and plunged headlong down hill to the left. This road leads through a sandy hollow, shaded by trees for about a quarter of a mile, where it crosses the bridge famous in goblin story..."

Approximately one-third of a mile north of Andre's Brook, the Post Road intersected with the Continental Road, identified on some period maps as the road to White Plains. The section of the Continental Road east of the Post Road is now Bedford Road; the section which extended west from the Post Road down to the Hudson River corresponds approximately to modern-day Beekman Avenue. (The segment leading to the river does not appear on the 1785 John Hill map, but it does appear on the "Tarwetown 1725-1795" map in the Historical Society's collection, as well as several other post-war maps or reproductions.)[90]

Ichabod wanted to turn right onto the Continental Road, which would have taken him northeast in the direction of the Mill Road, which corresponds to modern day Webber Avenue and Sleepy Hollow Road. Instead, Gunpowder bore to the left and continued north on the Post Road.

Where was the intersection of the Continental Road with the original Post Road, relative to the current Broadway/Bedford Road intersection?

Henry Steiner's estimate of the original route of the Post Road has it linking with what is now New Broadway[91]; consulting a modern Sleepy Hollow street map, this would put the Bedford Road crossing roughly 250 feet east of Broadway, or about halfway between Broadway and Pine Street.

Topographic maps do indicate a higher elevation at Bedford Road at this point, so bearing to the left toward what is now New Broadway could possibly correspond to Irving's account of Gunpowder "plunging down hill to left." New Broadway then passes between two slight hills, which *could* correspond to the "sandy hollow" described by Irving as the scene of Ichabod's final dash toward the bridge.

Edgar Mayhew Bacon, however, seemed to believe that the original intersection was about 500 feet further east, "somewhere near" the Old Croton Aqueduct crossing.[92] This seems to corroborate John Romer's statement linking the original Post Road to the aqueduct.

This theory is supported by at least two maps, one being the unsigned "Tarwetown 1725-1795" map, and the other a map in the Historical Society collection, published in September 1880 by "Geo. L. Wiley & Bro., C.E.," which depicted "Tarwe-town One Hundred Years Ago."[93]

Both of these maps show the old Post Road swinging far to the east, and skirting the southwest slope of Prospect Hill (now Cedar Hill) before curving back to the northwest to approach the bridge behind the Old Dutch Church.[94]

This corresponds very closely to the route of the Old Croton Aqueduct in the vicinity of Bedford Road and Cedar Hill. In fact, if one places a modern map showing the Old Croton Aqueduct Trail next to the "Tarwetown 1725-1795" map, the courses of the aqueduct and the Post Road match almost exactly – that is, assuming the "1725-1795" map is drawn to scale.

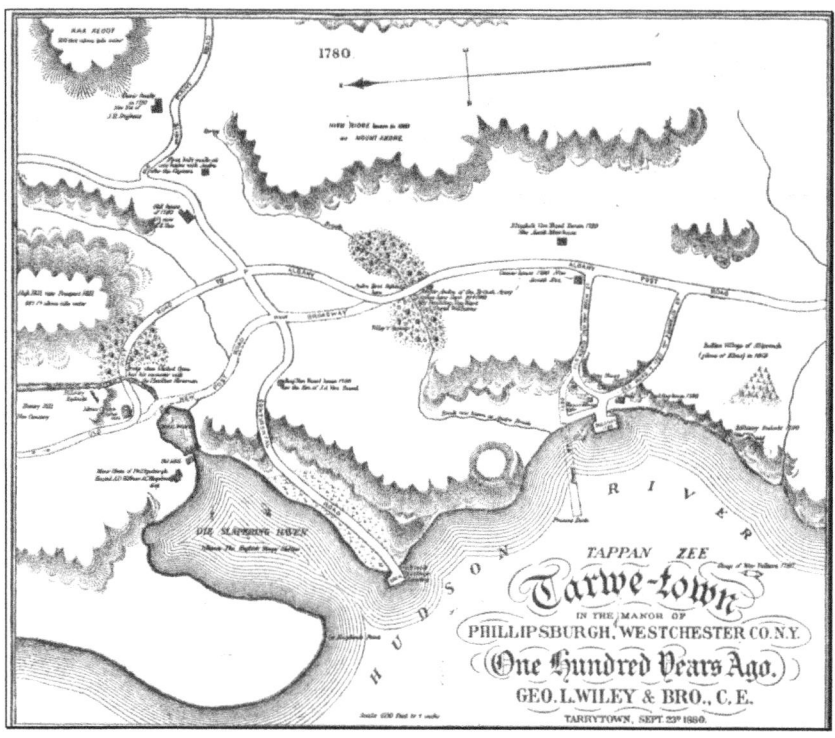

1880 George Wiley map showing the original route of the Albany Post Road swinging far to the east, "somewhere near" the Old Croton Aqueduct, and then skirting the base of Prospect Hill before crossing the Pocantico (Collection of The Historical Society, Inc., Serving Sleepy Hollow and Tarrytown)

Assuming the original Post Road did follow this route, then after crossing the Continental Road it would have continued along the southwest slope of Prospect Hill for approximately 750 feet. At this point the road would have been at an elevation of about 180 feet (as indicated by modern-day topographic maps), rapidly descending about 60 feet as it curved to the left toward what is now the Webber Park subdivision – could *this* have been the downhill "plunge" that Irving described?

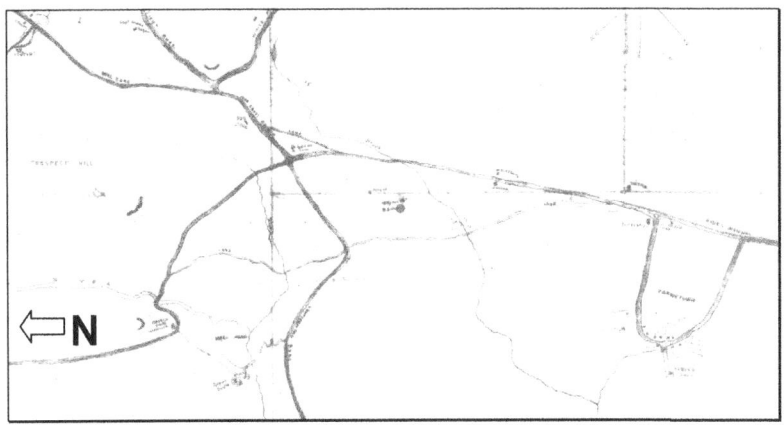

Detail from unsigned "Tarwetown 1725-1795" map also shows the original "King's Highway" swinging far to the east before curving back towards the church. (Collection of The Historical Society, Inc., Serving Sleepy Hollow and Tarrytown)

Throughout this section, we have referenced Washington Irving's descriptions of the roads about Tarrytown and Sleepy Hollow, including approximate distances between various landmarks. But how accurate were Irving's descriptions? In a word, *very*. Reporting to Irving in April 1820 on the public's reaction to his story, his friend Henry Brevoort declared, "The old people are surprised at your accurate recollections of the localities of the place and its inhabitants."[95]

Tarrytown journalist Daniel Van Tassel also commented in 1898, "how remarkably correct is the author as to the return trip of Ichabod Crane up the Highland Turnpike... the meeting of the roads, west down the hill to the old Dutch church, and east over the rising ground along Bedford Road on the way to Sleepy Hollow."[96]

Van Tassel also suggested that Irving's writings were "so accurate in detail" that they "must have come from notes taken on the spot," rather than from memory.[97] Irving's earliest known journal was kept during the summer of 1803, in which he documented his trip up the Hudson and westward through the New York wilderness, in the company of the Hoffman family – could he have also kept an as yet undiscovered (and therefore unpublished) journal of his 1798 visit to Sleepy Hollow? Possibly... but more likely, his brother-in-law, Tarrytown native Henry Van Wart, helped to jog his memory about some of the finer details.

"'If I can but reach that bridge,' thought Ichabod, 'I am safe...'"

From this point on, the route would cross, from east to west, Gory Brook Road, then New Broadway, then Anderson Avenue... ultimately ending up at the river crossing behind 47 Dell Street. (For the home stretch between Cedar Hill and the river, there is really no way to *directly* follow Ichabod's route without cutting through the yards of private residences – *not* recommended!)

"Just then he saw the goblin rising in his stirrups, and in the very act of hurling his head at him... he was tumbled headlong into the dust, and Gunpowder, the black steed, and the goblin rider, passed by like a whirlwind..."

Ichabod would have made his crash-landing in the vicinity of what is now the Old Dutch Church maintenance garage, in the dirt driveway known as Horseman's Ride. The goblin rider (who apparently *could* cross the bridge after all) presumably raced up the knoll behind the church, returning to his unmarked grave somewhere in the Old Dutch Burying Ground...

Chapter 3

A Knickerbocker Story

"There is a Knickerbocker story which may please from its representation of American scenes. It is a random thing, suggested by recollections of scenes and stories about Tarrytown. The story is a mere whimsical band to connect descriptions of scenery, customs, manners, &c."

- Washington Irving, 1819

So reads Washington Irving's exceedingly modest assessment of what was to become his best-loved story!

As discussed previously in Chapter 1, Irving's handwritten manuscripts for *The Sketch Book* were mailed from England to Irving's brother Ebenezer in America in seven volumes. "The Legend of Sleepy Hollow" was included in the sixth installment, mailed on December 29, 1819.

Volume 6 of *The Sketch Book* was published in March of 1820. In addition to "The Legend of Sleepy Hollow," it also contained "The Pride of the Village" and "John Bull."

But *when* and *where* was "The Legend of Sleepy Hollow" actually written?

Castle Von Tromp

In his biography of his Uncle Washington, Pierre Munroe Irving stated, "The outline of this story had been sketched more than a year before" the completed manuscript was mailed to America, which would put the drafting of the outline sometime in mid to late 1818.

Continuing Pierre's narrative, the story was outlined "at Birmingham, after a conversation with his brother-in-law, Van Wart, who had been dwelling upon some recollections of his early years at Tarrytown..."[1]

Irving's brother-in-law, Henry Van Wart, was only five months younger than Washington, born on September 25, 1783 in Tarrytown, New York. Henry married Irving's sister Sarah in 1804, and they moved to England to establish a branch of the Irving family business, eventually settling in Birmingham.

The Henry and Sarah Van Wart residence was located at the corner of Legge Lane and Frederick Street in the fashionable Camden Hill (now called Newhall Hill) section of Birmingham, about 100 miles Northwest of London. The house, which Irving nicknamed "Castle Von Tromp," became like a second home to him.

Following the bankruptcy of his family's business in England earlier that spring, Washington Irving was disheartened, broke, and probably more than a little homesick. As he often did, he sought solace in the company of his sister, her husband, and their four children, arriving in Birmingham in late June, 1818.

Years later, author Elihu Burritt discussed Irving's frame of mind with Henry Van Wart, observing, "He had lost all that inspiration and glow of intellectual activity which once stimulated and rewarded his ambition to excel as a writer... and feared that he never should be able to shake it off and resume his literary life."2

"Castle Von Tromp," the home of Irving's brother-in-law Henry Van Wart, where "The Legend" was outlined in the summer of 1818 (From a watercolor by Thomas Wakeman, 1870)

Henry, a fellow New York transplant who had also tasted bankruptcy as an associate of P. and E. Irving, could easily empathize with his brother-in-law. Wishing to raise him from his slump, Henry engaged Irving in conversation about their younger days in Tarrytown, recalling "the laughable incidents they themselves had witnessed there; the oddest characters of the valley, the ridiculous legends and customs, habits, and sayings..."3

Van Wart, according to Pierre Munroe Irving, "touched upon a waggish fiction of one Brom Bones, a wild blade, who professed to fear nothing, and boasted of his having once met the devil on a return from a nocturnal frolic, and run a race with him for a bowl of milk punch."[4]

Henry Van Wart (Library of Congress)

One should not underestimate just how significant Henry Van Wart's contribution to the writing of "The Legend of Sleepy Hollow" may have actually been. Having grown up in Tarrytown, Henry could probably recite most of the "local tales and twilight superstitions"; he knew the names of all the local heroes (including his own Uncle Isaac, one of the captors of the spy Major Andre); and he had likely explored many of the local haunted spots. In addition to the exploits of Brom Bones, Van Wart surely regaled Irving with a number of other stories, both fact and fiction. He probably also provided a few long-forgotten details, filling in the gaps of Irving's own boyhood memories of Sleepy Hollow.

Continuing Pierre's narrative, "The imagination of the author suddenly kindled over the recital, and in a few hours he had scribbled off the framework of his renowned story, and was reading it to his sister and her husband. He then threw it by until he went up to London, where it was expanded into the present legend."[5]

Ichabod Crane or Rip Van Winkle?

BUT – here we have a contradiction. In Pierre's account, presumably obtained directly from his uncle, the story "framework" which he read to the Van Warts was for "The Legend of Sleepy Hollow." However, Henry Van Wart told Elihu Burritt that the morning following their discussion, it was "Rip Van Winkle" that Irving read to the family at the breakfast table, wearing an expression of "hope and gladness that set his face aglow."[6]

Versions of this anecdote have appeared in most biographies of Irving, as well as numerous magazine articles published over the years. Some identify the story Irving read to his hosts as "The Legend of Sleepy Hollow," while others declare that it was "Rip Van Winkle"; a few versions seem to combine the two, or remain (deliberately?) vague.

Is it possible that the conversation between the two men resulted in BOTH stories? Or, did the pair spend more than one night reminiscing – after all, Irving was the Van Warts' houseguest for about six weeks – and the details of two (or more) evenings blurred into one?

Irving, who had been teaching himself the German language in early 1818, may actually have had parts of "Rip Van Winkle" already completed prior to his visit. English Professor and Irving Scholar Henry Pochman, in a paragraph-by-paragraph comparison published in 1930, demonstrated that portions of "Rip Van Winkle" were direct translations of the German-language tale of "Peter Klaus the Goatherd."[7]

Although Pochman believed Irving's source to have been the version of "Peter Klaus" contained in Otmar's *Volks-Sagen nacherzuhlt von Otmar* ("Folktales Re-Told by Otmar"), Walter Reichart, writing in 1957, determined that his actual source had been Johann Gustav Busching's *Volks-Sagen, Marchen and Legenden*, published in Leipzig in 1812. In fact, Irving's copy of the Busching work may still be found in his library at Sunnyside.[8]

The "Peter Klaus" story in its original German was written in a simple prose style, and could have been easily translated by Irving using his German dictionary. Did Irving's notebooks already contain a partial translation of "Rip Van Winkle" when he boarded the coach to Birmingham?

What Irving may have taken away from his reminiscences with Van Wart was the inspiration to set his retelling of an old German folktale in an old-fashioned New York Dutch community, thereby transplanting the story from Germany's Harz Mountains to the Catskills of New York. Was this the story that Henry Van Wart so vividly remembered Washington Irving reading at the breakfast table?

Likewise, Irving could have made notes, both written and mental, of Brom Bones and other Sleepy Hollow tales, as related to him by Van Wart, for use in the not-too-distant future. Pierre Munroe Irving was very clear that one of the subjects the two men discussed was Brom Bones, down to the detail of the horse race for a bowl of punch.

The episode of "running a race... for a bowl of milk punch" clearly found its way into the completed "Sleepy Hollow" story; at the frolic at Van Tassel's, Brom Bones bragged about having challenged the Headless Horseman to a race "for a bowl of punch, and should have won it, too..."[9]

86

Also, during this same Birmingham visit, Irving received a letter from his friend Washington Allston, dated July 24, 1818, which contained the phrase "linked sweetness long drawn out," from a poem by John Milton.[10]

Irving incorporated this phrase into "The Legend" to describe the sound of Ichabod Crane's "nasal melody... floating from a distant hill" as he would sing psalm tunes to ward off evil spirits. This may be considered a piece of "circumstantial evidence" which adds credence to the theory that Irving was at least *contemplating* his story during the summer of 1818. Could the "linked sweetness" phrase in Allston's letter have so struck a chord with Irving that he jotted it down among his other Birmingham "Legend" notes for later use?

Armed with several outlines and partial sketches, Washington Irving returned to London in mid-August of 1818 – refreshed, confident and determined to succeed as a writer.[11]

Westminster Bridge

Following Irving's death, author N. P. Willis published an account of the writing of "The Legend of Sleepy Hollow" which he apparently obtained from Irving himself during a visit to Sunnyside in the summer of 1857:

> "Walking with his brother, one dull foggy Sunday, over Westminster Bridge, he got to telling the old Dutch stories which he had heard at Tarrytown, in his youth – when the thought suddenly struck him" – 'I have it! I'll go home and make a memoranda of these for a book!' And, leaving his brother to go to church, he went back to his lodgings and jotted down all the data; and, the next day – the dullest and darkest of London fogs – he sat in his little room and wrote out 'Sleepy Hollow' by the light of a candle."[12]

> The Legend of Sleepy Hollow.
>
> (Found among the papers of the late Diedrich Knickerbocker)
>
> A pleasing land of drowsy head it was,
> Of dreams that wave before the half-shut eye;
> And of gay castles in the clouds that pass,
> Forever flushing round a summer sky.
>   Castle of Indolence.
>
> In the bosom of one of the spacious coves which indent the eastern shore of the Hudson, at that broad expansion of the river denominated by the ancient Dutch navigators ~~of those waters~~ the Tappaan Zee, and where they always prudently shortened sail ~~and implored the protection~~ of St. Nicholas when they crossed, there lies a small market town or rural port, which by some is called Greensburgh, but which is more universally and properly known by the name of

First page of the original hand-written manuscript of "The Legend of Sleepy Hollow" (Courtesy of The New York Public Library, Astor, Lenox, and Tilden Foundations, Berg Collection of English and American Literature)

Willis' account seems to agree with Pierre Munro Irving's version, which states that while Irving conceived the "framework" of the story in Birmingham, it was not "expanded into the present legend" until sometime later, in London.

When was "The Legend" completed?

It is possible to estimate the approximate dates that Irving was drafting some of his sketches by noting the dates on his 1819-1820 correspondence with Henry Brevoort or his brother Ebenezer. In his letters, Irving often detailed which volumes were in work at various times, and when they were sent to Ebenezer.

While Irving's notebooks undoubtedly contained a number of outlines and partial drafts, it is also apparent from his letters to Brevoort and Ebenezer that he did not have a stockpile of finished stories ready for publication; rather, he mailed installments of *The Sketch Book* to Ebenezer as quickly as he completed them. He did not maintain a regular writing schedule, choosing to write only when inspired to do so. In Irving's own words, his "writing moods" were "very precarious."[13]

Although the "Sleepy Hollow" story was apparently *outlined* in the summer of 1818 in Birmingham, Irving probably did not begin working diligently on the actual manuscript until after the Volume 5 essays had been completed and posted to his brother, which was on October 28, 1819. Irving's primary focus in September and October was the completion of the fifth installment, which consisted of four Christmas stories that he hoped would see publication in December.[14]

(Irving's September 21, 1819 letter to Henry Brevoort contains a curious statement: "My mind gets running away from me now & then and breaking into subjects which are not fitted for the number in hand."[15] Was Washington Irving anxious to complete his Christmas volume so that he could get started on his ghost story?)

Another piece of "circumstantial evidence," this time in support of the premise that Irving penned the manuscript of "The Legend" during the November-December 1819 timeframe, may be found in a November 3, 1819 letter to Walter Scott. Discussing one of Scott's neighbors, "Lauchie Long Legs," whom Irving had met during his 1817 visit to Abbotsford, Irving recalled seeing him "striding along the profile of the knoll... with his flimsy garments fluttering about him."[16]

Compare this to Irving's description of Ichabod Crane: "To see him *striding along the profile* of a hill... with his clothes bagging and *fluttering about him*..."[17]

Did Washington Irving's recollection of the gangly appearance of Lauchie Long Legs help to shape his concept of what Ichabod Crane should look like? He clearly recycled his vivid description of "Lauchie" when first introducing us to the scarecrow-like Ichabod.

Assuming Irving continued the pattern he established with the previous five installments, the manuscripts of "The Legend of Sleepy Hollow" and "The Pride of the Village" were probably not completed until a day or two before their mailing date, December 29, 1819. (The third essay which would make up Volume 6, "John Bull," had already been mailed to Ebenezer in early August – it was originally intended for Volume 4, but was bumped to a later volume in favor of "Rural Funerals.")

Based on the above rationale, it appears reasonable to assume that the actual manuscript of "The Legend of Sleepy Hollow" was most likely written sometime between October 28 and December 29, 1819.

Where was "The Legend" written?

Having established the most likely "when" the story was written, is it possible to determine "where" Washington Irving actually wrote it?

Upon relocating to London from Liverpool in August 1817, Irving rented a room from a Mrs. Holloway in her residence on Cockspur Lane, where he likely wrote some of his earlier sketches.[18] However, by July or August 1819, Irving had apparently relocated to *21 Edward Street, Portland Place, London,* as evidenced by his correspondence.

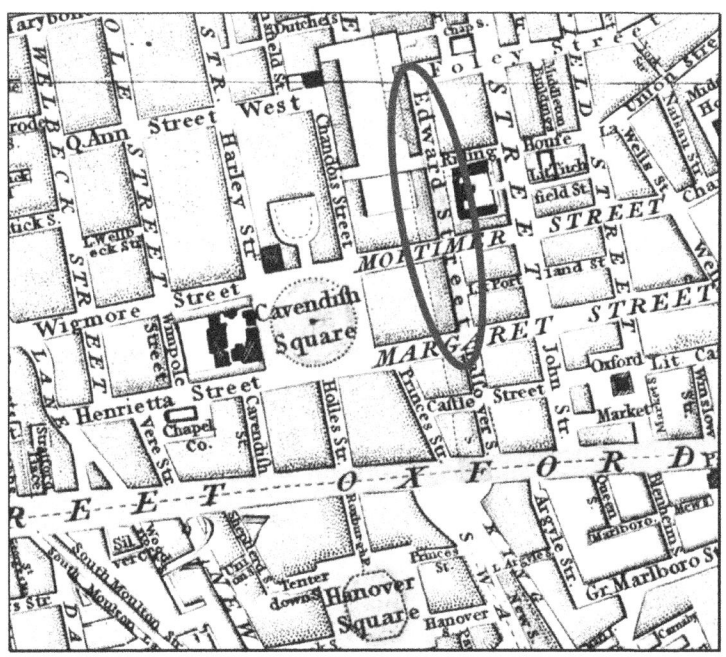

Detail from 1818 London map showing Edward Street – The Birthplace of "The Legend of Sleepy Hollow"!

The Edward Street address first appears on an August 20, 1819 letter to John G. Lockhart, and was used for the last time on a February 9, 1820 letter to Walter Scott.[19]

(Subsequent letters simply say "London," although Irving probably lived on Edward Street until August 1820 when he and his brother Peter left for an extended visit to Paris.[20])

Fortunately, Irving included the "Portland Place" qualifier on several of his letters, enabling us to distinguish *this* Edward Street from the seven other Edward Streets that existed in London at the time!

An 1818 London map shows the Edward Street close to Portland Place to have been only three blocks long, running north and south, and located one block east of still-existing Cavendish Square. It was bordered on the north by Foley Street (still-existing) and on the south by Margaret Street (also still-existing).

Edward Street was slightly less than two miles from Westminster Bridge – definitely a walk-able distance, albeit a long walk, for Irving to have made on that foggy morning he is said to have penned "The Legend."

Edward Street no longer exists. The three-block stretch that was once Edward Street is now part of modern-day Regent Street, adjacent to the University of Westminster (which did not exist in 1819 – originally Royal Polytechnic, it was built in 1838).

What exactly was located at 21 Edward Street? Was it a boarding house? A hotel? A friend's private residence? Efforts to find out have so far been unsuccessful.

And sadly, the precise location of the 21 Edward Street residence that might have been considered "The Birthplace of The Legend" appears to have also been lost to time...

Chapter 4

The Headless Horseman

"The dominant spirit, however, that haunts this enchanted region, and seems to be commander-in-chief of all the powers of the air, is the apparition of a figure on horseback without a head..."
- from "The Legend of Sleepy Hollow," 1820

When one hears the phrase "headless horseman," Washington Irving's "The Legend of Sleepy Hollow" usually comes to mind. Although Irving's Headless Horseman is probably the most famous, legends of headless ghosts, both on and off horseback, have been around for centuries.

Headless Horseman Legends

Headless ghost legends date as far back as ancient Egypt. In India, the Dund were headless ghosts on horseback with their heads tied to the pommel of their saddles. In Bengal, they were known as Skandhahata. Celtic legends of Ireland and Scotland feature headless apparitions on horseback called the Dullahan, who appear when someone is about to die.

In Arthurian legend, Sir Gawain lops off the head of the Green Knight, who then rides away carrying his head in his hand, vowing to return in a year and a day.

Sir Gawain and the Green Knight
(Medieval manuscript illumination)

Anne Boleyn, the second wife of England's infamous King Henry VIII, was beheaded in 1536, and to this day is said to haunt the Tower of London "with her head tucked underneath her arm."[1]

The most prevalent headless ghost legends seem to be from Germany. Some of these headless horseman folktales may be found in the writings of The Brothers Grimm and Johann Karl August Musaus.

The Headless Horseman

As the Europeans began to settle in North America in the 1600s and 1700s, they brought their customs and folklore with them. Headless horseman legends began to emerge throughout the American Colonies, including New York, Connecticut, New Jersey, Pennsylvania, and as far west as Kentucky.

In *Things That Go Bump in the Night*, Louis Jones describes an incident during the Revolutionary War where two British officers observed "one of their own hussars, elegant and soldierly" riding his horse down Alden's Lane in Philadelphia, carrying his own head in front of him on his saddle.[2]

"The Hesse-Cassel Corps of Field Jaegers, 1776-1783," painted by artist Don Troiani, pictures a company of Hessian soldiers crossing the mill bridge at Philipsburg Manor. (Copyright Don Troiani, WWW.HISTORICALIMAGEBANK.COM, used with permission)

It has been suggested that some headless horseman legends were imported to the United States from Germany by Hessian soldiers during the Revolutionary War. "Hessian" is a generic term for the approximately 30,000 mercenary soldiers, primarily from the Hesse province in Germany, who were hired by the King of England to supplement the British forces fighting in the American Colonies.

There was a strong Hessian presence in the Tarrytown region during the war. The "jaegers" ("hunters"), dressed in "green coats with carmine collars, cuffs, and lapels, with green vests trimmed with gold"[3] consisted of foot soldiers as well as mounted troopers, most notably the Jaeger zu Pferd ("mounted hunters") commanded by Captain Friedrich Heinrich Lorey.[4]

After the war, some 5,000 former Hessians married and settled in the United States and Canada, and "soon after they had done so, there sprang up a legend of the headless trooper who at night rose from his grave in the churchyard to ride through the countryside."[5]

Washington Irving himself published an anecdote in the April 1840 *Knickerbocker* magazine, stating that the Irish immigrants hired to build the Croton Aqueduct through Sleepy Hollow had found themselves "most grievously harried... by all kinds of apparitions." Submitted as a Letter to the Editor, Irving wrote that the Irish laborers "on their way home at night beheld misshapen monsters whisking about their paths, sometimes resembling men, sometimes boys, sometimes horses, but invariably *without heads*; which shows that they must be lineal descendants from the old goblins of the Hollow." Irving further informed the editor that "this is a true story and you may account for it as you please," adding that it had been told to him "last evening by one of the young engineers who was on a visit to the cottage."

(But – Was Irving truly relating a story that had been told to him, or is this another Knickerbocker-esque, tongue-in-cheek account poking fun at the Irish immigrants, much the same way his earlier writings had poked fun at Dutch stereotypes? Irving's letter seems to invoke the stereotype of the "hard-drinking Irishman" by hinting that these apparitions seemingly materialized when the workmen were on their way home from "certain whisky establishments"...)

Fifty-plus years after the March 1820 publication of "The Legend," the Headless Horseman of Sleepy Hollow was still making appearances. Edgar Mayhew Bacon related a story of how, in the 1870s, he overheard a woman telling her neighbors that while waiting outside one evening for her husband to come home, she saw "out there in the road, a big, black, shadder-like, without any head, an' him on horseback at that."[6]

The occasional headless horseman legend still surfaces from time to time. In *Mysterious California*, Mike Marinacci gives an account of a headless ghost who has been seen in Ventura County – except instead of riding a black steed, this spectre rides "a big prewar motorcycle."[7]

Irving's Headless Hessian

Could Washington Irving have based part of his Sleepy Hollow tale on an already existing legend? Irving himself implied as much in his essay "Sleepy Hollow," which appeared in the May 1839 issue of *The Knickerbocker* magazine. In this essay, Irving reminisced about his first trip to Sleepy Hollow in 1798 at the age of 15.

Irving wrote, "I believe it was the very peculiarity of the name and the idea of something mystic and dreamy connected with it that first led me in my boyish ramblings into Sleepy Hollow." He described "entering familiarly into the various cottages, and gossiping with the simple folk... while [he] conciliated the good-will of the old Dutch housewife, and drew from her long ghost stories, spun out to the humming accompaniment of her wheel."[8]

Irving continued, "I shunned, however, the populous parts of the Hollow, and sought its retired haunts far in the foldings of the hills, where the Pocantico 'winds it wizard stream.' " He described how he came upon "an old goblin-looking mill, situated among rocks and waterfalls, with clanking wheels, and rushing streams." (Irving was referring to Carl's Mill, located on a tributary far upstream on the Pocantico.) As he approached the old mill, "an old negro thrust his head, all dabbled with flour, out of a hole above the water wheel," and Irving "sat with him by the hour on a broken mill-stone, by the side of the waterfall."[9]

Carl's Mill – Is this where 15-year-old Washington Irving first heard the story of the Headless Hessian? (Engraving from June 11, 1853 issue of Gleason's Pictorial.*)*

Irving concluded his account by saying, "it was to [Knickerbocker's] conference with this African sage, and the precious revelations of the good dame of the spinning-wheel, that we are indebted for the surprising though true history of Ichabod Crane and the headless horseman."[10]

The Carl's Mill anecdote is repeated almost verbatim in Irving's *Wolfert's Roost,* an 1855 collection of newly revised essays that had previously been published in *The Knickerbocker.*

This account certainly seems plausible; it is easy to imagine the old gentleman, or the Dutch housewife, entertaining the young visitor with a local ghost story.

Another possible clue is provided in the Postscript of "The Legend," which was, of course, "found in the handwriting of Mr. Knickerbocker." Here we learn that "Knickerbocker" had originally heard the story from a "pleasant, shabby, gentlemanly old fellow" – could this be a nod to the "old negro" encountered at Carl's Mill?

Sleepy Hollow Legends

We know that Washington Irving wove one actual local legend into "The Legend of Sleepy Hollow," the story of the Lady in White of Raven Rock, which was previously discussed in Chapter 2. But were there also headless horseman legends circulating in the Sleepy Hollow region prior to the publication of Irving's story?

Apparently there were! According to Irving scholar Dr. Elisabeth Paling Funk, "belief in headless apparitions, including headless, ghostly animals, was rampant in the European areas that contributed to the Hudson River Valley population."[11]

Folklorist and storyteller Sandy Schlosser includes a story titled "The Headless Horseman" on her <AMERICAN-FOLKLORE.NET> website, which she believes to be "a retelling of the folktale which was used by Washington Irving to create his masterpiece, *The Legend of Sleepy Hollow.*"[12] A more detailed version of this story also appears in her book *Spooky New York* as "The Galloping Hessian."

In Schlosser's account, a local Dutchman is passing the Sleepy Hollow cemetery on his way home from a tavern in Tarrytown when he observes a mist rising from the graveyard, which transforms into a phantom horse with a headless rider. Fleeing on foot from the headless apparition, the Dutchman falls, and the horseman, who appears to be wearing a Hessian uniform, gallops past him. According to Schlosser, the Dutchman's story "was all over Tarrytown" by the next day.[13]

(Schlosser's research has also uncovered a headless horseman story from Troy, NY, but she does not believe the two stories to be related; the Troy story appears to have originated earlier, and rather than a Hessian in search of his missing head, the Troy horseman is a local man galloping toward his former home.)[14]

Although Irving's account of the Hessian soldier's decapitation by an American cannon ball refers only to "some nameless battle" of the Revolution, Sandy Schlosser's version places the Hessian at the Battle of White Plains in October 1776. Her research suggests that the headless horseman legend began circulating in the Sleepy Hollow region shortly after the White Plains battle.[15]

It should be noted that Schlosser's use of the Battle of White Plains in her story was primarily for dramatic effect, and was not based on historical fact... *or was it?*

A Real Headless Hessian!

The main Battle of White Plains took place on October 28, 1776, between 14,500 American soldiers under General George Washington and 13,000 British and Hessian troops under General William Howe. The Americans were forced to withdraw to a new position slightly further north, and over the next several days, a number of smaller skirmishes and artillery exchanges took place.

One such action occurred on November 1, when a combined force of British and Hessian artillerymen advanced on an American position, and were driven back by an artillery barrage from the Americans. American General William Heath witnessed the attack, and recorded in his journal, "A shot from the American cannon at this place *took off the head of a Hessian* artillery-man. They also left one of the artillery horses dead in the field."[16]

An actual Headless Hessian! And a dead horse, which might serve as his ghostly steed! (Located less than 10 miles from Sleepy Hollow, White Plains is also close enough for the phantom to "ride forth to the scene of battle in nightly quest of his head...")

Did the true story of the decapitated Hessian artilleryman find its way to Sleepy Hollow, eventually giving rise to a headless ghost legend, which was related 22 years later to a young Washington Irving by the "African sage" at Carl's Mill?

Another White Plains Casualty

There is one other recorded incident of a soldier having been "killed by a cannon ball from the enemy separating his head from his shoulders" at the Battle of White Plains, this time an American, Abraham Onderdonk. This was attested to by one of Onderdonk's neighbors, John P. Blauvelt, who witnessed the event.[17]

Irving biographer Andrew Burstein suggests that Irving's explanation of how his phantom horseman came to be headless may have been inspired by the cause of Onderdonk's death. Burstein surmises that Irving "may" possibly have heard of the incident from Aaron Burr, who was aide-de-camp to General Israel Putnam, Onderdonk's commanding general.[18]

This is certainly possible – Irving did know Burr, although not as well as did his brother, Peter, who had been editor of Burr's *New York Morning Chronicle* newspaper. Burr had been impressed with Washington's "Jonathan Oldstyle" letters published in 1802-03 in the *Morning Chron-*

icle, and requested Irving's legal services during his treason trial in Virginia in 1807 (probably hoping Irving would write a favorable article or two for the New York press!).[19]

While it is possible that Burr and Irving *may* have discussed the White Plains battle at some point, and that the Onderdonk incident *could* have come up, it does not seem as likely as the Carl's Mill scenario. Irving's own account of first hearing about the Headless Horseman from a local storyteller he met while exploring Sleepy Hollow seems to have more of a ring of truth to it.

The Headless Horseman's Grave?

Another oral tradition in the Sleepy Hollow region is that the body of a Hessian trooper (at least one version specifies "headless") was found after a skirmish, and was given a Christian burial in an unmarked grave in the Old Dutch Burying Ground. This was said to have been done as a gesture of gratitude by a local family whose daughter had once been saved by another Hessian soldier.

This "tradition" is usually linked to the *true* story of Cornelius and Elizabeth Van Tassel, and their infant daughter, Leah. The family's home, located on the Sawmill River Road just south of present-day Elmsford, was looted and set on fire on November 17, 1777 by a company of Hessian soldiers commanded by Major Andreas Emmerick. According to an account given in *Tales of the Old Dutch Burying Ground*, Elizabeth Van Tassel "discovered that their baby daughter Leah was missing. She ran back to the house, but was driven back by the flames. She collapsed, sobbing, when a young Hessian motioned her to follow him. Behind a shed, wrapped in a blanket, lay baby Leah, safe and warm."[20]

This story was corroborated by an account given in 1845 by Captain John Romer, who had married Leah Van Tassel in 1791. Romer's version of his future wife's rescue appears in the *Souvenir of the Revolutionary Soldiers' Monument Dedication at Tarrytown, N. Y., October 19th, 1894.*[21]

A slightly different version of this story appears in *Historical Sketches of the Romer, Van Tassel and Allied Families*, written in 1917 by John Lockwood Romer, grandson of Capt. John Romer. Romer wrote, "The wife of Cornelius Van Tassel sought refuge in an old dirt cellar in the farmyard, carrying her infant daughter in her arms. Here they were discovered, half-clad and shivering with the cold, by a Hessian trooper, who, touched by their pitiable condition, threw them a feather mattress that he had taken from the burning house – an act of mercy which undoubtedly saved their lives."[22]

Does the X mark the "traditional" location of the grave of the Headless Hessian?

Off the northeast corner of the church, there is a section of the graveyard that is conspicuously devoid of tombstones. It is located about halfway between the tombstone of Anna Van Tassel Bont and the double tombstone of Joseph and Susannah Youngs (roughly 20 feet northwest of the

Youngs' plot). Visitors to the churchyard are sometimes directed to this bare patch as the "traditional" location of the Headless Hessian's unmarked grave, in what was once a sort-of "potter's field." However, it is not clear (and no one is saying) how much of this story is actual local lore, and how much is recent fabrication, made up by well-meaning tour guides wishing to enhance some young visitor's Sleepy Hollow experience...

(Likewise, past visitors sometimes came across a small brass grave marker inscribed "HESSIAN SOLDIER, 1776-1783," planted by the cemetery staff for the entertainment of their guests. Unfortunately, this practice had to be discontinued because some tourists apparently thought the markers would make nice souvenirs, and it was getting too costly to keep replacing them...)

There is no official record of the Van Tassels, or anyone else, having provided a burial for an unknown Hessian soldier. Old Dutch Burying Ground records contain no documentation of any British or Hessian troops having been buried there. As pointed out by cemetery historian Jim Logan of the Friends of the Old Dutch Burying Ground, the graveyard contains the remains of many American veterans of the Revolutionary War, and "it is unlikely that an enemy mercenary could have been buried there without the knowledge of the congregation."[23]

(In the off chance that the Van Tassels *did* somehow secretly provide a Christian burial "out of gratitude" to an unnamed Hessian soldier, it could not have been for one of the casualties of White Plains – the Leah Van Tassel incident occurred in November 1777, a full year *after* the White Plains battle.)

One possible source of the "Hessian grave" story may be found in Romer's *Historical Sketches of the Romer, Van Tassel and Allied Families*: "On one occasion a marauding Hessian, hiding behind a large boulder, on the farm of Lieutenant Van Tassel, was shot and killed, and his body buried under an apple tree standing near; and later still, in a sharp skirmish near the Van Tassel home, five more Hessians were killed and their bodies likewise buried under the same tree."[24]

Could the *true* story of the six Hessians' graves on the Cornelius Van Tassel property have morphed over a number of generations into a more fanciful tale of a lone Hessian trooper having been buried, by the very same Cornelius Van Tassel, in the Old Dutch Burying Ground?

What about Kinderhook?

While there are no known headless horseman legends in the immediate Kinderhook vicinity, there is a house in Claverack, NY, about 14 miles south of Kinderhook, which boasts a legend of a phantom coach with a headless driver. The Claverack residence, named Talavera by the original owner, was built around 1799 by William W. Van Ness, first cousin of Washington Irving's friend William P. Van Ness. A long driveway which crosses the front lawn is the scene of the ghostly visitations.

A Van Ness descendant, identified only as Mrs. Van Ness Philip, related the Claverack legend in a 1953 *YANKEE* magazine article: "Strange thing about that drive, none of the family use it... You see, there is a tradition in the Van Ness family that a headless horseman drives a coach about this house, around and around the drive every night. In it there is a screaming girl. Just a Van Ness tradition of course, but it makes it very hard for me to keep servants."[25]

Which brings us to the usual question – was this Van Ness family legend already in existence in 1809 when Washington Irving was a guest at Kinderhook? Or, did the Claverack legend appear later, possibly influenced by Irving's tale of the Headless Horseman of Sleepy Hollow?

Like headless horseman legends, phantom coach stories have been around for centuries, probably having their origins in Europe. It is entirely possible that the phantom coach legend could have found its way to Claverack prior to Washington Irving's visit to Kinderhook.

However, the Sleepy Hollow and Claverack tales are very different, and it seems unlikely that one would have directly spawned the other. While Irving may have indeed heard the phantom coach legend while staying with the Kinderhook Van Ness family, it seems there would have had to have been additional influences at work in order for him to morph the coach driver into a Hessian trooper.

It is interesting to note that Mrs. Philip used the term "headless horseman" in her retelling of the family legend. Technically, the driver is not a horseman at all, he is a coachman! The use of the term "horseman" appears to be a more recent embellishment by Van Ness descendants wishing to link their story to Washington Irving. Folklorist Sandy Schlosser suggests that, possibly, even the "headless" aspect may have been a "post-Irving enhancement."[26]

An English Headless Horseman

While it is not certain which Headless Horseman tales may have been related to Washington Irving during his sojourn in Sleepy Hollow in 1798 (or Kinderhook in 1809), we know that he heard at least one while living in England a few years before writing "The Legend of Sleepy Hollow."

On a sightseeing trip with his brother Peter through Derbyshire in the summer of 1816, the two took shelter in a cave with some other tourists while waiting for a rain storm to pass, and the travelers entertained each other with songs and stories. Irving's August 5, 1816 notebook entry recalled, "Old woman tells a long (ghost) story about a ghost she saw when a girl 12 years old. The ghost was on horseback, without a head but with bright spurs. He used to haunt their neighborhood, *asked a young man to ride behind him* which he did – carried him to his home but the door being fast ghost horse and all *jumped over the house* – young man died shortly after."[27]

This tale may have partially inspired the story of "Old Brouwer" which is embedded in the text of "The Legend of Sleepy Hollow," where the guests of the Van Tassels are exchanging ghost stories at the quilting frolic: "The tale was told of old Brouwer, a most heretical disbeliever in ghosts, how he met the horseman returning from his foray into Sleepy Hollow, *and was obliged to get up behind him*; how they galloped over bush and brake, over hill and swamp, until they reached the bridge; when the horseman suddenly turned into a skeleton, threw old Brouwer into the brook, and *sprang away over the tree-tops* with a clap of thunder."[28]

(Dr. Elisabeth Paling Funk has a theory about Irving's use of the name "Brouwer" in his story: Irving's brother Ebenezer was married to Elizabeth Kip (1786-1827); her mother's maiden name was Jane Brouwer.[29] Could the "Old Brouwer" tall tale have been based in part on an old Brouwer family tradition, eventually reaching Washington's ears through his sister-in-law, Elizabeth? Or – probably more likely – did he simply borrow the name Brouwer from Elizabeth's family?)

While the Derbyshire tale appears to be the only English headless horseman story that rated a mention in Irving's journals, it is quite possible that he heard others. Headless horseman legends are plentiful in England, known in Abington, Aylsham, Ballymena, Baschurch, and Prestbury, to name a few.

Other European Sources

Irving's "Haddon Hall Notebook," which he kept in 1821 while compiling notes and early drafts for *Bracebridge Hall*, contains an entry on page 111 where the author was asked about American superstitions. Irving replied, "Our superstitions in America were pretty generally reflections of the superstitions of Europe singularly blended together. As we had settlers from all nations. Those of NY were partly from Dutch, English & Germans though the Dutch predominated – and now and then were mingled some traces of the old indian legends & superstitions which were feebly handed down."[30]

Washington Irving certainly had ample access to legends and folklore of all three sources cited. New York, predominantly of English descent when Irving was born, had originally been colonized by the Dutch as New Netherland in the early 1600s, and still had a large Dutch population when Irving was coming of age in the late 1700s; and many German immigrants were already present in the Hudson River region by the early 1700s, drawn by inexpensive farmland, with additional former Hessian soldiers settling there after the Revolutionary War.

Most literary scholars agree that Irving indeed incorporated elements of European folklore in *The Sketch Book*. Prof. Susan Manning, English Literature Professor at the University of Edinburgh, Scotland, suggested, "Important literary sources are the demonic horseback chase through Kirk Alloway in Robert Burns' *Tam O'Shanter*, and Burger's 'Der Wilde Jager' ('The Wild Huntsman'). The throwing of the false head occurs in the Rubezahl legends of Germany."[31]

Tam O'Shanter

"Tam O'Shanter – A Tale," a narrative poem by Robert Burns, first appeared in *Edinburgh Magazine* in Scotland in March 1791. In "Tam O'Shanter," the title character Tam flees from a coven of witches he encounters at the ruins of Alloway Kirk, an ancient church in Ayr, Scotland. There are a number of similarities between Tam's flight from the witches and Ichabod Crane's encounter with the Headless Horseman of Sleepy Hollow.

*Tam O'Shanter escapes across the Brig O'Doon
(19th Century engraving by Scottish artist John Faed)*

As Tam O'Shanter begins his journey home astride his horse Maggie, he begins to croon an "auld Scot's sonnet"[32]; Ichabod Crane, riding Gunpowder, "began to whistle," and later, "broke forth with involuntary fervor into a psalm tune."[33]

Tam passes a series of landmarks, which he recognizes as the scenes of various gruesome deaths – one where someone had frozen in the snow, another where a woman had hanged herself, and yet another where the body of a murdered child had been discovered[34]; Ichabod similarly encounters places "where many of the scenes of ghost stories had been laid," including Major Andre's Tree and Wiley's Swamp, where a log bridge crosses a "haunted stream."[35]

Tam's horse Maggie comes to a stop at one point, "til by the heel and hand admonish'd"[36]; likewise, Ichabod "rained a shower of kicks and blows upon Gunpowder."[37]

At the height of the chase, one of Tam's supernatural pursuers is "hard upon" his horse's tail[38]; the Headless Horseman's steed is "hard on [Gunpowder's] haunches," and Ichabod "fancied that he felt his hot breath."[39]

Tam ultimately escapes by crossing a bridge (the "Brig O'Doon," a medieval stone bridge which may still be seen near Alloway), leaving his pursuers behind because witches (and ghosts) are said to be unable to cross running water.[40] This mirrors the account in "The Legend of Sleepy Hollow," where the Headless Horseman is unable to cross the churchyard bridge. However, where Tam O'Shanter makes it to safety – except the witch has pulled off poor Maggie's tail, leaving only a stump – Ichabod Crane is struck down by the pumpkin "head" hurled at him by the Headless Horseman.[41]

We know Irving was familiar with Robert Burns' work; in "Abbotsford," his 1835 memoir of his 1817 visit with Sir Walter Scott, he described a day trip to Alloway Kirk, Burns' birthplace, where he passed the morning with Burns' "tender little love verses running in [his] head."[42]

German Influences

German literature saw a surge in popularity in England in the late 1700s through early 1800s. This did not go unnoticed by Washington Irving, who wrote in 1810, "About this time the passion for German literature raged in all its violence in Great Britain, and the literary world was completely infatuated by the brilliant absurdities of the German muse..."[43]

Upon assuming the editorship of the *Analectic Magazine* in 1813, it became necessary for Irving to keep up with current literature trends in rival publications, including *The Portfolio*, which was noted for its German literature content. He also actively sought out periodicals from England, France and Germany, looking for material he could reproduce in the *Analectic*.

Following his arrival in England in 1815, Irving discovered *Blackwood's Edinburgh Magazine* and the *Foreign Quarterly Review*, both of which regularly featured material from Germany.

Sir Walter Scott is often credited with having steered Washington Irving toward German folklore during his August 1817 stay with the Scott family at Abbotsford in Scotland. Scott was highly enthusiastic about German legends and folktales, having translated several collections himself, and Irving was no doubt impressed by the 300+ German titles on the shelves of Scott's library. Scott almost certainly encouraged Irving to look to Germany for ideas and inspiration.

Shortly after his visit with Scott, Irving set out to teach himself the German language. While the Irving family business was going through bankruptcy hearings in early 1818, Washington "shut himself up from society, and was studying German, day and night, in the double hope that it would be of service to him, and tend to keep off uncomfortable thoughts."[44]

Irving described his German studies in a May 1818 letter to his friend Henry Brevoort, saying, "It is a severe task, and has required hard study; but the rich mine of German literature holds forth abundant reward."[45]

One of the "abundant rewards" Irving alluded to was the old German legend of Peter Klaus, which he essentially retold as "Rip Van Winkle," a fact that Irving himself acknowledged. Most critics, however, agree that he greatly improved on the original by infusing his own humor, while at the same time moving the story to an American setting.

Could one of the other "rewards" have been Irving's source for "The Legend of Sleepy Hollow"?

Der Wilde Jager (The Wild Huntsman)

One suggested German influence is "Der Wilde Jager" ("The Wild Huntsman"), a poem written in 1778 by Gottfried August Burger. This poem is essentially a narrative of a supernatural chase on horseback, where the main character is doomed to continue riding "till time itself shall have an end," as is the Headless Horseman in Irving's tale.

"Odin as the Wild Huntsman"
(1873 engraving, artist unknown)

The poem has an eerie backdrop typical of Gothic literature, and the chase itself maintains a fast-paced, frantic tone, much like the flight of Ichabod Crane from his headless pursuer. But there the similarity ends – the over-all storyline of "Der Wilde Jager" is very different from that of "The Legend of Sleepy Hollow."

Sir Walter Scott had translated "Der Wilde Jager" from German to English in 1796. If Irving was not already familiar with Scott's translation, he could have learned of it during his 1817 stay with the Scott family.

Otmar's "Wild Huntsman of Hacklenburg"

Comparisons have also been made to another "Wild Huntsman" tale, this one by Johann Karl Christoph Nachtigal, writing under the pen name Otmar. In "The Wild Huntsman of Hacklenburg," the huntsman throws a half-eaten thigh bone of a horse at his victim, not unlike the use of a pumpkin as a projectile in Irving's story.

"Hacklenburg" appears in *Volks-Sagen nacherzuhlt von Otmar* ("Folktales Re-Told by Otmar"), published in Bremen in 1800. The Otmar edition was the most popular collection of German folktales at the time, so there is a good chance that Irving may have been familiar with it.[46]

Christoph Martin Wieland's influence

Washington Irving's 1818 Notebook contains an entry on page 5 that says, simply, "Light tales in the manner of Wieland."[47] It is unclear exactly what Irving meant when he wrote this – perhaps it was a sort-of "note to self" that he should endeavor to create his own stories in Wieland's style?

The Wieland he refers to is Christoph Martin Wieland (1733-1813), a German poet and novelist noted for light-hearted satiric stories. Walter Reichart suggested that Wieland's style was influenced by the writings of Clara Reeve (1729-1807). Reeve included elements of the supernatural, typical of the Gothic style that was extremely popular in England in the late 1700s and early 1800s, but concluded her stories with rational explanations for all seemingly supernatural occurrences. Horace Walpole (1717-1797), generally credited with inventing the Gothic style of writing with his 1764 novel *The Castle of Otranto*, referred to Reeve's rationalized creations as "tame ghosts."[48]

A copy of Wieland's *Die Abenteuer des Don Sylvio von Rosalva (The Adventures of Don Sylvio von Rosalva)* still exists in Irving's library at Sunnyside. This book, translated into English in 1773, was given the very telling sub-title "A History in Which Every Marvellous Event Occurs Naturally."

Dr. Elisabeth Paling Funk believes that Irving's main Gothic influence was in fact Ann Radcliffe (1764-1823), even more so than Wieland or Reeve.[49] Radcliffe, who published a number of novels in the 1790s, followed this same formula, known as *supernatural explique*, of introducing supernatural themes and then rationalizing them.

Could this increasingly popular method of explaining away the supernatural have influenced Irving to conclude his own tale with the implication that his ghostly Headless Horseman may not have been a ghost at all, but may actually have been Brom Bones in disguise?

Rubezahl Legends

Although several European sources may have influenced Irving, the most significant appear to be the German legends of Rubezahl.

Rubezahl is the name of a gnome or "mountain spirit" who is the subject of many European legends and folktales, especially of Germany. The earliest collection of Rubezahl tales was published in 1662 by Johannes Praetorius. Later, Johann Karl August Musaus included five Rubezahl legends ("Legenden von Rubezahl") in his book *Volksmarchen der Deutschen* (*Folk Tales of the Germans*), published in five volumes between 1782 and 1786.

Specifically, it is Musaus' "Fifth Legend of Rubezahl" that describes an encounter with a headless ghost. In this story, the character Johann is traveling by carriage with

Countess Cecilia and her two daughters when he sees a headless apparition carrying his head under his arm. When Johann addresses the ghost, it throws its "head" at him, hitting him in the forehead and knocking him off the carriage.[50]

The "ghost" is later discovered to be a real person, a rival of Johann, wearing a costume; this parallels Irving's version where he implies that his own Headless Horseman is really Brom Bones, Ichabod's romantic rival, in disguise. Rather than a pumpkin, the severed "head" in the Musaus tale is identified as a "huge hollowed out gourd filled with sand and stones."[51]

An 1804 German edition of Musaus' *Volksmarchen der Deutschen* still exists in Irving's library at Sunnyside. This 1804 edition was revised and edited by C. M. Wieland. Could this also partially explain Irving's cryptic 1818 Notebook entry, "Light tales in the manner of Wieland"?

In addition to this German edition, a two-volume English-language version, translated in 1791 by William Beckford as *Popular Tales of the Germans*, was also available to Irving at the time he was working on *The Sketch Book*.

In the July 1930 issue of the magazine *Studies in Philology*, Henry Pochman noted some interesting similarities between passages from Musaus' Rubezahl story and "The Legend of Sleepy Hollow." Indeed, much of the detail of Ichabod Crane's encounter with the Headless Horseman appears to have been "borrowed" from the Fifth Rubezahl legend.

Pochman presented the Rubezahl passages in their original German; the corresponding English translations presented here are from the 1791 William Beckford edition. (In the Beckford translation, the character name Johann is anglicized to become John, and the name Rubezahl is translated as Number-Nip – roughly, "Turnip Counter.")

A comparison of "Rubezahl" to "The Legend of Sleepy Hollow"

In both stories, the local people spend winter evenings telling ghost stories:

> Rubezahl: "The common people amused themselves with absurd stories, which the fancy of the old housewives, in winter evenings, spun out as long and as slender as the threads from their distaffs..."52
>
> Sleepy Hollow: "They are given to all kinds of marvelous beliefs... to pass long winter evenings with the old Dutch wives, as they sat spinning by the fire, with a row of apples roasting and spluttering along the hearth, and listen to their marvelous tales of ghosts and goblins..."53

Both John and Ichabod Crane are affected by the ghost stories they had heard earlier that evening:

> Rubezahl: "All the stories of Number-Nip, which he had formerly devoured with such eager attention, came rushing at once into his mind, now he was traveling the stage where these adventures had happened."54
>
> Sleepy Hollow: "All the stories of ghosts and goblins that he had heard in the afternoon, now came crowding upon his recollection... He was, moreover, approaching the very place where many of the scenes of the ghost stories had been laid."55

John's and Ichabod's fears are described in a similar fashion:

> Rubezahl: "A cold shudder ran down his back, and his hair grew stiff like bristles."56
>
> Sleepy Hollow: "The hair of the affrighted pedagogue rose upon his head with terror."57

Both stories have similar descriptions of the appearance of a large, shadowy apparition:

>Rubezahl: "He saw, to his utter confusion, stalking on about a stone's throw before the coach, a jet-black figure, of a size exceeding that of man..."[58]
>
>Sleepy Hollow: "In the dark shadow of the grove, on the margin of the brook, he beheld something huge, misshapen, black and towering... He appeared to be a horseman of large dimensions."[59]

Seeing that their unwanted companions are keeping pace with them, both John and Ichabod vary their speed to try to lose them:

>Rubezahl: "If the coach halted, the figure also halted; and when the postilion drove on, it proceeded also."[60]
>
>Sleepy Hollow: "Ichabod... quickened his steed, in hopes of leaving him behind. The stranger, however, quickened his horse to an equal pace. Ichabod pulled up, and fell into a walk, thinking to lag behind – the other did the same."[61]

Both John and Ichabod note that the apparently headless apparition does indeed possess a head, but instead of being set "on his shoulders," it is being carried:

>Rubezahl: "It was now plain to be seen that John's eye had taken a false measure – the man on foot had a head as well as other people, only he did not wear it, according to the usual fashion, between his shoulders, but carried it under his arm, just as if it had been a lap-dog."[62]
>
>Sleepy Hollow: "Ichabod was horror-struck, on perceiving that he was headless! – His horror was still more increased, on observing that the head, which should have

rested on his shoulders, was carried before him on the pommel of the saddle."63

In both stories, the headless apparition throws its head at John/Ichabod, hitting them in the head and knocking them to the ground:

Rubezahl: "The monster took his head from under his arm, and hurled it at John; it struck him right on the forehead, and the blow was so severe that he *tumbled headlong* from the box over the fore-wheel..."64

Sleepy Hollow: "Just then he saw the goblin rising in his stirrups, and in the very act of hurling his head at him. Ichabod endeavored to dodge the horrible missile, but too late. It encountered his cranium with a tremendous crash—he was *tumbled headlong* into the dust..."65

The most significant clue here is Irving's use of the phrase "tumbled headlong." It seems far too coincidental for this specific term to have been used independently in both stories to describe the characters being knocked to the ground after being struck in the head by a flying projectile. Irving clearly referred to the Beckford translation of the Rubezahl tales, borrowing some of the fine detail (and at least one specific phrase) to enhance his own story.

Rubezahl, the Musical?

On October 6, 1819, right about the time of Irving's epiphany on Westminster Bridge that led to the writing of "The Legend," a musical titled "The Gnome King; or, the Giant Mountains" was performed at London's Covent Garden Theater. Adapted by William Coleman, the two-act play was based on the "First Legend of Rubezahl."

Could Irving, an avid theater-goer, have seen it? If so, could it possibly have inspired him to seek out other

Rubezahl/Number-Nip stories, ultimately leading him to the headless apparition sequence in Legend Number Five?

To Summarize...

Washington Irving clearly did not invent the Headless Horseman; these legends had been around for years, and Irving likely either heard or read about them – probably both. The Headless Horseman of Sleepy Hollow was most likely a composite of legends Irving heard as a youth in New York, with the chase sequence embellished with details borrowed from "Tam O'Shanter" and "The Fifth Legend of Rubezahl," specifically the 1791 William Beckford translation.

It has been suggested that Irving's decision to make his goblin rider a Hessian was a "nod to the ghost's ancestry in German folklore."[66] It may have also served to make the horseman extra terrifying – the Hessian mercenaries fighting in the Revolutionary War had a reputation for being especially ruthless and bloodthirsty, with some Americans believing they would eat their children![67]

Postscript – An Old Millstone

In March 2011, Pocantico Hills resident Lucas Buresch, a part-time historian and blogger, set out to find the original site of Carl's Mill. With an 1867 map providing the general location, he proceeded up the Pocantico River until he came across a location that, even after 150+ years, was still recognizable as the view of the mill which had appeared in *Gleason's Pictorial* in 1853.[68]

The wooden structure was long gone, but Buresch did find some ancient pieces of rusted metal to attest to the fact that a man-made structure had indeed once occupied the site; he also found fine sand and gravel at the spot where, as pictured in the engraving, a waterwheel had once stood.

Is this the former location of Carl's Mill? Compare this view of the Pocantico to the 1853 engraving pictured earlier in this chapter on page 98. (Photo courtesy of Lucas Buresch)

But most significantly, "by the side of the waterfall," right where Irving said it was, Buresch discovered... *a millstone*!

Could this be THE millstone where 15-year-old Irving sat "by the hour" absorbing local legends – including the tale of the Headless Horseman – as recited by the "African sage" he met at Carl's Mill?

Is the THE millstone?? (Photo courtesy of Lucas Buresch)

Chapter 5

A Worthy Pedagogue

> *"In this by-place of nature, there abode, in a remote period of American history, that is to say, some thirty years since, a worthy wight of the name of Ichabod Crane; who sojourned, or, as he expressed it, 'tarried,' in Sleepy Hollow, for the purpose of instructing the children of the vicinity."*
> — from "The Legend of Sleepy Hollow," 1820

Who was Washington Irving's inspiration for the literary character Ichabod Crane? Several individuals have been suggested, including Jesse Merwin, Samuel Youngs, and... *Ichabod Crane??*

Colonel Ichabod B. Crane

It may come as a surprise to some readers to learn that there was indeed a real person who lived in Irving's time with the (some would say unfortunate) name Ichabod Crane. However, while this Ichabod may have lent his name to Washington Irving's gangly schoolmaster, the two characters were nothing alike.

Ichabod Bennett Crane was born on July 18, 1787 in Elizabethtown, NJ, the son of Revolutionary War General William Crane and the former Abigail Miller.

Colonel Ichabod Bennett Crane (Library of Congress)

Crane enlisted in the Marine Corps in January 1809 and was promoted to Lieutenant. He served aboard the 44-gun frigate *USS United States* under then Captain Stephen Decatur.

Crane resigned from the Marines and joined the Army, was appointed Captain of the Third Artillery in April

1812, and took part in several battles in Canada against the British during the War of 1812, including the captures of Fort York and Fort George in the spring of 1813.

Captain Ichabod Crane, then 27 years old, was stationed in 1814 at Fort Pike in Sackets Harbor, NY, on the shores of Lake Ontario. It was at Sackets Harbor that Captain Ichabod Crane is believed to have met Washington Irving, who was then a Colonel in the New York State Militia and aide-de-camp to Governor Daniel D. Tompkins. Col. Irving had been dispatched in September 1814 to Sackets Harbor and put in charge of bolstering defenses against an expected attack by the British (which never happened). While there is no documentation that the two indeed met – no mention is found in journal entries by either of them – it is highly likely that the two officers' paths crossed while stationed at the same location.

Requisition order issued by then Major Crane while stationed at Fort Preble, Maine, in December 1815 – signed "I. B. Crane, Major Commanding"

Capt. Crane was named commander of Fort Woolcott in Newport, Rhode Island, in 1820. He was promoted to Major in 1825, and reassigned to Fort Monroe, VA. He saw action in the Black Hawk War in 1832.

Promoted to Lieutenant Colonel in November 1832, Crane was transferred to the "Buffalo Barracks" in Buffalo, New York, which was the largest military installation in the United States at the time, housing more than 600 men and their dependents.

Col. Ichabod Crane monument in Asbury Methodist Cemetery, New Springville, Staten Island, New York (Photo courtesy of Friends of Abandoned Cemeteries of Staten Island)

Lt. Col. Crane next served in Florida under Col. Zachary Taylor during the Second Seminole War, returning to the Buffalo Barracks in 1837.

Crane was promoted to the rank of Colonel in mid-1843. From 1851 to 1853, Col. Ichabod Crane served as governor of the Military Asylum, later renamed the Soldier's Home, in Washington, DC, which had been established after the Mexican-American War as a retirement home for homeless or disabled veterans.

Colonel Crane's final assignment, from 1853 through 1857, was as post commander of Governors Island, located in New York Harbor.

On a personal note, Col. Ichabod Crane married Charlotte Rainger (1798-1878) on August 27, 1825. They had three children, two sons and a daughter. One son, Charles Henry Crane, became Surgeon General of the Army in 1882.

Colonel Ichabod Crane died on Staten Island, NY, on October 5, 1857. He is buried in an almost inaccessible corner of Asbury Methodist Cemetery in New Springville, Staten Island, NY. His grave is marked by a white obelisk adorned with a pair of crossed cannons and inscribed, "He served his country faithfully 48 years and was much beloved and respected by all who knew him."

Washington Irving very likely remembered the odd-sounding name "Ichabod Crane" from his chance meeting with the young Captain Crane in the fall of 1814, and later appropriated it, without his knowledge, for his soon-to-be-famous schoolmaster.

As for Colonel Crane's reaction to the news that his name had been used for the comical character? He was furious!

(One "oral tradition," yet to be verified, states that Colonel Crane later complained to Irving about the use of his name – the story does not specify whether the protest was by letter or in person – to which Irving characteristically replied that Crane should write a story and name one of his characters "Washington Irving.")[1]

Jesse Merwin

If the fictional Ichabod Crane's namesake was an army artillery officer, where did Irving find the inspiration to transform him into a Connecticut-born schoolmaster? Irving historians have long pointed to one of Irving's close friends, long-time Kinderhook resident Jesse Merwin.

Jesse Merwin was born August 25, 1784 in Durham, Connecticut. He was the youngest of seven children born to Revolutionary War veteran Daniel Merwin (1746-1820) and the former Rebecca Seward (1743-1815).

Jesse Merwin (Photo courtesy of David Trafton)

Jesse's parents, along with Jesse and two of his brothers, relocated to Columbia County in New York State in 1808.[2] Jesse became the first teacher at the tiny one-room schoolhouse located on what is now Route 9H.

On October 16, 1808, Jesse Merwin married Jane Van Dyck (1786-1882), the daughter of a wealthy Kinderhook farmer.

Like Ichabod Crane, Merwin was, "according to country custom in those parts, boarded and lodged at the houses of the farmers, whose children he instructed. With these he lived successively a week at a time..."[3]

This apparently continued even after his marriage to Jane Van Dyck, which seems an unusual arrangement, and is not addressed in any of the various books or articles which profile Merwin. Perhaps this was done as a matter of convenience in order to be closer to the schoolhouse during the week? Or maybe it was intended as a temporary arrangement while Jesse and Jane saved money for a home of their own? All we can do is speculate.

Whatever the circumstances, May of 1809 found Merwin "boarded and lodged" at Kleinrood, the Kinderhook estate of Judge William P. Van Ness, where he made the acquaintance of then 26-year-old burgeoning author Washington Irving. The two men quickly formed a close friendship that would be maintained, primarily through letters, throughout the rest of their lives.

Jesse's great-granddaughter, Mrs. Gertrude Raup, offered, "Grandpa liked to talk better than work. That is why he and Washington Irving were friends. They both liked to talk politics and Jesse Merwin did not like to teach school, but he liked farming less."[4]

Jesse Merwin's father-in-law died in 1810, and Jesse and Jane inherited his farm, located south of Cochran Lake (later renamed Merwin Lake). It is believed that Jesse gave up teaching around this time and became a full-time farmer.[5]

On October 16, 1810, Jesse and Jane's first child Peter Van Dyck Merwin was born. They would have a total of eleven children; their youngest, born in 1834, was named Washington Irving Merwin after Jesse's famous writer friend.[6]

Beginning in 1813, Merwin also served as Justice of the Peace for many years, "the duties of which office he discharged with scrupulous fidelity and conscientious regard to the just claims of suitors, ever frowning upon those whose vocation it is to 'foment discord and perplex right.' "[7]

In 1843 Jesse was elected one of seven trustees of Kinderhook's newly founded Methodist Episcopal Church. The following year, Merwin and his son Daniel were two of the four people elected Inspectors of Elections at Kinderhook.[8]

Jesse Merwin died on November 8, 1852 at the age of 68. Active in his community and the church, Jesse Merwin was said to have "secured the love and esteem of all who knew him."[9] His obituary offered, "Mr. Merwin was well known in this community as an upright, honorable man, in whom there was no guile."[10]

Merwin is buried in the Old Kinderhook Cemetery, and residents of Kinderhook still take pride in pointing out "the grave of Ichabod Crane" to visitors.

Irving's References to Jesse Merwin

Jesse Merwin is mentioned in several of Irving's published letters, as well as journal entries; however, in many cases, Merwin's name is misspelled, appearing as Jesse (or Jessy) Marvin or Marron. This is probably due to the transcriber's difficulty reading Irving's infamously poor handwriting. (In the Introduction to Volume II of *Washington Irving Journals and Notebooks*, the editors described the challenges of transcribing Irving's hand-written notes: "Entries are most often in pencil and badly deteriorated... Irving's handwriting is nearly illegible, and transcription approaches the art of cryptography."[11])

Despite the misspellings, it is generally clear who Washington Irving was referring to in the various entries where Merwin is mentioned. (To avoid confusion, the various letters and journal entries quoted here will use the correct spelling of Jesse Merwin's name, rather than the erroneous spellings found in the original publications.)

Jesse Merwin is first mentioned in a letter from Irving to his friend Henry Brevoort, sent from Van Ness's in Kinderhook on May 11, 1809. Irving wrote, "The only Country acquaintance I have made, is a schoolmaster who teaches the neighborhood children – a pleasant good natured fellow, with much native, unimproved shrewdness and considerable humour – as he is a kind of inmate at Van Ness's we have become very great friends, and I have found much entertainment in his conversation."[12]

On May 19, 1809, Irving wrote to Mrs. Hoffman, Matilda's mother, "My honest acquaintance the Schoolmaster also, who is possessed of a considerable portion of good sense and native humour, (and who, according to the custom of the country, passes part of the time at Van Ness's in consequence of teaching his children) yields me occasionally an hour of very entertaining conversation."[13]

On December 18, 1809, Irving wrote a letter to Judge Van Ness inviting him to come to visit him in New York City. Irving advised Van Ness, "leave your farm and its cares behind you: put your household under the ghostly superintendence of the evangelical sinner Jesse Merwin…"[14]

Two paragraphs later in the same letter, Irving asked, "How does my friend Partridge and his Academy? Do the flesh and the spirit still keep up their hostilities within him?" In the footnote for this statement in *Washington Irving Letters*, Volume I, the editors assumed that "Partridge was apparently one of the teachers at Kinderhook."[15] I believe, however, that Irving was still referring to Jesse Merwin, jokingly comparing him to the schoolmaster "Partridge" from the novel *Tom Jones* by Henry Fielding.

In the closing paragraph of his letter, Irving mentioned Merwin once again, saying "let my friend Jesse know that I still recollect him with great consideration."[16]

Washington Irving mentioned Jesse Merwin one more time in a letter to Henry Brevoort, written from Liverpool, England on June 7, 1817. Irving's letter was in reply to a letter written to him by Brevoort on April 30, 1817, which (apparently) contained details of a conversation between Brevoort and their mutual friend, Mrs. Archibald Campbell. Irving wrote, "When next you see her, tell her I am infinitely gratified by her friendly recollection. I do not remember the circumstances you allude to of her veto against *the story of Jesse Merwin*, but it could not help being good as she was concerned in it. I dare say it was some joke at my expense, and I always take care to forget such jokes as soon as possible."[17]

Unfortunately, the original April 30, 1817 letter from Henry Brevoort seems to have been lost to history; the footnote in *Washington Irving Letters,* Volume I stated that the letter had not been located, nor does it appear in *Letters of Henry Brevoort to Washington Irving*, compiled in 1916 by George S. Hellman.

What "story of Jesse Merwin" did Mrs. Campbell jokingly veto? Without the original Brevoort letter, it is impossible to say, and any possible ties to "The Legend of Sleepy Hollow" would be pure speculation (and wishful thinking!).

A Life-Long Friendship

In a February 26, 1898 letter to the editor of *The New York Times*, Harold Van Santvoord erroneously placed Irving in Kinderhook from May 1809 through the following fall and winter. Van Santvoord wrote, "Irving and the whimsical pedagogue whiled away many an hour, fishing in the stream that flowed through the verdant meadows, shooting partridges and squirrels in the woods, gathering nuts and apples in the Fall, and, when the pumpkins were ripe, making raids on the farmers' cornfields; and then, during the long Winter evenings, cracking jokes and spinning yarns with Katrina Van Tassell and Brom Bones in the quaint old Dutch kitchen of a neighboring farmhouse, before a roaring log fire."[18]

Van Santvoord's claims here are in error; Irving spent less than two months with the Van Nesses in Kinderhook, returning to New York City in June. This is attested to by a letter written by Irving to Judge Van Ness from New York, dated June 24, 1809, in which he wrote, "As to your inquiries as to what I am doing in the city, I can simply answer *nothing...*"[19]

This was followed by another letter from New York City to his friend Rebecca Gratz, dated July 4, 1809.[20]

Later that July, Irving made a sixteen-day trip to Canada with Henry Brevoort; August and September found him at the Hoffman's "retreat" at Hellgate, where he hoped to put the finishing touches on *Knickerbocker's History*.[21]

On October 23, 1809, Irving wrote to Henry Brevoort from Philadelphia, where he had been doing research for his *Knickerbocker's History* in the Philadelphia Library.[22] Irving was still in Philadelphia on November 2, as indicated by a letter to John Howard Payne.[23]

Irving's December 18 letter to Judge Van Ness makes it further apparent that he had not been back to Kinderhook, stating "I long once more to visit your little empire: and am only deterred by the austerity of old Winter..."[24]

Washington Irving's own correspondence confirms that his 1809 sojourn in Kinderhook was limited to May and part of June. His activities and whereabouts in the subsequent months can be easily traced by the dates and locations provided in the headings of his letters.

There is a record of Irving having *possibly* made one other trip to Kinderhook, in 1810, following a brief stay in Albany. In a letter sent from Albany to Mrs. Hoffman, dated February 26, 1810, Irving wrote, "I shall remain here some days longer, and then go to Kinderhook. What time I shall return to New York I cannot tell... perhaps I cannot be more agreeably or profitably employed than in Van Ness's library."[25]

Irving's next published letter shows he was in Philadelphia on June 5, 1810; no other letters or journal entries have yet been located to confirm that this planned 1810 Kinderhook visit indeed took place, or if Irving made any other visits to Kinderhook prior to publication of "The Legend of Sleepy Hollow."

Irving is known for certain to have visited Jesse Merwin in Kinderhook in 1833, some 13 years after the publication of "The Legend of Sleepy Hollow," while Irving was touring New York State with future President Martin Van Buren. Irving's September 10, 1833 Journal entry contains the brief notation, "Visit Jesse Merwin – trees loaded with fruit about the house."[26]

The brief time spent in Kinderhook in the spring of 1809 was apparently sufficient time for Irving and Merwin to form a life-long friendship. According to Van Santvoord, the two exchanged a number of letters over the years. He stated that these letters had been preserved by Merwin's youngest son David, but "were unfortunately destroyed by a careless servant during the annual spring housecleaning period."[27]

Only one letter from Washington Irving to Jesse Merwin, written in February 1851, appears to have survived. First published by Irving's nephew Pierre in *The Life and Letters of Washington Irving*, Volume I, the content of this letter is reproduced here in its entirety.

"Sunnyside, February 12, 1851

"You must excuse me, my good friend Merwin, for suffering your letter to remain so long unanswered. You can have no idea how many letters I have to answer, besides fagging with my pen at my own literary tasks, so that it is impossible for me to avoid being behind hand in my correspondence. Your letter was indeed most welcome – calling up, as it did, the recollection of pleasant scenes and pleasant days passed together in times long since at Judge Van Ness's, in Kinderhook. Your mention of the death of good old Dominie Van Nest recalls the apostolic zeal with which he took our little sinful community in hand, when he put up for a day or two at the Judge's; and the wholesome castigation he gave us all, one Sunday, beginning with the two country belles who came fluttering into the school-house during the sermon, decked out in their city finery, and ending with the Judge himself, in the strong hold of his own mansion. How soundly he gave it to us! How he peeled off every rag of self-righteousness with which we tried to cover ourselves, and laid the rod on the bare backs of our consciences! The good plain-spoken, honest old man! How I honored him for his simple, straightforward earnestness, his homely sincerity. He certainly handled us without mittens; but I trust we are all the better for it. How different he was from the brisk, dapper, self-sufficient little apostle who cantered up to the Judge's door a day or two after; who was so full of himself that he had no thought to bestow on our religious delinquencies; who did nothing but boast of his public trials of skill in argument with rival preachers of other denominations, and how he had driven them off the field and crowed over them. You must remember the bustling, self-confident little man with a tin trumpet in the handle of his riding whip, with which I presume he blew the trumpet in Zion!

"Do you remember our fishing expedition, in company with Congressman Van Alen, to the little lake a few miles from Kinderhook; and John Moore, the vagabond admiral of the lake, who sat crouched in a heap in the middle of his canoe in the centre of the lake, with fishing-rods stretched out in every direction like the long legs of a spider? And do you remember our piratical prank, when we made up for our own bad luck in fishing, by plundering his canoe of its fish when we found it adrift? And do you remember how John Moore came splashing along the marsh on the opposite border of the lake, roaring at us; and how we finished our frolic by driving off and leaving the Congressman to John Moore's mercy, tickling ourselves with the idea of his being scalped at least? Ah, well-a-day, friend Merwin, those were the days of our youth and folly. I trust we have grown wiser and better since then; we certainly have grown older. I don't think we could rob John Moore's fishing canoe now. By the way, that same John Moore, and the anecdotes you told of him, gave me the idea of a vagabond character, Dirk Schuyler, in my 'Knickerbocker History of New York,' which I was then writing.

"You tell me the old school house is torn down, and a new one built in its place. I am sorry for it. I should have liked to see the old school house once more, where, after my morning's literary task was over, I used to come and wait for you occasionally until school was dismissed, and you used to promise to keep back the punishment of some little, tough, broad-bottomed Dutch boy until I should come, for my amusement – but never kept your promise. I don't think I should look with a friendly eye on the new schoolhouse, however nice it might be.

"Since I saw you in New York, I have had severe attacks of bilious intermittent fever, which shook me terribly; but they cleared out my system, and I have ever since been in my usual excellent health, able to mount my horse and gallop about the country almost as briskly as when I was a youngster. Wishing you the enjoyment of the same inestimable blessing, and begging you to remember me to your daughter, who penned your letter, and to your son, whom, out of old kindness and companionship, you have named after me,

"I remain ever, my good friend,
"yours very truly and cordially,

"Washington Irving." 28

Page from February 12, 1851 letter from Washington Irving to Jesse Merwin

Several important points may be inferred from this letter. First, it clearly refers to only one visit to Kinderhook, in the spring of 1809, as indicated by Irving's reference to his *Knickerbocker's History of New York*, which he "was then writing." This appears to contradict Harold Van Santvoord's statement that Irving "was a frequent visitor" to Kinderhook; at the same time it supports Edgar Mayhew Bacon's rebuttal, in which he stated that prior to the publication of his *Sketch Book*, Irving only visited Kinderhook once, in 1809.[29]

Also, Irving's letter seems to refute another of Harold Van Santvoord's assertions, that in addition to *Knickerbocker's History of New York*, Irving wrote part of *The Sketch Book* at Kinderhook.[30] Irving only mentioned *Knickerbocker's History*; had he indeed written material for *The Sketch Book*, particularly "The Legend of Sleepy Hollow," wouldn't he have mentioned it? Especially in a letter to the man believed by many to have been the inspiration for the Ichabod Crane character?

Merwin had apparently seen Irving in New York City at some point, as indicated by Irving's comment in the second to last paragraph, but the exact date of this visit is unknown; Irving's journals do not contain any mention of it.

We know that except for the occasional brief visit to Sunnyside, Irving spent the majority of his time from December 1847 through June 1849 in John Jacob Astor's library in New York City, where he was busy revising his earlier works for republication by George Putnam, as well as conducting research for the first volume of his *Life of Washington*. The "bilious fever" mentioned in his letter occurred during the summer of 1850, so Merwin's visit apparently took place prior to that.[31]

Irving's letter contains one phrase that is especially interesting because it is almost identical to one used in "The Legend of Sleepy Hollow." He reminded Merwin, "you used to promise to keep back the punishment of *some little tough broad bottomed dutch boy* until I should come, for my amusement..."

In "The Legend of Sleepy Hollow," Irving described how Schoolmaster Crane would occasionally find cause to apply his birch rod to *"some little, tough, wrong-headed, broad-skirted Dutch urchin..."*[32]

Coincidence? Or could Irving have possibly subconsciously paraphrased a passage from a story he had written more than 30 years earlier? Or a third possibility – could Irving's choice of words have been intended as a sort of inside joke between the author and the "worthy pedagogue" of his own story?

(Note: Irving's letter to Jesse Merwin, at one time in the possession of Merwin's son, David, resurfaced in November 2007 when it was listed in an auction by Stair Galleries of Hudson, NY, but it was apparently withdrawn from sale with no explanation provided. Its current location is unknown, presumably in a private collection.)

Jesse Merwin as Ichabod Crane

It is not known if Washington Irving ever discussed the origins of the "Ichabod Crane" character with Jesse Merwin, but Merwin himself apparently made the connection. Harold Van Santvoord offered, "It was in a spirit of playful humor... that Irving caricatured Jesse Merwin, and the pedagogue seemed to enjoy the grotesque humor of the portraiture as much as the author himself."[33] Merwin's 1852 obituary seems to confirm this, declaring that Jesse had "long most heartily enjoyed the reputation the legend gave him."[34]

Possibly the earliest published assertion that the Crane character was based on Merwin appeared in the January 30, 1835 *New York Sun* article announcing Irving's purchase of Sunnyside (discussed previously in Chapter 2). The article, which was reprinted from the *Westchester Herald*, reads, "The original of the sagacious schoolmaster, was not the individual generally considered as such, who still resides in this country, but Jesse Martin, a gentleman who bore the birchen away at the period of which the Legend speaks, and who afterwards removed further up the Hudson, and is since deceased."[35]

The 1835 *Sun* article contains several errors, the most obvious being the use of the name "Martin" vice "Merwin." Secondly, having been born in 1784, Merwin would have been much too young to have taught in Sleepy Hollow "at the period of which the Legend speaks," specifically, the 1790s. And finally, while the article correctly places him "further up the Hudson" (Kinderhook *is* about 100 miles north of Sleepy Hollow), Merwin was not dead in 1835, but rather lived another 17 years.

Curiously, the story that Merwin first taught in Sleepy Hollow before relocating to Kinderhook still persisted as late as 1898, when Edgar Mayhew Bacon wrote, "The firm belief of the people of Tarrytown, where the affair occurred, is to the effect that when the unfortunate pedagogue escaped with his life from the pumpkin of his rival he took refuge in Kinderhook, and under that name of Merwin set himself to overcome those eccentricities of manner which were his only title to immortality."[36]

Bacon's assertion here is that Merwin originally taught under a different name (Crane?), and changed his name after fleeing Sleepy Hollow to Kinderhook. This is definitely false; Kinderhook's Harold Van Santvoord countered, "As the family record proves, and as living descendants of Ichabod Crane (Jesse Merwin) stoutly affirm, the pedagogue never taught school in Tarrytown. There is no evidence to show that he ever spent a day in Tarrytown in his life."[37]

Van Santvoord, for all his erroneous claims regarding Merwin, was correct in this case. He is known to have been acquainted with Jesse Merwin's son David, who was probably his source of information regarding Jesse's background. In addition, modern-day Merwin descendants have traced their (and Jesse's) lineage back to a common ancestor, Miles

Merwin (1623-1697), who emigrated from England to the New World in 1630.[38]

Jesse Merwin was next referenced in an article in the December 19, 1844 issue of the *Christian Advocate and Journal*, in which former President Martin Van Buren described the Kinderhook schoolhouse, mentioned Irving's 1809 visit, and alleged that "our friend Merwin sat for the picture of Ichabod Crane."[39]

On May 19, 1846, the Methodist Episcopal Church of Kinderhook, of which Merwin was a trustee, sent a letter to supporters in New York City explaining that Merwin had been asked to "come down to your city *in the caricature of Ichabod Crane* for the purpose of collecting money for said church, by lecturing on temperance at the Tabernacle, or at such place or places as you may think proper."[40]

This would seem to imply that Merwin *did* indeed believe himself to have been the model for the fictional schoolmaster – why else would he perform this task as "Ichabod Crane" unless he identified himself with the character?

The bottom of the Methodist Episcopal Church letter is appended with the following notation in the hand of former President Martin Van Buren:

> "This is to certify that I have known Jesse Merwin, Esq., of Kinderhook for about a third of a century, and believe him to be a man of honor and integrity; and that he is the same person celebrated in the writings of Washington Irving under the character of Ichabod Crane in his famous 'Legend of Sleepy Hollow.'
> "M. Van Buren" [41]

It has been suggested that the Van Buren endorsement means little, that all it really says is that the former President *believed* Ichabod to have been patterned after Jesse Merwin.[42] The implication is that, despite his stature,

Martin Van Buren's "belief" in something does not make it an indisputable fact.

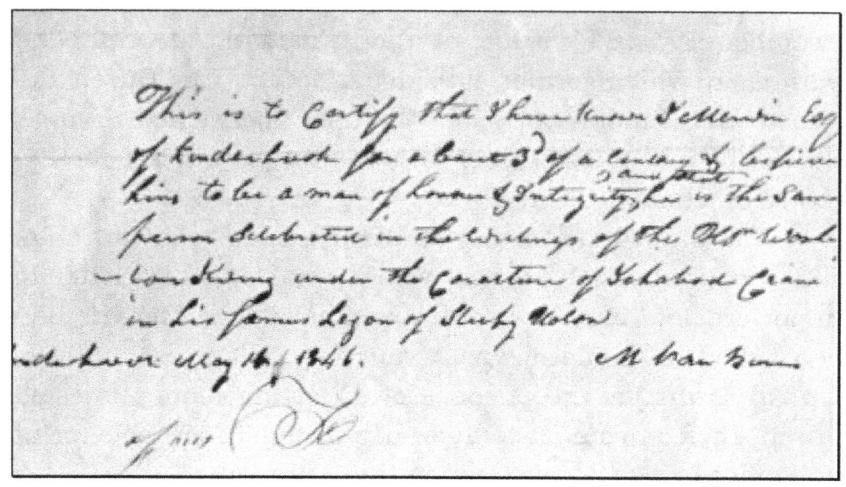

President Martin Van Buren's endorsement of Jesse Merwin as the original of Ichabod Crane

But was Martin Van Buren in a position to know the true identity of Ichabod Crane? Where does Van Buren fit in with Washington Irving and Jesse Merwin?

The Martin Van Buren Connection

Martin Van Buren was born in Kinderhook, NY, in 1782, the son of a farmer and tavern keeper. He studied law under Irving's friend William P. Van Ness. Van Buren was not living in Kinderhook in 1809 while Irving was there, so they did not have an opportunity to meet; Van Buren was actually residing in the village of Hudson at the time, where he was employed as County Surrogate.

Washington Irving first met Martin Van Buren in England in September 1831 when Irving was serving as Secretary to the U.S. Legation in London. (Van Buren had been nominated Ambassador to Great Britain, which ultimately fell through when he was rejected by the Senate the following January.)

This is pure speculation, but one can easily imagine that during one of the initial conversations between the two men, Van Buren would have likely mentioned that he was from Kinderhook, which would have been Irving's cue to reply that he had spent time there, and to possibly inquire as to whether they had any mutual friends in Kinderhook. Irving probably would have learned that Van Buren had studied law under their mutual friend William P. Van Ness; this *may* have even prompted Irving to bring up the name of Jesse Merwin, whom he had befriended while staying with Van Ness in 1809.

President Martin Van Buren (Library of Congress)

Upon resigning from the American Legation in September 1831, Irving moved in with Van Buren in London and the two men were essentially room-mates for several months, touring England together in December. In a March 1832 letter to his brother Peter, Irving described his new friend Van Buren as "one of the gentlest and most amiable men I have ever met with."[43]

After his return to the United States and his "tour on the prairies," Washington Irving spent the winter of 1832-33 in Washington, DC, where he again had the opportunity to spend time with Van Buren, who had just been elected Vice President under President Andrew Jackson. (Van Buren would, of course, go on to become the eighth President of the United States, serving one term from 1837 through 1841.)

September 1833 found Irving and Van Buren as traveling companions once again on a tour of New York State, which included a stop in Kinderhook. Irving is known to have visited Jesse Merwin during this trip – possibly in the company of Van Buren, as the two men were traveling together, and both knew Merwin.

The point of this exercise is to illustrate that Martin Van Buren knew Washington Irving very well, and that the two men spent a good deal of time together from 1831 through 1833. If Jesse Merwin had indeed been the model for Ichabod Crane, Irving had ample opportunity to reveal this fact to Van Buren; it is entirely possible that Van Buren's 1844 and 1846 statements to this effect could have been based upon information he had received from Irving himself.

Of course, an argument could also be made regarding what Martin Van Buren did *not* say; he never explicitly stated that *Irving had told him* that Jesse Merwin had been the inspiration for Ichabod Crane. Is it possible that despite the countless hours the two men spent together, they never discussed "The Legend of Sleepy Hollow" at all?

Washington Irving Identifies Jesse Merwin as Ichabod

As indicated by the opening sentence of Irving's February 1851 letter to Jesse Merwin, which reads, "for suffering your letter to remain so long unanswered," this letter was actually a reply to one previously written to Irving by Merwin. Merwin's letter to Irving was mentioned briefly by Irving's nephew and biographer, Pierre Munroe Irving, who stated that "Merwin had called on him at New York, but, not finding him, had afterward written to him."[44]

No date is given for the Merwin letter, which had apparently been "penned" by one of Jesse's daughters, nor is a date given for Merwin's attempted meeting with Irving.

This letter was apparently found among Washington Irving's papers after his death. According to Pierre Munroe Irving, the back of the letter from Merwin was "indorsed in Mr. Irving's own handwriting: *'From Jesse Merwin, the original of Ichabod Crane.'* "[45]

In a 1925 newspaper interview, Jesse's grandson George Merwin mentioned "a letter that [his] grandfather wrote Irving, and signed with the name of Ichabod."[46] It is not clear if this is a different letter which Jesse himself had signed "Ichabod," or if this refers to the same letter which Irving had annotated. It is possible that George Merwin, being unfamiliar with the two men's respective handwritings, may have presumed the "original of Ichabod Crane" notation to have been written by his grandfather, rather than by Washington Irving.

It is interesting to note that according to Wayne R. Kime, writing in *Pierre M. Irving and Washington Irving: A Collaboration in Life and Letters*, it was the original intent of Pierre Munroe Irving to *deny* that Jesse Merwin was the prototype of Ichabod Crane! [47] Kime cited Pierre's manuscript outline, located in the Berg Collection of the New York Public Library.

However, his Uncle Washington's reply to Merwin is listed in the *Life and Letters* Table of Contents, as well as in the heading of Chapter 14, as "Letter to Jesse Merwin, the Original of Ichabod Crane."[48] Did Pierre change his mind after discovering the letter from Jesse Merwin bearing his Uncle Washington's hand-written endorsement?

(Note: Efforts to locate the letter from Jesse Merwin to Washington Irving which bears Irving's hand-written notation have so far been unsuccessful. We can only hope that it still exists, either preserved in a private collection, or buried in the archives of one of the several historical societies or libraries which maintain collections of Irvingiana. Perhaps someday, someone will come forward and share this relic with present, as well as future, "Legend" aficionados.)

Samuel Youngs

Many residents of Tarrytown and Sleepy Hollow have long believed that the character of Ichabod Crane was largely inspired by Westchester County native Samuel Youngs. They note that after the Revolutionary War, Youngs "became a schoolteacher, lawyer and state assemblyman."[49]

This roughly parallels the career path of the fictional Ichabod Crane following his encounter with the Headless Horseman. Irving related that several years after Ichabod's disappearance from Sleepy Hollow, a farmer visiting New York City brought back the news that he had seen Ichabod, alive and well; that Ichabod "had kept school and studied law at the same time, had been admitted to the bar, turned politician..."[50]

The belief that Ichabod Crane was modeled after Samuel Youngs may date back to the years immediately following the publication of "The Legend of Sleepy Hollow." The same January 30, 1835 *New York Sun* article which named Jesse "Martin" (Merwin) as the inspiration for Ichabod also included the intriguing statement that the original of the schoolmaster "was not *the individual generally considered as such*, who still resides in this country..." Although he was not named in the article (possibly because Youngs was indeed still alive at the time of its publication?), could this have been a reference to Samuel Youngs?

Samuel Youngs was born on December 4, 1760, the son of Joseph Youngs (1722-89) and Susannah Arden (1732-83). Samuel also had a brother, Abraham, and a sister, Mary. The Youngs family home was a 152-acre farm in Mount Pleasant, about four miles east of Sleepy Hollow. The farmhouse was situated on the road to White Plains at what was known as "Youngs Corners," the intersection of Lower Cross Road and Unionville Road, approximately where modern-day Sprain Brook Parkway crosses Route 100C.[51]

Revolutionary War Hero

During the Revolutionary War, the Youngs house was used as a headquarters and gathering place for the Continental army and local militia. Youngs Corners was attacked on February 3, 1780 by a British force of about 1,000 troops commanded by Colonel Chapple Norton. The Americans, under Lt. Colonel Joseph Thompson, were overrun, with 14 killed, 37 wounded and 76 taken prisoner. Youngs' house and outbuildings were then burned by the British.[52]

Samuel Youngs was a volunteer in the Westchester County Militia. He served as a "Westchester Guide," drawing upon his familiarity with the unmapped roads and countryside of the Tarrytown region to guide American soldiers on their forays against the British.[53]

After Lt. Col. Aaron Burr assumed command of the American forces in Westchester County in the fall of 1778, Youngs served as an unpaid volunteer in Burr's newly-formed mounted corps. The duties of this corps included acting as couriers and relaying intelligence about enemy troop movements.[54]

In an 1814 letter, Youngs described his role in the destruction of a block-house, or small fort, which had been built by the British "on a rising ground below Delancey's bridge." Youngs was one of about 40 men who attacked the position with incendiary "hand grenades" or "canteens filled with inflammable materials."[55]

In 1782, Youngs was commissioned a Lieutenant "in a company attached to Sheldon's Dragoons."[56] Lt. Samuel Youngs' name appears in the officers' section on the West side of the Revolutionary Soldiers Monument erected in 1894 in Sleepy Hollow Cemetery.

The Schoolmaster

According to Thomas Scharf's *History of Westchester County*, Samuel Youngs began teaching school in 1790 in School District Number Two in Eastchester township, about 10 miles southeast of Sleepy Hollow.[57]

It is not known if Youngs ever taught in Sleepy Hollow as well; few, if any, such records were kept in the Sleepy Hollow region prior to the mid-1830s. The very existence and locations of the early schoolhouses are in dispute, much less the names of the presiding schoolmasters.

Youngs probably viewed teaching as a way of temporarily supporting himself while preparing for a legal career. He taught from about 1790 to 1792, at which time he was replaced by Andrew Dean.

Unlike modern-day schoolteachers, small-town schoolmasters in the 1700s were not required to possess college degrees or special certifications. Like the fictional Ichabod Crane, whose primary qualification seems to be that he "had read several books quite through," the fact that Youngs was studying law was probably deemed sufficient by the local Dutch farmers to entrust their children to his instruction in the basic "Three Rs."

Youngs' Legal Career

Samuel Youngs began practicing law in 1793. He was appointed Surrogate of Westchester County for five separate terms: October 31, 1800 through January 28, 1802; February 19, 1807 through March 10, 1808; February 16, 1810 through February 12, 1811; March 19, 1813 through March 26, 1815; and July 8, 1819 through February 17, 1821.[58] (Note: A Surrogate is a judicial officer with jurisdiction over matters such as wills and the settlement of estates.)

Youngs was also a Master of Chancery,[59] which is, basically, an assistant to the judge of a court involved with non-criminal cases, such as lawsuits. Similarly, Ichabod Crane's ultimate vocation was "justice of the Ten Pound Court," which is a judge authorized to resolve lawsuits involving property valued at less than ten pounds.[60]

Samuel Youngs served two terms as a New York State Assemblyman representing Westchester County, first in 1796 and again from 1809-10.

Youngs was residing in Mount Pleasant at this time, which contradicts tradition that, like Ichabod, he disappeared to parts unknown after leaving his teaching position. He did move to White Plains at some point, still only a few miles away, where he lived for 15 years, and then to Greenburgh (present-day Elmsford).[61]

Youngs would later assist many Westchester County Revolutionary War veterans with their pension applications, providing "abundant testimony" regarding their service, thereby indirectly providing a wealth of historical data regarding wartime activities in the area.[62]

Samuel Youngs was described as "of a genial disposition and very good company. He had seen service during the

Revolution and he delighted in telling anecdotes of the war..."63

Youngs never married, nor did he have any children. He died on September 12, 1839, at the age of 78. He was originally buried in the Old Dutch Burying Ground in Sleepy Hollow, next to his parents. However, when Dale Cemetery in nearby Ossining was dedicated in October 1851, the local cemetery association sought a notable citizen to be the first burial there. Youngs seemed a logical choice – he had been very highly regarded as a patriot and as a public servant... but possibly more importantly, he had no heirs to object to it. His body was disinterred and re-buried in Dale Cemetery, where his grave is marked by a large obelisk.

Samuel Youngs monument in Dale Cemetery, Ossining, New York (Photo courtesy of Patrick Raftery)

(Note: Youngs' original grave site in the Old Dutch Burying Ground is indicated by a small brass grave marker, inscribed "Samuel Youngs, 1760-1839," placed immediately to the right of his parents' double tombstone. Next to Youngs' marker is a second marker, inscribed, simply... "ICABOD.")

Connection to Washington Irving

So what then is the connection, if any, between Washington Irving and Samuel Youngs? Samuel's sister Mary Youngs (1761-1815) was married to Abraham Van Wart; Mary and Abraham had a son, Henry Van Wart, who married Washington Irving's sister, Sarah. Therefore, Washington Irving's brother-in-law Henry Van Wart – the very same Henry Van Wart who kindled Irving's imagination one night in Birmingham with his "waggish fiction of one Brom Bones" – was the nephew of Samuel Youngs!

It is not known if Irving ever met Samuel Youngs in person. Irving's published correspondence only contains one reference to Youngs, in a January 1840 letter to Irving's old friend Gouverneur Kemble, then a U.S. Congressman. The letter requests that Kemble support a claim submitted by Youngs for remuneration for the destruction of his father's farm by the British during the war. Since Samuel had died several months earlier, Irving's letter appears to have been written on behalf of the "other heirs" of Joseph Youngs – possibly at the request of Irving's brother-in-law, Henry Van Wart?[64]

Conspicuously missing from Irving's letter is a personalized character reference for Samuel Youngs; instead, the letter contains an almost generic-sounding endorsement of the Youngs family having been "active in the service of the country." One might infer that Irving did not know Samuel Youngs personally, or if he did, he must not have known him very well.

It is well-documented that while living in England from 1815-26, Irving spent a great deal of time at the Birmingham residence of Sarah and Henry Van Wart. It seems quite plausible, then, that Irving could have at least heard *of* Youngs, simply from hearing Henry speak of his Uncle Samuel.

Samuel Youngs' career may indeed have been Irving's inspiration for the ultimate fate of Ichabod after he was chased out of Sleepy Hollow. The other, more well-documented candidate, Jesse Merwin, was married and still a schoolteacher when Irving befriended him in 1809; Irving needed a different ending to Ichabod's story, and therefore may have borrowed from the life of the other schoolteacher he knew (or at least knew *of...*).

Fleshing Out the Character of Ichabod

It appears that the Ichabod Crane character was based loosely on Kinderhook schoolmaster Jesse Merwin, possibly including elements of Samuel Youngs' life as well, with the name provided by Col. Ichabod Bennett Crane. How, then, did Washington Irving flesh out the character of his fictional Ichabod Crane?

Henry Fielding's "Partridge"

Irving biographer Stanley T. Williams suggested "this caricature derives traits from Fielding's Partridge and from the schoolmaster in *The Deserted Village.*"[65]

The "Partridge" that Williams was referring to is a schoolmaster who becomes the title character's traveling companion in Henry Fielding's 1749 novel *Tom Jones.*

There are indeed some similarities between the characters of Partridge and Crane. For one thing, Fielding's Partridge is very self-serving, often having ulterior motives for his actions. For example, when Partridge volunteers to accompany the title character Tom Jones on his journey, it is primarily because he believes Tom to be a runaway and expects to be "well rewarded for his pains" if he can eventually persuade Tom to return home.[66]

Ichabod Crane, too, is shown to have a self-serving side, his ulterior motives illustrated several times in the "Sleepy Hollow" story. For instance, Irving relates how Ichabod would sometimes walk some of his younger students home from school, especially those with pretty sisters or whose mothers were good cooks – "noted for the comforts of the cupboard."

Probably the best example of Ichabod's self-serving nature is his infatuation with Katrina Van Tassel. He is clearly charmed by Katrina's beauty, but is obviously just as enchanted by the prospect of one day inheriting her father's abundant estate: "From the moment Ichabod laid his eyes upon these regions of delight, the peace of his mind was at an end, and his only study was how to gain the affections of the peerless daughter of Van Tassel."[67]

But the most noteworthy similarity between Partridge and Ichabod Crane is that each exhibits an extremely superstitious nature. In one scene in *Tom Jones*, Partridge and Tom become lost while traveling at night, and Partridge becomes convinced that a witch has cast a spell on them; they later see a light in the distance, which further terrifies Partridge, until it is discovered to be a gypsy encampment.[68]

Partridge also relates several "certainly true" ghost stories, including one where a devil carries a man off through the keyhole of a door, stating that "evil spirits can carry away anything without being seen."[69] In one particularly humorous passage, Partridge and Jones attend a performance of Shakespeare's *Hamlet*, and upon seeing the ghost in the play, Partridge "fell into so violent a trembling, that his knees knocked against each other."[70]

Ichabod Crane is likewise a firm believer in the supernatural, spending many evenings in the company of "the old Dutch wives" listening to "their marvelous tales of ghosts and goblins, and haunted fields... and particularly of the headless horseman." Returning home from these evening gatherings, "every sound of nature... fluttered his excited imagination," and Ichabod's nasal voice can be heard throughout the Hollow, singing psalm tunes in order to keep the evil spirits away. (Ichabod's superstitious nature apparently did not go unnoticed by Brom Bones, who would later use his fear of ghosts against him.)

There may be something to the Partridge analogy. As discussed previously, in a December 1809 letter to Judge Van Ness in Kinderhook, Irving mentioned Jesse Merwin twice by name, and then asked, "How does my friend Partridge and his Academy?" In this context, I believe Irving's reference to "Partridge" was actually directed at Merwin. Could Partridge have been a nickname Irving gave his schoolteacher friend, after the comical character in the Fielding novel?[71]

One final observation: "Partridge" and "Crane" are both types of birds! Could Irving's choice of the name Crane have been a subtle nod to the Partridge character in *Tom Jones*, whom he also associated with his friend Jesse Merwin?

Oliver Goldsmith's schoolteacher

The other part of Stanley Williams' suggestion, that Irving may also have been inspired by *The Deserted Village*, refers to a poem by Oliver Goldsmith, first published in 1770. Goldsmith's schoolteacher, who remains nameless, appears very briefly, his description contained in 24 lines out of the entire 430-line poem.

Of his schoolteacher, Goldsmith wrote, "A man severe he was, and stern to view... yet he was kind."[72] Similarly, Ichabod Crane, while not averse to the application of the birch rod, "administered justice with discrimination rather than severity."[73]

But the main similarity to be noted between Goldsmith's unnamed schoolteacher and Irving's Ichabod Crane is that both characters are highly regarded by their respective townspeople for their seemingly superior knowledge and speaking abilities. Goldsmith says of his schoolmaster, "The village all declared how much he knew; 'Twas certain he could write, and cypher too."[74] Likewise, Ichabod Crane is "esteemed... as a man of great erudition, for he had read several books quite through."[75] Both Goldsmith and Irving paint their townspeople as simple "rustics," much in awe of those having had formal education, which is seemingly defined as an ability to read.

Also, both Goldsmith and Irving compare the knowledge possessed by their respective schoolmasters to that of the village parson. In *The Deserted Village*, only the parson is able to out-argue the schoolteacher; in "The Legend of Sleepy Hollow," Ichabod is "inferior in learning only to the parson."[76]

Lauchie Long Legs

"Lauchie Long Legs" was one of Walter Scott's neighbors in Scotland. He was a poor farmer, or "cocklaird," whose "bleak-looking" property was located just to the east of Scott's residence, Abbotsford. His ancestral family estate, meager as it was, was formally named Lochbreist, and following Scottish tradition, he was named after it – Laird (or Lord) Lochbreist – but was better known by his nickname Lauchie Long Legs, "from the length of his limbs."[77]

During Irving's August 1817 visit to Abbotsford, Scott pointed out Lauchie from a distance, and entertained Irving with a story of how, following his return from a trip to France, Scott had been questioned by Lauchie about the French people. Lauchie had apparently been under the impression that France was inhabited by illiterate barbarians, and he seemed "quite astonished" to learn that they were "nearly" as civilized as the Scots! [78]

In a November 3, 1819 letter to Scott, Irving recalled observing "the *worthy wight* Lockie Longlegs... *striding along the profile* of the knoll... with his flimsy garments *fluttering about him*."[79]

Irving's letter to Scott was penned during the period he was in the process of writing the final version of "The Legend of Sleepy Hollow." Irving clearly recycled his description of Lauchie, only very slightly modified, to describe Ichabod Crane: "A *worthy wight* of the name of Ichabod Crane... *striding along the profile* of a hill on a windy day, with his clothes bagging and *fluttering about him*..."[80]

Although the fictional Ichabod apparently inherited Lauchie's lanky physique, their personalities were quite different. Ichabod Crane was worldly and sophisticated (or at least appeared that way to the "country bumpkins" of Sleepy Hollow), possessing "vastly superior taste" and "superior elegance." Lauchie, on the other hand, was "ignorant" and "knew nothing of the world beyond his neighborhood."[81]

Was it Irving's original intent for Ichabod to be "exceedingly lank," or did his recollection of Lauchie Long Legs, which occurred right about the time that he was committing "The Legend" to paper, influence his concept of Ichabod's appearance?

Don Quixote

Comparisons have also been made between Irving's Ichabod Crane and Miguel de Cervantes' Don Quixote, from his 1605 novel of the same title.

In particular, Irving's description of Ichabod riding his borrowed "broken-down plough-horse," Gunpowder, on his way to the Van Tassel's quilting frolic, is highly reminiscent of Don Quixote astride his old work horse, Rocinante, whom he transforms, if only in his mind, into a steed worthy of a knight.

Don Quixote refers to himself several times as a "knight-errant," and is described as "sallying forth in quest of adventures." Irving used almost the exact same words in describing how Ichabod "issued forth, like a knight-errant in quest of adventures" on his way to the Van Tassel farm on that fateful night...[82]

Thomas Anburey's Influence

When Irving was compiling material in 1817-18 for *The Sketch Book*, he began copying passages from various books containing accounts of travel in the United States, presumably to draw from for descriptions of scenery and backgrounds for his American-themed stories. One of them, *Travels through the Interior Parts of America*, written in 1789 by Thomas Anburey, contained a colorful paragraph ridiculing the appearance of New Englanders on horseback, which Irving transcribed into one of his 1817 notebooks:

> "In short you cannot possibly form a just idea of it unless you were mounted on N England Rosinante which title they justly merit for I assure you they are very much a la Quixote and to meet a New Englander riding in the woods... you might mistake him for a Knight of the Woeful Countenance. Their horses are of a very slender make and not over fat... the master with his long leg bestrides it which are in Stirrups that the toe can but just reach. Then his upright position with his long lank visage... picture to yourself such a man thus mounted, of such outre appearance & forbear to laugh if you can." [83]

This excerpt is similar to Irving's description of Ichabod Crane astride Gunpowder; could this descriptive passage have inspired Irving's account of his own New Englander mounted on his borrowed "not over fat" steed as he made his way to the party at Mynheer Van Tassel's house?

Trends in American Literature

Although living in England during the writing of *The Sketch Book*, Washington Irving's target audience was the American book-reading public. To be successful, he needed to make his stories appealing to the American tastes in literature that were prevalent in 1819. In a letter to Henry Brevoort dated April 1, 1819, Irving asked him, "what themes &c would be popular and striking in America?"[84]

Unfortunately, Brevoort's reply, assuming one existed, appears to have been lost to time. His earliest known letter written subsequent to Irving's inquiry was dated September 9, 1819, in which he referenced two of Irving's other letters, dated July 10 and July 28; no mention was made of Irving's April 1 letter.[85]

The Yankee Stereotype

An increasingly popular character type in stories and plays published in the late 18th and early 19th centuries was the "Yankee." The Yankee character was a native of New England, particularly the state of Connecticut.

The Yankee stereotype first appeared in 1787 as a comic character in the play *The Contrast* by Royall Tyler. Other Yankees followed in *The Yorker's Stratagem* by J. Robinson in 1792, *Jonathan Postfree* by L. Beach in 1806, *Love and Friendship* by A. B. Lindsley in 1809, and *The Bucktails* by Irving's close friend James Kirke Paulding in 1815.[86]

These early Yankees, most of whom seemed to be named Jonathan, were typically portrayed as country bumpkins who found themselves out of their element in the big city. The early stereotype Yankee was a simple backwoods character who used common sense to get the better of his more sophisticated city-dwelling rivals.

However, with the introduction of Ichabod Crane in "The Legend of Sleepy Hollow," the Connecticut Yankee character is more akin to what we would refer to as a "city slicker," with the backwoodsman persona going to Ichabod's rival, Brom Bones. Irving is thereby credited as having been the first to introduce a conflict between East and West, the refined and cultured Connecticut Yankee vs. the rough-hewn frontiersman.[87] In a classic conflict of city vs. country, Irving's educated city slicker is bested by the country dweller.

Originally, the Yankee was assigned "heroic qualities that elevate him from buffoon to folk hero."[88] However, in "The Legend of Sleepy Hollow," where the Yankee and backwoodsman roles are reversed, these heroic attributes are instead given to Brom Bones.

Dutch–Yankee Conflict

Setting his tale in New York's Hudson River Valley, Irving also took the opportunity to draw upon the anti-Yankee sentiments held by the Dutch residents in the early 19th century. Ichabod's Connecticut Yankee character reflects the influx of New Englanders into New York in the early 1800s, "impressing their stamp on regional commerce, politics and culture." From 1800 through 1820, such Yankee immigrants resulted in a 130% increase in the population of New York State.[89]

Ichabod Crane is clearly an interloper into the rustic setting that is Sleepy Hollow.

Irving had previously addressed this conflict in 1809 in his *Knickerbocker's History of New York*, writing about "the people of Connecticut, who bordered upon the eastern frontier of New-Netherlands... gangs of these marauders, we are told, penetrated into the New-Netherland settlements, and threw whole villages into consternation by their unparalleled volubility, and their intolerable inquisitiveness – two evil habits hitherto unknown in those parts."[90]

This "intolerable inquisitiveness" stereotype, further defined by American Literature Professor Donald Ringe as "the Yankee's propensity to talk and to question his neighbors and acquaintances about their business,"[91] is also demonstrated by Ichabod Crane: "He was a kind of travelling gazette, carrying the whole budget of local gossip from house to house."[92]

Perhaps the worst Yankee "trait" was their purported love of money, as epitomized by the shrewd and greedy "Yankee peddler" stereotype. Ichabod is shown to possess this trait as well, scheming about how Katrina's inheritance "might be readily turned into cash..."[93]

(Irving touched upon this subject once again in an 1839 essay for *The Knickerbocker* magazine titled "Conspiracy of the Cocked Hats." In the postscript to his essay, Irving informed The Editor that a "smooth-tongued" Yankee had infiltrated the traditional Dutch stronghold of Communipaw, and had persuaded a Dutch heiress to elope with him. The enterprising groom subsequently divided his bride's prized cabbage garden into town lots and advertised them for sale – sound familiar?)[94]

Irving had also written in his 1809 *Knickerbocker's History*, "Great jealousy did they likewise stir up, by their intermeddling and successes among the divine sex; for being a race of brisk, likely, pleasant-tongued varlets, they soon seduced the light affections of the simple damsels from their ponderous Dutch gallants."[95]

Irving revisited this romantic rivalry theme in "The Legend of Sleepy Hollow," describing Ichabod Crane as "peculiarly happy in the smiles of all the country damsels... sauntering, with a whole bevy of them, along the banks of the adjacent mill-pond; while the more bashful country bumpkins hung sheepishly back, envying his superior elegance and address."[96]

This is, of course, Ichabod's undoing when he sets his sights on Katrina Van Tassel, and finds himself the target of her other jealous suitor, Brom Bones...

Anti-Puritanical Sentiments

As he did with the Dutch-Yankee conflict, Washington Irving also seems to have drawn upon the anti-Puritanical sentiments of post-war New York that were prevalent at the time.

Ichabod Crane is described as being "a perfect master of Cotton Mather's history of New England witchcraft, in which, by the way, he most firmly and potently believed."[97] Cotton Mather was a very well-known Puritan minister, probably best remembered for his role during the infamous Salem Witch Trials of the late 1600s.

Irving presented a few other more subtle hints to Ichabod's puritanical attitudes. Describing his methods in the classroom, Irving related that Ichabod "ever bore in mind the golden maxim, 'Spare the rod and spoil the child,' " which is a variation of a Biblical quote from Proverbs 13:24.[98]

Also, Irving stated that one of Ichabod's other vocations was singing master, leading the church choir on Sundays "where, in his own mind, he completely carried away the palm from the parson." Sometimes finding himself walking home alone at dusk, Ichabod would imagine he was being besieged by ghosts and witches, and would "sing psalm tunes" to "drive away evil spirits."[99]

Part of Irving's seemingly negative attitude toward Puritanism may have been due to his own upbringing. Irving's father, William Irving, had been a strict no-nonsense Presbyterian. Characterized as stern and virtually humorless, he required Washington and his siblings to attend church every morning and afternoon, with a lecture in the evening.

Of his father's unyielding religious views, Irving later said, "I was led to think that somehow or other everything that was pleasant was wicked."[100] In an 1825 letter, Irving wrote, "religion was forced upon me before I could understand or appreciate it; I was taxed with it; thwarted with it; wearied with it in a thousand harsh and disagreeable ways; until I was disgusted with all its forms and observances."[101]

Irving's disdain for religion was clearly present when he was a young man touring Europe in 1804-06, long before writing "The Legend of Sleepy Hollow." His April 17, 1805 journal entry, written in Italy, refers to "the miracles and fables of the Romish religion" as being "silly superstition." A few pages later, in his April 19, 1805 entry, he recounted observing a religious service, stating that he and his travel companions "left the church disgusted with the climax of superstition we had witnessed."[102]

(It should be noted that Irving's attitudes toward religion apparently changed dramatically later in life. He joined Christ Episcopal Church in Tarrytown in 1848, eventually becoming a church vestryman and warden. The original pine pew which Irving occupied every Sunday is still on display in the Christ Church baptistry.)

Near the end of "The Legend of Sleepy Hollow," following the schoolmaster's disappearance, Ichabod's copy of Cotton Mather's *History of New England Witchcraft* is "consigned to the flames" – perhaps as a symbolic gesture, with the Mather volume serving as a representation of religious intolerance.

Postscript – An Early Schoolmaster-to-Politician Story Idea?

One of the small notebooks Irving kept in England in 1817, a year or more before his "nostalgic conversation" with Henry Van Wart, contains a curious entry on page 6: *"Story of Member of Congress originally Schoolmaster etc."*

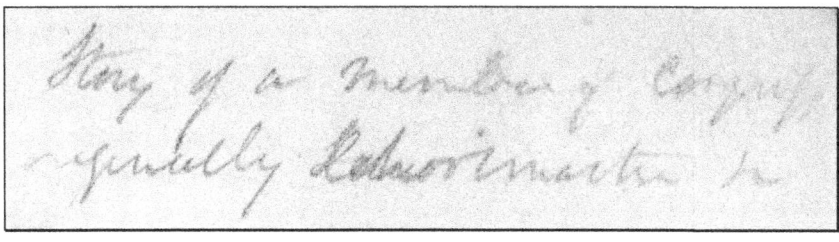

Washington Irving's hand-written notebook entry from 1817 (Photo courtesy of The New York Public Library, Manuscripts and Archives Division; Astor, Lenox, and Tilden Foundation; Washington Irving papers)

The 2½ by 4¾-inch notebook consists of a number of random, seemingly unrelated notes with no discernible theme; previous pages contain references to Daniel Boone, a "Chop House" in Soho, London, and the Missouri River![103]

Was this the seed of a story idea that Irving quickly jotted down in a moment of inspiration, which was later expanded and woven into "The Legend"?

Chapter 6

A Blooming Lass of Fresh Eighteen

> *"She was a blooming lass of fresh eighteen; plump as a partridge; ripe and melting and rosy cheeked as one of her father's peaches, and universally famed, not merely for her beauty, but her vast expectations..."*
> - from "The Legend of Sleepy Hollow," 1820

Unlike Ichabod Crane, Washington Irving's inspiration for the character of Katrina Van Tassel is a little harder to identify. Irving was reportedly very evasive about who had been the model for Katrina; when pressed by the ladies of Sleepy Hollow, Irving was said to reply that they *each* would have made a perfect Katrina!

Let's explore a few of the theories about the "true identity" of the original of Katrina Van Tassel...

Catriena Ecker Van Tassel

There is a much-photographed tombstone in the Old Dutch Burying Ground which is inscribed with the name Catriena Ecker Van Tassel. This Catriena was born on November 10, 1736, to Sibert Ecker (sometimes spelled Acker) and the former Aeltje DeRonde. The ninth of eleven children, Catriena was the grand-daughter of the original Wolfert Acker of "Wolfert's Roost" fame. An Ecker by birth, she became a Van Tassel upon marrying Petrus (Peter) Van Tassel in 1765.

Tombstone of Catriena Ecker Van Tassel in the Old Dutch Burying Ground (Photo courtesy of Patrick Raftery)

Catriena and Peter owned a farm on the Saw Mill River Road, adjacent to the farm owned by Peter's cousin Cornelius and his wife, Elizabeth – the same Cornelius and Elizabeth discussed in Chapter 4 – and their farm was also looted and burned during the same raid on the night of November 17, 1777.

Catriena Ecker Van Tassel died in 1793 at age 56.

This Catriena Van Tassel has been presumed by some to have loaned her name to the fictional "Katrina Van Tassel" after Washington Irving read it on her tombstone during his 1798 visit to Sleepy Hollow. Indeed, Irving describes in his 1839 essay "Sleepy Hollow" how he and his friends would "turn down the weeds and brambles that obscured the modest brown grave-stones, half sunk in earth, on which were recorded, in Dutch, the names of the patriarchs of ancient days, the Ackers, the Van Tassels..."[1]

While it is certainly possible for Irving to have appropriated the name of his heroine from a tombstone, it is more likely that he simply heard the name spoken during his stay in Tarrytown. "Catriena Van Tassel," or one of its variants, such as Catrina or Catharina, was a very common name in the area. A cursory investigation of Westchester County birth records turned up no fewer than a dozen "Catrina Van Tassels" born between 1700 and 1785!

Eleanor Van Tassel Brush

The predominant local tradition in Tarrytown regarding the "true identity" of Katrina Van Tassel is that she was modeled after Eleanor Van Tassel, the niece of Catriena Ecker Van Tassel. According to this theory, Washington Irving supposedly based Katrina's persona on Eleanor, but appropriated her name from Eleanor's Aunt Catriena's tombstone.

Eleanor, known as "Lena" or "Laney," was born on June 22, 1766. She was the eldest child, and only daughter, of Jacob Van Tassel of Wolfert's Roost and his wife, Hester Van Tassel (1734-1811).[2]

Eleanor apparently inherited some of her father's belligerent attitude toward the British. Thomas Scharf, in his *History of Westchester County*, offered an illuminating anecdote about young Laney, who he referred to as Katrina Van Tassel: "She was the happy possessor of a fine flock of geese that were led about under the guidance of a stalwart gander. She was very proud of them; but the Hessians encamped in the neighborhood viewed them with covetous eyes and in a different light, and several times attempted to steal them. Katrina's eye, however, was too watchful to permit their success. She warned off the marauders with a menacing wave of her hand and the expression of a chilling, prophetic hope that the old gander would eat grass from the grave of any Hessian who dared to touch one of them."[3]

Following then 13-year-old Eleanor's father's capture in 1779, the Roost was left virtually unprotected – a situation the British soon exploited. Washington Irving's 1839 "Chronicles of Wolfert's Roost" includes the following account of the subsequent raid on the Van Tassel home: "An armed vessel came to anchor in front; a boat full of men pulled to shore. The garrison flew to arms; that is to say, to mops, broomsticks, shovels, tongs, and all kinds of domestic weapons; for unluckily, the great piece of ordnance, the goose-gun, was absent with its owner. Above all, a vigorous defense was made with that most potent of female weapons, the tongue. Never did invaded hen-roost make a more vociferous outcry. It was all in vain. The house was sacked and plundered, fire was set to each corner, and in a few moments its blaze shed a baleful light far over the Tappan Sea..."[4]

Irving continued, "The invaders then pounced upon the blooming Laney Van Tassel, the beauty of the Roost, and endeavored to bear her off to the boat. But here was the real tug of war. The mother, the aunt, and the strapping negro wench, all flew to the rescue. The struggle continued down to the very water's edge; when a voice from the armed vessel at anchor, ordered the spoilers to desist; they relinquished their prize, jumped into their boats, and pulled off, and the heroine of the Roost escaped with a mere rumpling of the feathers."[5]

Eleanor "Laney" Van Tassel's monument in the Old Dutch Burying Ground (Author's photo)

Eleanor Van Tassel married Caleb Brush (1763-1856) on August 26, 1789. The couple had nine children: Joshua, John, James, Mahala, Catharine, Benjamin, Caleb, Jacob and William.[6]

Eleanor died October 27, 1861. She is buried with her husband in the Old Dutch Burying Ground, on the south side of the church, their graves marked by a large white monument.

So how did Eleanor become associated with Katrina Van Tassel? It appears that this theory originated simply because Irving wrote about her! She was the only young Van Tassel girl he included in any of his other writings, and she did, after all, once live in one of the houses long associated with "The Legend." It probably didn't hurt that Irving referred to Eleanor as "the beauty of the Roost," which of course mirrors his assertion that his fictional Katrina had been "famed not only for her beauty but for her vast expectations."

Typical of most "oral traditions," the story appears to have been embellished over the years. Some versions state that while attending a service at the Old Dutch Church in 1798, the teenage Washington Irving became enchanted by the "beautiful 18-year-old" Eleanor when he noticed her singing with the choir. He also supposedly (simultaneously?) looked out the window and saw the sun illuminating the name of Eleanor's Aunt Catriena on her tombstone. While a romantic notion, this tradition is quickly debunked when one does the math and discovers that Eleanor was actually 32 years old in 1798, with several children of her own, having been married for nine years.

The real question then becomes: When did Washington Irving first hear the story of Eleanor Van Tassel? Did he know anything at all about her prior to the 1819 writing of "The Legend of Sleepy Hollow"?

On that summer evening in 1818 in Birmingham that Irving spent reminiscing with Henry Van Wart – the night he first heard of Brom Bones' race with the devil for a bowl of punch – might he have also been told the story of the beautiful young Van Tassel girl who was almost carried off by a group of British sailors? Possibly...

It is equally possible that Irving knew *nothing at all* about Eleanor until he interviewed her father, Jacob Van Tassel, in the late 1830s – nearly 20 years *after* he wrote "The Legend." As discussed previously in Chapter 2, Irving "had a long conversation" with Jacob at his home in New York City, where he "gathered some of the particulars... since recorded" in his "Wolfert's Roost" essay, published in the April 1839 issue of *The Knickerbocker*.[7] Did "the particulars" gathered from Jacob include the story of the attempted abduction of Eleanor? We can only guess...

There is nothing concrete in Irving's writings or other contemporary accounts which directly link Eleanor Van Tassel to Katrina; any such theories appear to be based purely on speculation.

Yes, an essay written by Washington Irving almost 20 years after "The Legend" did include a two-paragraph anecdote about a teenage girl who happened to have the surname Van Tassel – but is this really enough to lead one to conclude that she *must have been* the prototype of Katrina?

Catharine Van Tassel

As discussed in Chapter 2, the most likely inspiration for the Baltus Van Tassel farm was the Revolutionary War-era Van Tassel Tavern, later known as the Mott House under the proprietorship of Jacob and Sarah Mott.

In the mid-1830s, after having settled into Sunnyside, Washington Irving reportedly told his new friends the Motts that their residence was the structure that he "had in mind" for the castle of Baltus Van Tassel when he wrote "The Legend of Sleepy Hollow." Some versions of the story specify that Irving said this in confidence to Jacob; others say it was to his wife. Edgar Mayhew Bacon further offered that Irving persuaded Jacob to refrain from altering the building, so that it might retain the same appearance as it did in the days when "Katrina" entertained her suitors.

At the time of Washington Irving's 1798 visit to Tarrytown, the Van Tassel Tavern was owned by John Van Tassel (1737-1807), who indeed had a daughter named Catharine. She was born November 29, 1773, the sixth of seven children.

This Catharine Van Tassel was the niece, as well as god-daughter, of Peter and Catriena Ecker Van Tassel, discussed in a previous section. She was also the first cousin of Eleanor "Laney" Van Tassel.

Catharine would have been 24 years old in 1798, the summer Irving spent in Tarrytown. Could Irving have met her? Quite possibly, especially if he happened to venture into the Van Tassel Tavern for a cup of cool apple cider during a break from his "boyish ramblings" through Sleepy Hollow…

Catharine Van Tassel never married. She died on June 9, 1820 at the age of 48, apparently after a long illness. Her epitaph reads:

> "Her months of affliction is over,
> Her days and nights of distress,
> We see her in anguish no more,
> She has gained her happy release."[8]

"The Legend of Sleepy Hollow" had just been published in Volume 6 of *The Sketch Book* a few months prior to Catharine's death; however, we will probably never know if she ever learned that "her" name (that is, the Dutch version of it) had been immortalized in Irving's story.

Irving's purported comments to the Motts more or less fall under the "oral traditions" category, having been passed down verbally through several generations before being set in print by various historians, including Scharf and Bacon.[9]

Irving's exact words have, unfortunately, been lost to time. Was he speaking figuratively, meaning that *in his imagination*, his fictional Katrina Van Tassel lived in the house in his story? Or did he mean, literally, that Katrina/Catharine Van Tassel had once been a real, flesh and blood occupant of the house?

Helen Van Alen

As we discussed briefly in Chapter 2, the prevailing "local tradition" in Kinderhook, New York, regarding Katrina Van Tassel is that the character was based on a local "coquette" named Helen Van Alen.

Like the Van Tassels of Sleepy Hollow, the Kinderhook Van Alens can trace their lineage back to their ancestral Holland. The family patriarch in North America was Laurentius Van Alen, born in 1632 in Oldenzaal, Holland, who arrived in Kinderhook in the late 1660s.

Laurentius and his wife Elbertje Evertse Backer (1646-??) had ten children. One of their sons, Luykas (1682-1747) and his wife, Elizabeth Truijt (1701-1790) are credited with having constructed Kinderhook's historic Luykas Van Alen House in 1737.[10]

Helen Van Alen was the youngest of six children born to David Van Alen (1752-1846), a grandson of Luykas, and his wife Maria Van Alen (who was also David's second cousin). Helen's family inherited the Luykas Van Alen House in the early 1800s – thus the "local tradition" that it was once the home of Katrina Van Tassel.

Historical marker outside Luykas Van Alen House, Kinderhook, New York, erected by State Education Department in 1932; recently toppled by a snowplow... (Photo courtesy of Glenn Fisher)

The earliest published record found thus far linking Katrina Van Tassel to Kinderhook came from, not surprisingly, Harold Van Santvoord. In his series of letters to the editor of *The New York Times*, published in the spring of 1898, he stated that the real name of Katrina (as well as that of Brom Bones) was "known to older residents of the village."[11] He further explained that "an aged lady of tenacious powers of memory and who was well acquainted with all the facts of the case gave [him] a few years before her death a minute description of the personal charms of Katrina Van Tassel, whom she had known quite well in her youth."[12]

Curiously, however, Van Santvoord did not provide the *name* of Katrina's prototype, although one of his letters did allude to her having resided in "a neighboring farmhouse" – presumably the Luykas Van Alen House?[13]

A year later, July 16, 1899, a feature article by John P. Ritter titled "The Real Ichabod Crane – When and Where Irving Discovered Him" appeared in *The New York Herald*. According to Ritter, "Among the older inhabitants of Kinderhook are several who remember *Katrina Van Alen* well, and those minds are stored with traditions of her beauty and her coquetry."[14] The article included a photograph of the Luykas Van Alen House, and asserted that it was a "well established fact" that Washington Irving and Jesse Merwin had "passed many evenings" in Katrina's company.

Despite his use of the name Katrina, was Ritter actually referring to Helen Van Alen? Was he calling her Katrina in error, or could he have been simply quoting the "older inhabitants" of the village who may have referred to Helen colloquially as "Katrina," much as Jesse Merwin was (and to this day, still is) sometimes referred to as Ichabod Crane?

Helen was again referred to as Katrina Van Alen in an October 23, 1925 *Frederick Post* article titled "Ichabod Crane's Grandson Tells About Sleepy Hollow." In this article, Jesse Merwin's grandson, George Merwin, credited Mrs. Maria Van Alen Herrick with providing the knowledge that "Irving had called upon Katrina [Van Alen] and thus drew a first-hand picture of her charms."[15] Given Mrs. Herrick as the source, the article was apparently referring to Helen Van Alen, who was Mrs. Herrick's great-aunt. Maria Van Alen Herrick was to become the leading proponent of the Helen Van Alen version of the Katrina Van Tassel tradition.

In an article published in 1953 in *YANKEE* magazine, statements by Mrs. Herrick confirmed that it was indeed her Great-Aunt Helen whom Van Alen family tradition maintains was the prototype of Katrina, and whom Irving and Merwin "were wont to call on."[16] (The authors were apparently quoting an earlier article, as Mrs. Herrick had died in 1935.)

However, Mrs. Herrick seemed to remember her great-aunt differently than the "older residents" quoted in earlier articles; her comments imply that Helen was not quite the beautiful coquette as was described in the story, although she apparently "made herself a little more lovely for Irving." According to Mrs. Herrick, her aunt "died an old maid, you know. Everyone thought she'd marry Washington Irving, but..."[17]

(Note: In some versions of the story, Helen Van Alen has been referred to as *Helena*, with an "a," possibly confusing her with a cousin born in 1782. However, her cousin Helena (with the "a") did not die "an old maid," but married one John Stevenson, circa 1805. Helena and John made their home in Phelps, NY, according to her father's 1847 will, and were never associated with the Luykas Van Alen House.)[18]

Where Does Maria Van Alen Herrick Fit In?

Who exactly was Maria Van Alen Herrick, and was she in a position to know the family's history?

Maria Van Alen (1866-1935) was the daughter of John D. Van Alen (1821-1869), the son of Helen's older sister, Elizabeth Van Alen (1797-1878). John D. Van Alen was therefore Helen's nephew, making Maria her great-niece. (Maria took the name Herrick after marrying William C. Herrick in 1884.)

After Maria's father died in March 1869, when she was three years old, her great-uncle Peter Van Alen, Helen's brother, was named her guardian. Also, both Maria and her brother, John D. Van Alen, Jr., were named in Helen's will.

The point of all this is to demonstrate that Maria Van Alen Herrick was indeed very close to her grandmother Elizabeth's brothers and sisters, including Helen, most of whom still resided in the Van Alen House into the 1860s. Maria grew up around her great-aunt Helen and her family; any family lore would likely have been heard first-hand, possibly from her Aunt Helen herself, as opposed to having been passed down through more distant relatives. This does give some measure of credibility to Maria's statements regarding Helen and her apparent fondness for Washington Irving.

According to Local Tradition...

There are several variations of the Helen Van Alen tradition. Some versions have Irving observing the rivalry between Jesse Merwin and "Brom Bones" for Helen's affections. This seems quite unlikely, as Merwin was already married in May 1809, having wed Jane Van Dyck the previous October.

Other versions state that it was Irving himself who had been the one smitten with Helen Van Alen, with his visits frequently interrupted by the unexpected arrival of "Brom Bones" at the Van Alen farm.

This romantic angle has appeared in print (and online) numerous times. In 1967, a *New York Times* article reporting the restoration of the Van Alen House in Kinderhook featured the headline, "House Where Ichabod Crane Went a-Courtin' Is Preserved." The article went on to describe the house "where Washington Irving courted the girl who inspired his fictional character, Katrina Van Tassel."[19]

Then in 1976, Allen Keller wrote in *Life Along the Hudson* that when Irving visited in 1809, "he walked and talked with Helen Van Alen, whose character seems to have inspired the fictional figure of Katrina Van Tassel..."[20]

This scenario also seems unlikely – remember, Irving was in Kinderhook grieving the death of his fiancée, Matilda Hoffman, which had occurred just a few short weeks earlier. Romancing another woman was probably the furthest thing from his mind at that point in his life. Of this period, Irving later wrote, "I cannot tell you what a horrid state of mind I was in for a long time – I seemed to care for nothing – the world was blank to me... Months elapsed before my mind resumed any tone."[21]

The unlikelihood of these other scenarios notwithstanding, there is a much bigger problem with the Helen Van Alen tradition: *Helen Van Alen was only three years old!*

Born on June 17, 1805, Helen was just a few weeks shy of her fourth birthday at the time of Irving's visit in May 1809. Young Helen obviously would not have been a romantic interest of either Irving or Merwin... and she could hardly have been "the original" of Katrina Van Tassel.

(It should be noted that some articles have suggested that Helen *or one of her older sisters* had been the original of Katrina. Helen did have two sisters who were in their teens in early 1809: Jane, who was 16, and Maria, 15. However, Helen's own great-niece, Maria Van Alen Herrick, was very specific in her assertion that it was *Helen,* as opposed to another family member, whom the Van Alens had long believed to have been Irving's muse.)

So how, then, did this "family tradition" linking Helen Van Alen to Washington Irving originate?

We know that Washington Irving visited Kinderhook on at least two more occasions, in 1833 and 1855 – could he have met Helen Van Alen on one of these later trips? In 1833, the still-single Helen would have been 28 years old; could she have met, and become infatuated with, the also single Washington Irving, thereby sparking a family tradition that was passed down through subsequent generations?

It may also have been at this time that Helen "made herself a little more lovely" for him, per her niece's commentary... although any romantic feelings were apparently unrequited, as Irving made no mention whatsoever of Helen Van Alen in any of his published letters or journals.

Assuming that the two *could* have met during one of Irving's later visits, could the actual dates have become blurred over time? Did Helen's descendants, probably unfamiliar with the timing of the writing and publication of "The Legend," simply assume that it was possible for her to have served as the model for Katrina Van Tassel?

Helen's Connection to the Luykas Van Alen House

As discussed in Chapter 2, the Luykas Van Alen property passed to Luykas' son, Laurens, after Luykas' death in the mid-1700s, and then eventually to Laurens' son David, who was Helen's father. However, it is not clear when, or how, David came into possession of the property.[22]

While Laurens' 1805 will originally provided for his son David, the two evidently had some sort of falling-out. Two codicils, dated 1807 and 1809, effectively disinherited David, although provisions were made for his wife, Maria, and their children.[23]

Might the apparent difficulties between Laurens and David have precluded them from having shared the residence? Laurens lived until 1812, and a November 27, 1815 advertisement in *The Hudson Bee* indicated that the farm had been "lately in the possession of Lawrence Van Alen" – might this indicate that David and his family, including young Helen, did not occupy the house until about 1815 or later, after Laurens' death?[24]

An August 1821 map by surveyor Augustus Tremain is the earliest record of David and family residing in the Van Alen house. (Although David had been disinherited by his father, his wife Maria was also a Van Alen, descended from Luykas Van Alen's brother Jacobus, and it is believed that ownership of the property passed to the family through her.)[25]

So, in addition to having been much too young to have been Irving's (or Merwin's) romantic interest, is it possible that young Helen Van Alen did not even reside in the Van Alen House in 1809 when Irving was said to have spent time there with her?

Wishful Thinking?

Did Washington Irving know the Van Alen family? Yes, without a doubt – in his 1851 letter to Jesse Merwin, he recalled going fishing with Congressman James Isaac Van Alen, who was Helen's cousin. Kinderhook in the early 1800s was not very large, and was the type of place where everyone knew everyone else. Genealogical records show numerous intermarriages between the Van Alens, the Van Burens and the Van Nesses. Irving quite likely met most of the Van Alen family during his month in Kinderhook... possibly even a little girl named Helen.

Prior to the 1819 publication of "The Legend of Sleepy Hollow," Washington Irving had only visited Kinderhook once, in May 1809. (Another trip had been planned for early 1810, but there is no evidence to show that this second visit actually took place.) Irving then left for England in 1815, and remained in Europe until 1832.

At three years of age, Helen Van Alen was certainly much too young in 1809 to have been romantically involved with Irving. There is also a *possibility* that Helen and her family did not even live in the Luykas Van Alen House at the time, not having taken possession of the home until "about" 1815, several years after Irving's visit.

Irving did return to Kinderhook on two more occasions, in 1833 and again in 1855, at which times he could have become acquainted with the then-adult Helen Van Alen. However, both of these visits took place a number of years *after* the publication of "The Legend," too late for her to have inspired one of the characters.

The Helen Van Alen connection to Irving and "The Legend" therefore appears to have been more the product of wishful thinking than historical fact. Kinderhook residents, aware of Jesse Merwin's association with Irving, assumed that Ichabod Crane's love interest *must have been* from Kinderhook as well, and set their sights on a local "coquette" who seemed to fit the description.

Catherine Van Alen

Writing in 1900 in *Columbia County at the End of the Century*, two years after his *New York Times* editorials, Harold Van Santvoord finally provided the name "known to older residents" of Kinderhook – he identified her as "one Katrina Van Alen who lived in a farmhouse near Lindenwald, built of brick imported from Holland."[26]

Then two years later, in his 1902 *Genealogical History of the Van Alen Family*, Benjamin Taylor Van Alen wrote, "Among the older inhabitants of Kinderhook, there may be found several who recall the traditions of Katrina Van Alen, a girl renowned for her beauty and coquetry... it is a fair inference that she was a cousin of Congressman Van Alen, probably being Catherine, the daughter of Dirck Van Alen, and *at that time an inmate of the old home*."[27]

Who was Catherine (or Catharina) Van Alen? Could she possibly have lived in the Van Alen House in 1809?

Catherine Van Alen was the youngest of five children born to Dirck Van Alen (1757-??) and the former Elbertje Van Buren (1760-??). No birth or baptismal records for her have been located thus far; her birth year is *estimated* to have been approximately 1795, based on the birth dates of her four older siblings: Evert (born in 1786), Dirck (1788), Margarietje (1791) and Lourens (1793).

Although genealogical records for Catherine are scant, to say the least, we know that she existed because she was mentioned by name, along with two of her siblings, in the September 1802 will of her maternal grandfather, Dirck Van Buren.[28]

Catherine's father, Dirck Van Alen, was a grandson of Johannes Van Alen; Johannes was the brother of Luykas, the original owner of the historic Van Alen House. In 1809, the house was owned and occupied by Laurens Van Alen; Dirck was the son of Laurens' first cousin, Evert Van Alen, making him Laurens' first cousin once removed.

No documentation has been located to indicate property ownership, or to even link Dirck to a specific residence. In fact, a Real Estate Assessment Roll for Kinderhook dated May 27, 1809 lists one Dirck Van Alen as owning no property, and having a net worth of only 10 pounds, quite destitute compared to the other residents listed.

Could Laurens Van Alen have possibly taken in his apparently down-on-his-luck cousin Dirck and his family, including 14-year-old Catherine? This is, of course, just one of several theories, and 200 years after the fact, virtually impossible to either prove or disprove. (It is also entirely possible that Catherine did not live with her father at all; the 1810 Census indicates no females living with Dirck, but does list one female between the ages of 10 and 16 residing in a household headed by one Evert Van Alen – possibly her older brother?)

Perhaps John P. Ritter was not in error when he wrote in 1899 that there were several "older inhabitants of Kinderhook" who remembered "Katrina Van Alen... who lived in the old mansion while Irving was sojourning at Lindenwald."[29] It would certainly help to explain the persistence of the identification of *Katrina* Van Alen as the original of Katrina Van Tassel... at least until Helen Van Alen's great-niece, Maria Van Alen Herrick, began promoting her Aunt Helen as having been Katrina's prototype.

Other Catherine Van Alens?

Genealogical records list several other Catherine/Catharina Van Alens living in the Kinderhook area around the turn of the 19th century; however, none were associated with the Luykas Van Alen House, nor were any of them implicated by "local lore."

One theory that should be mentioned, however, is the suggestion that Katrina Van Tassel may have been inspired by a much earlier Catherine Van Alen, the wife of Adam Van Alen (1700-1748), Luykas' nephew. Born Catherine Van Alstyne in 1713, she took the name Van Alen upon her marriage to Adam in 1731. (Widowed in 1748, she remarried in 1753 and took the last name Wyngard.)

This Catherine/Katrina theory appears to have been based on the erroneous belief that she had been "the original mistress" of the Van Alen House. This can be traced to an incorrect statement in Edward Collier's 1914 *A History of Old Kinderhook*, which identified Adam as the builder of the house, rather than Luykas.[30]

Adam was the eldest son of Luykas' brother, Johannes Van Alen (1675-1745). Adam and his wife Catherine inherited the house originally built by his grandfather, family patriarch Laurentius Van Alen (1631-1714). This house was nearby the Luykas Van Alen House, but much closer to Kinderhook Creek. It was destroyed by fire in the 1820s.[31]

This Catherine, the wife of Adam, never lived in the Luykas Van Alen House. Regardless, having been born in 1713, she was likely deceased (genealogical records are incomplete) by the time of Irving's 1809 visit; if not, she would have been quite advanced in years... and not very likely to have been the prototype of Irving's "blooming lass of fresh eighteen."

Jane Van Dyck

Surprisingly, very few people have suggested that the inspiration for the Katrina Van Tassel character may have been the one person *known for certain* to have been linked romantically to "the original of Ichabod Crane." For all of the theories about the various Van Alens, perhaps we should take a closer look at Jesse Merwin's only *verifiable* love interest: his wife, Jane Van Dyck.

Jane's Family History

The Kinderhook Van Dycks can trace their lineage back to Hendrick Thomasse Van Dyck, who was born in 1617 in Utrecht, The Netherlands, and died in 1687 in New York City. Hendrick, accompanied by his wife Dwertje Botjagers and their first child, daughter Ryckie, emigrated to New Netherland in the 1640s where he served as colonial Fiscaal (Treasurer) and Attorney General under Governor Peter Stuyvesant.

One of Hendrick's sons, Dr. Cornelius Van Dyck (1642-1687) relocated to Beaverwyck (later renamed Albany), where he married Elizabeth Laeckens (1638-1682) and is credited with having founded the "upstate branch" of the Van Dyck family tree.

Cornelius' eldest son, Hendrick Van Dyck (1665-1707) followed in his father's footsteps and became a surgeon. He married the former Maria Schuyler in 1689. Hendrick accidentally drowned in Albany in 1707; his widow, Maria, relocated their family to Kinderhook in 1718.

Hendrick and Maria had eight children. One of them, Pieter (1697-??), married Catherine Wederwax (1707-??), with whom he had four sons, one of whom died in infancy.

Here is where the genealogical records often become confusing: Pieter's surviving three sons – Hendrick, born April 1, 1733; Arent, born March 3, 1739; and Cornelius, born February 13, 1743 – *each* named one of their own sons Peter, following the Dutch tradition of naming a son after his grandfather.

Of these three first cousins, all named Peter Van Dyck, Jane's father has been identified as Peter C. Van Dyck (1767-1810), the son of Cornelius.[32]

A Wealthy Farmer's Daughter

Like the fictional Baltus Van Tassel, Peter C. Van Dyck owned a "substantial" farm, consisting of 160 acres.[33] The May 1809 Kinderhook Real Estate Assessment Roll shows Peter C. Van Dyck to have been moderately wealthy (as compared to other property values listed), with an assessed Value of Real Estate of 1,800 pounds (using the old English monetary system) and Value of Personal Estate of 300, for a total worth of 2,100 pounds.

Jane Van Dyck was born on September 30, 1786, to Peter and his wife, the former Maria Volandt (1765-1865).

Unlike the fictional Katrina, who was an only child, Jane Van Dyck had several younger siblings, including a set of twins, Catherine and Hendrick, born in 1792, and a brother Cornelius, born in 1798.[34]

Curiously, only one Peter Van Dyck is listed in the 1810 Federal Census for Kinderhook. We cannot be certain which of the three Peters – Jane's father or one of his two cousins – is represented by this entry, but it does list an appropriate number of household members consistent with

Peter C. Van Dyck's family in 1810. The household of *this* Peter also included two slaves.

Jane married local schoolteacher Jesse Merwin on October 16, 1808.

Peter C. Van Dyck died in 1810 at the unusually young age of 43, and Jesse and Jane inherited his farm. Their first son, born in 1810, was named Peter, after his grandfather. Over the next 24 years, the Merwins would have a total of 11 children, eight sons and three daughters. Rooms were added to the farmhouse as the family grew.

Jane and Jesse Merwin's farmhouse
(Photo courtesy of Miles Merwin Association)

Jane's mother, Maria, who lived to be 100 (a fact engraved on her tombstone), shared the house with them. One family tradition states that former President Martin Van Buren used to visit the Merwin Farm regularly to visit with Jane's mother in her native Holland Dutch (as opposed to the American Dutch dialect spoken by the majority of Kinderhook residents of Dutch descent). When Van Buren would leave in the afternoon heat, he would sometimes pluck a leaf from a head of cabbage in the Merwin garden, and place it on his bald head, under his hat, to help keep him cool on his walk back to Lindenwald.[35]

Jane's younger sister, Catherine, may have also moved in with them at some point. An extensive genealogy titled *The Merwin Family in North America*, published in four volumes by the Miles Merwin Association, contains a statement that Jesse and Jane's eldest son Peter, as an adult, "lived on the Van Dyck farm with his mother *and an aunt*" – probably Catherine.[36]

Catherine is buried next to her mother, Maria, in the Kinderhook Reformed Church Cemetery, and her name is engraved on the same tombstone.[37]

Jane Van Dyck Merwin and family, photographed about 1875.
Seated from left: Jane E., Jane Van Dyck Merwin, Peter, Asher;
Standing: Albertine, Samuel, David, Catherine, Washington Irving.
(Photo courtesy of Miles Merwin Association)

Following Jesse's death in November 1853, Jane, who never remarried, lived on at the Merwin farm for another 28 years, cared for by her adult children and surrounded by numerous grandchildren. One of Jane's grandsons, George B. Merwin, recalled in 1925 how "the youngsters of the family saved pennies and bought snuff" for her.[38]

Jane Van Dyck Merwin died on April 14, 1882, at the age of 95. She is buried next to Jesse in the Kinderhook Reformed Church Cemetery.

Jane the Heiress

At least superficially, Jane Van Dyck seems to fit the description of Katrina – she was the daughter of an affluent Dutch farmer; she was certainly romantically involved with "Ichabod," a.k.a. Jesse Merwin; and she stood to one day inherit her father's farm.

But personality-wise, was Jane anything at all like Katrina Van Tassel? Was she really a flirt, famed for her "coquettish tricks"? Was she truly indecisive, "beset with a labyrinth of whims and caprices"? We have no way of knowing...

As previously mentioned, several "local traditions" state that there was a rivalry between Jesse Merwin and the (suspected) prototype of Brom Bones, a local farmer named Abraham Van Alstyne (who will be discussed in detail in the next chapter). Most "traditions" have the two men vying for the attentions of Helen (or Catharina) Van Alen, but a few variations implicate Jane Van Dyck instead. So far, no contemporary documentation – letter, diary, journal, etc. – has been located to support *any* of these rivalry stories.

Since Jesse was already married to Jane at the time Irving met him in 1809, is it possible that the two men discussed how Jesse would one day inherit the Van Dyck farm? (And knowing Irving's sense of humor, might he have even engaged in a gentle ribbing of Merwin, insinuating that the impoverished schoolmaster had only married Jane so that he could someday appropriate her father's farm?)

Although Irving chose to give the fictional romance of Ichabod and Katrina an unhappy ending, could he have at least gleaned the *idea* of Ichabod scheming to "one day be lord of" Katrina's father's farm from the true history of Jesse and Jane Merwin?

Quite possibly... and if Jesse Merwin indeed maintained a regular correspondence with Washington Irving over the years, as Harold Van Santvoord alleged, then Jesse certainly would have informed his author friend that he had inherited his father-in-law's farm and had abandoned teaching. This occurred in 1810, some eight years before "The Legend" was written.

Did the true story of Jane the heiress give rise to the concept of Katrina the heiress? Perhaps those seeking the "true identity" of Ichabod's love interest need search no further than Jesse Merwin's own wife, Jane Van Dyck. This theory seems as plausible, perhaps even more so, than some of the other local traditions about the origins of Katrina Van Tassel...

Chapter 7

A Burly, Roaring, Roystering Blade

> *"He was broad-shouldered and double-jointed, with short curly black hair, and a bluff, but not unpleasant countenance, having a mingled air of fun and arrogance. From his Herculean frame and great powers of limb, he had received the nickname of BROM BONES, by which he was universally known."*
>
> - from "The Legend of Sleepy Hollow," 1820

As with the characters of Ichabod Crane and Katrina Van Tassel, local traditions of both Sleepy Hollow and Kinderhook have long maintained the "true identity" of the fictional Brom Bones as having been one of their own local residents. These largely undocumented "facts" have been passed down orally from generation to generation.

Let's take a look at a few of these Broms...

Brom Byce

Possibly the earliest speculation of the identity of Brom Bones came from Washington Irving's close friend Henry Brevoort, who wrote to him in April of 1820 soon after receiving a copy of the sixth volume of *The Sketch Book*. He commented, "The last number is highly relished, particularly the Legend, which in my opinion is one of the best articles you have written – It unites all the excellencies of your old & new manner of writing. The old people are surprised at your accurate recollections of the localities of the place & its inhabitants. – My old uncle Abm. a mighty warrior of the olden time, entertained me with a commentary on every name that you have mentioned, even to Brom Bones *whom he recognizes for his first friend Brom Byce.*"[1]

The surname "Byce" as used by Brevoort may be a variation of the name "Boyce," or it may simply be a misspelling; in the Introduction to *Letters of Henry Brevoort to Washington Irving*, the editor pointed out that Brevoort's letters contain "numerous misspellings both as to proper and common names, errors which have been preserved in the text of these volumes."[2]

While no one with the name "Byce" has been found in published records, several rolls of Westchester County militiamen exist, including one dated July 8, 1778, which include the names Abraham BOYCE and Abraham Boyce, Junior. Other records show variations in spelling, such as Buice, Bice or Boice. (Interestingly, Ensign Thomas Boyce, the brother of one of the two Abrahams, signed his name "Buyes" on the July 1778 roll.)[3]

Abraham Boyce (1745?-1780)

The first of the two Abraham Boyces listed on the various militia rosters was born "about" 1745, the son of Jacob

Boyce (1716-1755) and the former Catherine Storms (1719-1805).

The names of two of Abraham's brothers, Jacob and Thomas, can also be found on the militia rosters; Abraham and Jacob are both listed as privates, where Thomas' name appears in the officers' section as an Ensign. All were members of Colonel James Hammond's regiment.

Very little seems to have been recorded about the brothers' wartime exploits, but it is known that all three received wounds in battle. Jacob and Thomas apparently both recovered; in fact, Thomas went on to become a Justice of the Peace after the war. Abraham Boyce, however, died of his wounds on December 10, 1780.[4]

Although two Abraham Boyces are named in the militia rosters, only one "Abraham Boyce" appears on the Revolutionary Soldiers' Monument erected in 1894 in Sleepy Hollow Cemetery. The inscription presumably refers to *this* Abraham Boyce, as his brother Thomas is also listed.

The intent of the Revolutionary Soldiers' Monument was primarily to honor those patriots buried in the adjacent graveyard; the names of those known to have been buried elsewhere were therefore not included. Also, as explained in the *Souvenir of the Soldiers' Monument Dedication* published in 1894, there were no tombstones to mark the graves of several local Revolutionary War veterans, "the evidence of their burial place not being ascertained until too late" for their names to be included in the inscription.[5]

Abraham Boyce, Jr. (1760?-1839)

Abraham Boyce, Jr., whose name also appears on the various Westchester Militia rolls, was *not* the son of the Abraham Boyce discussed in the previous section. No genealogical data has yet been located which positively identifies this Abraham Jr.'s parents; Old Dutch Church marriage records do list a February 2, 1758 wedding between one Abraham BUYS and the former Maria Rasel, which is certainly within the correct timeframe, but no other documentation has been located to link this couple to this Abraham Jr.

(Note: This Abraham Jr. should not be confused with another Abraham Boyce Jr., who was christened on September 7, 1766; assuming this "other" Abraham Jr. was probably born earlier that same year, he would have been not quite 9 years old when the first shots of the war were fired in 1775, much too young to have been a militiaman. Also, this "other" Abraham Jr. went on to father four children, where the subject of this section was childless.)[6]

Writing in 1848 in his *History of the County of Westchester*, Robert Bolton provided a very brief biography of a possible candidate for the second Abraham Boyce listed on the rolls. "The noted Brom Boyce," wrote Bolton, "at the early age of sixteen, enrolled himself among the minute men of the American army. He was soon distinguished for his bravery and daring, and was recognized as the best guide to be procured in the vicinity." Bolton continued, "Boyce, after the Revolution, followed the business of a carman in the city of New York. He was a member of the Bedford Street church about thirty-five years, and died in 1839, aged eighty-two years. His remains were interred at Tarrytown."[7]

An application for a government pension was filed on February 5, 1827, by one Abraham Boyce; this was probably the same individual profiled by Bolton. According to his application, this Abraham Boyce enlisted in May 1776 in Captain Stephen Oakley's company of the Westchester County Militia. Boyce transferred to several different companies throughout the war, serving at various times under Capt. Seibert Acker, Capt. Daniel Williams, and Capt. Jonathan

Paulding. According to his account, Boyce took part in the fighting "at the time the British landed at Staten Island" (presumably July-August 1776).

Boyce also stated that he "was in a skirmish" at the Youngs house "when Captain Williams was taken prisoner." The skirmish Boyce referred to took place on Christmas Day 1778, when British forces led by Major Mansfield Bearmore raided Joseph Youngs' farm at Four Corners, where about 40 American soldiers under Captain Daniel Williams were quartered. Williams and Youngs were among the prisoners taken, and Youngs' barn was burned and his cattle seized by the British.[8]

As part of a detachment guarding a shipment of grain intended for the Continental Army, Boyce received a wound to the wrist by a broadsword wielded by a "light horseman." He was captured by the British and imprisoned in Manhattan's infamous "sugar house," the former Rhinelander Sugar Warehouse, which had been converted by the British to house American prisoners-of-war. Boyce was freed after eleven months as part of a prisoner exchange.

Following his release, Boyce ventured to Elizabethtown, then to Fishkill in Dutchess County, where he again enlisted in the American forces, traveling "as far as the falls of Niagara."

Boyce was honorably discharged in 1783, after which he made his home in White Plains, later moving to Mount Pleasant. He ultimately relocated to New York City, where, in Boyce's words, he "drove a cart" until forced to retire due to rheumatism. This seems to agree with Bolton's account, which specified Boyce's profession as a "carman," the minor difference likely being a matter of semantics.

Abraham Boyce's pension application states that he was married; he did not provide his wife's name, but did say that she would "be sixty-two years of age in March [1827]," putting her date of birth sometime in March 1765. The application further stated that he had no children.

There is one inconsistency between Bolton's account and Boyce's application: Bolton stated that Boyce died in 1839 at age 82, which indicates that he was born in 1757; however, Boyce's own account stated that he had enlisted in the militia in May 1776, which, if one accepts Bolton's assertion that Boyce enlisted at age 16, would put his birth year at 1760. Could Bolton have simply been mistaken about Boyce's age at either the time of his enlistment or his death?

Which Abraham Boyce?

To which, then, of the two Abraham Boyces was Henry Brevoort referring in his April 1820 letter to Washington Irving?

Henry's "old uncle" Abraham Brevoort was born in 1745; it seems logical that the man he referred to as his "first friend" would have been close to his own age, possibly someone he had grown up with, and the first Abraham Boyce was indeed born in 1745 as well. However, one cannot exclude the possibility that the older Uncle Abraham may have indeed befriended the younger of the two Boyces, particularly later in life when differences in age often become fairly irrelevant.

Irving's May 13, 1820 reply to Henry Brevoort's letter offered no additional information. In it, Irving simply stated, "I will reply more at length by another opportunity. The Sketch Book is doing very well here."[9] Unfortunately, it appears to have slipped Irving's mind to provide a more detailed response. His next two recorded letters to Brevoort, dated August 15 and September 22, 1820, made no mention whatsoever of "The Legend of Sleepy Hollow" or of "Brom Byce."[10]

Could the exploits of either (or both) of the men named Abraham Boyce been one of the "recollections" discussed by Irving and his brother-in-law Henry Van Wart that evening in the summer of 1818 when "The Legend" was conceived? Possibly – but it is equally possible that Uncle Abraham Brevoort's "recognition" of Byce/Boyce as the original of Brom Bones is simply a testament to Washington Irving's ability to so bring his characters to life that his readers are able to see themselves, or people they know, in them.

Abraham Martling

Currently, the prevailing theory in Tarrytown and Sleepy Hollow regarding the prototype of Brom Bones is that he was most likely Abraham Martling, identified as having been the post-Revolution village blacksmith. This hypothesis does not seem to be based on a generations-old "local tradition," however, but appears to have originated much more recently, possibly within the past 15 or 20 years.

Although Washington Irving did not specify Brom Bones' occupation, he did tell us that Brom was "famed for great knowledge and skill in horsemanship," paired with "great powers of limb." This combination has led some to conclude that Brom *must have been* a blacksmith, reasoning that one of a blacksmith's primary duties would have been shoeing horses, and that he therefore would have become proficient at working with them.

One of the main proponents, and possibly the originator of this theory, was the late Bill Lent (1929-2013), long-time sexton of the Old Dutch Church and well-known church and graveyard tour guide. Lent can be found quoted in a number of online and print articles explaining how, in trying to identify the original of Brom Bones, he and other (unnamed) local historians had "looked for" a local Revolutionary War era blacksmith named Abraham – or, "according to the Dutch abbreviation," Brom. They eventually settled on Abraham Martling as the most likely candidate.

But which Abraham Martling? In what we will see as a recurring theme throughout this chapter, it is not unusual to have to sort through a number of individuals of multiple generations, all sharing the same name. This is due to an old Dutch custom of naming children after their grandparents, and then after their uncles or aunts. It can be difficult to discern *which one* is the person we are seeking, further complicated by the fact that they are often closely related.

In the case of Abraham Martling, Grenville Mackenzie's *Families of the Colonial Town of Philipsburgh* lists no fewer than seven Abrahams born between 1740 and 1765, all of them "of age" to have fought in the Revolution at some point.[11] It is easy for historians and genealogists to confuse their respective wartime exploits.

Let's discuss a few of these Abrahams, especially those singled out by Bill Lent and his compatriots as the "probable" inspiration for the fictional Brom Bones character. Did any of these Abrahams exhibit "Bones"-like behavior? *(And which, if any, were actually blacksmiths?)*

Abraham Martlenghs (1693-1761)

The progenitor of the Martling family in Westchester County, Abraham Martlenghs, was the son of Johannis Marteling, who was born about 1650 in the Dutch West Indies and emigrated to what is now New York City in 1675. Abraham, who chose to use the Dutch spelling of the family name, was born on Staten Island on September 5, 1693, and moved to Tarrytown in 1714.[12]

As discussed in Chapter 2, Abraham is credited with having constructed, "around" 1714, the stone farmhouse on the Albany Post Road that was to become the Van Tassel

Tavern during the Revolutionary War, and later known as the Jacob Mott House.

Martlenghs married Rachel DeVouw (1695-??), the daughter of one of his neighbors, on April 16, 1715. They had nine children, including Abraham Martling (1719-1786) and Isaac Martling (1741-1779), who would later become known as "Isaac the Martyr" after being ambushed and killed by a local British sympathizer during the Revolution.[13]

Abraham Martlenghs made his living as *a blacksmith*. He became the first recorded town clerk of Philipsburgh (1742-1747) and a justice of the peace. Martlenghs was also a deacon and an elder of the Old Dutch Church.

Abraham Martlenghs died on April 22, 1761, at the age of "67 years, 7 months and 17 days," as engraved on his tombstone, which is located directly behind the Old Dutch Church.[14]

Dutch-language tombstone of Abraham Martlenghs (1693-1761), progenitor of the Martling Family, in the Old Dutch Burying Ground (Photo courtesy of Patrick Raftery)

Abraham Martling (1719-1786)

This Abraham Martling was born April 21, 1719, the second son of the previously discussed Abraham Martlenghs.

Abraham Martling, who used the anglicized spelling of his family name, was *a boatman* by trade. He was part of the family business owned by his brother, Captain Daniel Martling (1737-1788), the proprietor of Martling's Landing (later called Requa's Dock), which was located near the foot of modern-day White Street in Tarrytown. The Martling brothers would have navigated their Dutch market-sloops, typically laden with locally-milled grain, between the Tarrytown docks and the New York City markets.

Martling lived on Main Street in Tarrytown on "a bluff" which overlooked his brother Daniel's house, among a dozen or so other early homes clustered in what is now the waterfront section of Tarrytown, and close by the family's dock.[15]

He married Jannettje Ackerman (1724-1782) on March 19, 1739. The two had eight children, including a son named, according to Dutch custom, Abraham, born June 30, 1742.

Like his father, Martling served as town clerk of Philipsburg from 1748 through 1749.

When the Revolutionary War broke out, Abraham Martling joined the militia. He took part in an August 1776 attack by a small number of American galleys on two British frigates, the 44-gun *Phoenix* and the 20-gun *Rose*, which were sailing down the Hudson toward Tarrytown. He was one of the 14 Americans wounded in the "Galley Fight," as it became known.[16]

(Or was he? One of Martling's contemporaries, Captain John Romer, the husband of Leah Van Tassel Romer, in an 1845 interview with James MacLean Macdonald, indicated that a *different* Abraham – this one's nephew, Abraham B. Martling, born in 1761 to Barent Martling and the former Sarah Bell – was actually the one who had been wounded in the naval engagement.[17])

One of the several Abraham Martlings was wounded in the "Galley Fight" between American sloops and the British Frigates Phoenix and Rose... but which Abraham? (1778 engraving by Dominic Serres, from a sketch by Sir James Wallace; Library of Congress)

This Abraham Martling (1719-1786) has also been credited by some as having been one of the leaders of a November 25, 1777 raid on British General Oliver De Lancey's mansion in Bloomingdale (now part of Manhattan's Upper West Side).[18] The attack was in retaliation for the November 17 burning of the Cornelius and Peter Van Tassel residences by Col. Emmerick's jaegers (previously discussed in Chapter 4).

Captain John Romer, in his 1845 interview, described how several whaleboats proceeded down the Hudson "with muffled oars," carrying "volunteers from Westchester County." They slipped past the British, looted the De Lancey house, and set it on fire. Burdened with "considerable plunder," they once again avoided the British warships patrolling the Hudson and returned safely to Tarrytown.[19]

Abraham Martling's work experience as a "boatman" and his knowledge of the river would have made him a natural choice to have led, or at least participated, in the De Lancey raid. However, other historians credit yet another nephew, also named Abraham Martling (1763-1841), as having planned and led the expedition. This other Abraham, the son of "Isaac the Martyr," will be discussed in a later section of this chapter.

Apparently, recent applicants to the Daughters of the American Revolution have also confused the various Abrahams and their wartime activities. The DAR website <WWW.DAR.ORG> listing for Abraham Martling (1719-1786) has been flagged in red with the notation "Future Applicants Must Prove Correct Service," followed by "The proof of service used to establish this person as a patriot is no longer valid." Possible explanations listed for the discrepancy included "the service belongs to another person of the same name" and/or "multiple people have claimed the same service." Sadly, it appears that enough confusion exists to cast doubt on this Abraham's status as a Revolutionary War Veteran.

Abraham Martling died on June 16, 1786, at age 67. He is buried in the Old Dutch Burying Ground in Sleepy Hollow, near his father and several other Martling family members, directly behind the Old Dutch Church. His name appears on the Revolutionary Soldiers Monument on Battle Hill in Sleepy Hollow Cemetery.

Abraham Martling, Jr. (1742-1830)

The third Abraham Martling we will examine was the son of the Abraham Martling (1719-1786) discussed in the previous section. This Abraham was born in Tarrytown on June 30, 1742.[20]

Martling relocated to New York City in the early 1760s. On June 21, 1765 he married Maria Couwenhoven (1744-1821). They had eight children, two of whom died in infancy. In keeping with tradition, their eldest son, born January 8, 1766 was named – what else? – Abraham Martling...

Martling made his living as a cordwainer, or *shoemaker* (as opposed to a "cobbler," who repairs shoes).[21]

Abraham Martling moved back to Tarrytown with his family in 1772.

Very little is known of his service during the Revolutionary War. The 1926 edition of *The Old Dutch Burying Ground of Sleepy Hollow* states that he was "a Revolutionary soldier," their information presumably based on church or other local records.[22] However, his name does not appear on published militia rosters, nor did he apply for a government pension after the war.

The names of two "Abram" Martlings are engraved on the Revolutionary Soldiers Monument in Sleepy Hollow Cemetery. This Abraham Martling (1742-1830) is generally believed to have been the one listed as "junior," below his father's name.

Martling died on November 3, 1830 "after a short and painful illness," as inscribed on his tombstone, which is located not far from those of his father and his grandfather.[23]

Abraham Martling (1763-1841)

The final Abraham Martling under consideration was a cousin of the previously discussed Abraham Martling (1742-1830) and nephew of Abraham Martling (1719-1786). Born "about 1763" (and baptized May 8, 1764), this Abraham was the son of "Isaac the Martyr" Martling (1741-1779) and the former Elizabeth Hicks.[24]

Published biographical sketches usually state that he lived "on Beaver Hill, overlooking the Sawmill River Valley," but this was probably later in his life; in his youth, Abraham presumably would have lived with his father, Isaac, in his Franklin Avenue house in Tarrytown, close to the Martling family docks.

When the Revolutionary War came to the Hudson Valley, this Abraham Martling, purportedly known locally as "Brom Marlin,"[25] was barely into his teens. However, as discussed in an earlier section of this chapter, he is sometimes credited with having planned, as well as commanded, the attack on General De Lancey's Bloomingdale residence in November 1777.[26] Could the planning and leadership of such a dangerous mission really have been entrusted to a 14-year-old boy? Or did some biographers simply confuse young "Brom Marlin" with one of his older relatives?

Captain John Romer, in his detailed 1845 account, stated that he did not know who had led the raid, but he *believed* it to have been "Captain Buchanan of the water guards."[27] Captain Romer (1764-1855) was the brother of Abraham Martling's wife, Frena Romer Martling – wouldn't he have known if his brother-in-law Abraham had played such a major role in the expedition?

Likewise, Captain Romer's testimony concludes by telling us that "*one man* when they came to re-embark had a pair of brass andirons slung across his shoulders."[28] Later accounts attribute this to Martling himself – but had this individual been Martling, it seems that his brother-in-law would have heard the story at some point, and he would not have credited a nameless "one man" with the action. This appears to be a classic example of how tales of wartime exploits often become embellished, even *romanticized*, as they are retold through the years.

As discussed previously in Chapter 2, the Water Guard mentioned by Romer had a base at none other than Lt. Jacob Van Tassel's "Wolfert's Roost." Romer described it as an "aquatic corps… composed of nautical men of the river and *hardy youngsters of the adjacent country*, expert at pulling an oar and handling a musket."[29] So while it does seem a stretch for 14-year-old Abraham Martling to have commanded the expedition, it is entirely believable for him to have *participated* – the Water Guard apparently welcomed strapping teenage boys to man the oars and otherwise assist the more senior combatants.

Moving past the speculation, what is *known* of Martling's military service may be derived from his application for a government pension, dated April 17, 1818. Martling stated that he had enlisted in the Continental Army in October 1779 at the age of 16. He served as a dragoon, or cavalryman, in Captain George Schaffner's Company, attached to the regiment commanded by former French cavalry officer Colonel Charles Armand Tuffin, known colloquially as "Colonel Armand."

(One of Martling's descendants stated in his 1965 membership application to the Sons of the American Revolution that Abraham had been "seriously wounded" at the Battle of Brandywine; however, this battle took place in September 1777, two years before Martling enlisted in Armand's regiment – more confusion involving yet another Abraham Martling?)

According to Martling's pension application, he took part in the Battle of Yorktown "at the taking of Lord Cornwallis" in the fall of 1781. He was discharged from service "sometime in May or June" of 1783 in Charleston, South Carolina.

Abraham Martling then returned to Westchester County, where, on November 28, 1784, he married Frena "Fanny" Romer (1758-1849) with whom he fathered 5 children (none of them named Abraham!).

Martling "obtained a few acres of ground upon the extreme westerly end" of the farm owned jointly by his brother-in-law, John Romer, and Cornelius Van Tassel, in what is present-day Elmsford. He built "a small dwelling up against the rocks," and in an apparent effort to take up farming, "set out some fruit trees, and cultivated what little of the soil was available."[30]

The various published biographical sketches of this Abraham Martling make no mention of his ever having been a blacksmith, although it could certainly be argued that his wartime experience as a dragoon would probably have made him an expert horseman!

Martling appears to have fallen on hard times at some point. In his original April 1818 application for a government pension, he stated that he was 55 years of age, "in reduced circumstances" and "in need of the assistance of his country for support."

Although his 1818 application was approved and he began receiving a pension (of $8 per month), it was apparently suspended for some reason in early 1821. Martling submitted another application on May 28, 1821, in which he reiterated his military service and stressed that he had no other means of support. He described his home as "one room underground with a roof," situated on "land almost covered with rocks." An itemized list of his worldly belongings included five old chairs, one table, and two pots...

The application further stated that Martling had "no occupation," and he described himself as "a cripple very much bowed down with a rheumatic affliction." Martling's second pension application was approved in June 1821, and his payments resumed.

Grave of Abraham Martling (1763-1841) in the Reformed Church Cemetery, Elmsford, New York (Photo courtesy of Patrick Raftery)

Abraham Martling died at his home on January 1, 1841. He is buried in the Reformed Church Cemetery in Elmsford.

Brom the Blacksmith?

While Irving did not specify how his fictional Brom Bones made his living, he did tell us that he was very muscular and a skilled horseman – two traits which some concluded adds up to *blacksmith*.

BUT – Since the primary modes of overland transportation in the 1700s were by foot, horse, or wagon, wouldn't most colonial New Yorkers have been proficient at working with horses, not just blacksmiths? Likewise, most rural occupations of the Colonial period – farming, lumbering, carpentry, to name a few – involved manual labor, and those making their livings in these professions could indeed develop "prodigious strength," also a trait not limited to blacksmiths.

Surely dozens of brawny horsemen named Abraham (including a few blacksmiths) could be found in any of the Dutch villages which lined the Hudson in the 18th century. The identification of an individual as the original of Brom Bones simply because he may have been a blacksmith is still just speculation, as Irving never provided any additional clues as to Bones' occupation.

Giving the blacksmith theorists the benefit of the doubt, we can state that of the three Tarrytown Martlings under consideration, the only one known for certain to have been a blacksmith was the first Abraham Martlenghs (1693-1761), and he died 22 years before Washington Irving was born.

The other two Tarrytown Martlings (the first one's son and grandson) were a *boatman* and a *shoemaker*, respectively. It is these two, either Abraham (1719-1786) or his son, Abraham Jr. (1742-1830) who are alternately pointed out to Old Dutch Burying Ground visitors as having been the inspiration for the Brom Bones character; the most recent version of this theory suggests that Bones may have been "a composite" of both of them. (A small brass grave marker inscribed "BROM" may be found adjacent to the tombstone of Abraham Jr., 1742-1830.)

(Note: The local blacksmith during the war, and presumably the years that immediately followed, was actually one Abraham *Reviere*; his blacksmith shop was located south of the Van Tassel Tavern, at the site of the current Citibank – the former Westchester County Savings Bank building – at the southeast corner of modern-day Broadway and Neperan Road.[31])

The irony is that of the several Abraham Martlings discussed in this chapter, the one who was probably the most "Bones"-like was the last one, Abraham (1763-1841), who is the only one *not* pointed out to graveyard visitors, as he is not buried in Sleepy Hollow – he was buried in Elmsford!

Abraham Van Tassel

The *Souvenir of the Revolutionary Soldiers' Monument Dedication* book published in Tarrytown in 1894 contains a reproduction of an original Revolutionary War Muster Roll, titled "Capt. Gabriel Requa's Company of East Philipsburg." Near the bottom of the list may be found an intriguing entry: "*Abram Van Tassel (Bones).*"[32]

Abraham "Bones" Van Tassel was born in 1754, the youngest son of Johannes Van Tassel (1709-??) and Annetje Ecker (1714-??).

Daniel Van Tassel (1841-1930) – genealogist, historian and editor of the *Tarrytown Argus* newspaper – was the great-nephew of Abraham Van Tassel; Abraham was the younger brother of Daniel's great-grandfather, John Van Tassel. In his *Genealogy of the Van Texel – Van Tassell Family in America 1625-1900*, Daniel wrote, "Abraham was a tall, raw boned man and was early nicknamed 'Brom Bones' to distinguish him from other Van Tassels bearing the same name, who lived in the neighborhood and attended the

Sleepy Hollow Church at that time. Abraham lived in Sleepy Hollow a little north of Carl's Mill."[33]

Other than his enlistment in the Westchester County Militia First Regiment, little is known of Abraham Van Tassel's wartime activities. His participation was likely limited to local skirmishes; writing about his uncle in the May 28, 1898 *New York Times*, Daniel Van Tassel offered, "While his pugnacious brother John fought in the French war and afterward from start to finish in the Revolution, Abraham never left the Hollow."[34]

"Brom Bones" Van Tassel was married twice, first circa 1778 to Hester DeVoe (1759-1799), with whom he had eight children: Johannis, or John (born in 1779); Hannah (1783); Leah (1784); Isaac (1786); Catrina, or Catherine (1789); Abraham (1791), who was nick-named "Indian Brom" and is sometimes confused with his father as having been the original "Brom Bones"; Helena (1793); and Ann (1796).

Following Hester's death in 1799, Abraham was remarried in 1802 to Sarah Minnerly, with whom he had two daughters, Rebecca (born 1804) and Emeline (1806).

Edgar Mayhew Bacon provided a humorous account of Abraham Van Tassel's reaction to hearing "The Legend of Sleepy Hollow" for the first time, presumably in the spring of 1820:

> "Brom Bones, who figures in the courtship of 'Sleepy Hollow' as the practical joker who impersonated the Headless Horseman, was in Mr. William See's store, with a lot of other ancient cronies, when the first copy of the immortal Legend reached Tarrytown. No longer 'Brom, the devil,' but old uncle Abr'm Van Tassel, the patriarch listened in great wrath when someone told him that Washington Irving had put him in a book. Grasping his ponderous stick, he started for the door.

" 'Hole on, Uncle Brom! Where you goin' so fast'? they cried.

" 'Goin' to lick that writin' feller till he can't see!' roared the newly immortalized." 35

Bacon's anecdote suggests that Van Tassel, who would have been in his mid-sixties at the time of this incident, had possessed a wild streak in his younger years (not unlike the fictional Brom Bones), and his bad temper apparently still surfaced on occasion.

William See's Store, where Abraham "Brom Bones" Van Tassel first learned he had been immortalized in Washington Irving's story (Photo courtesy of The Historical Society, Inc., Serving Sleepy Hollow and Tarrytown)

This characterization is contradicted by Daniel Van Tassel's 1898 account, which stated, "Abraham Van Tassel was a man of gentle disposition, with a decidedly religious turn... He quietly cultivated his fields, reared a moderately large family, and regularly of a Sunday attended the services held at the Old Dutch Church of Sleepy Hollow, of which he was a member, and for some years its voorleser. [Note: A voorleser is a leader in singing and reading.] A quiet, exemplary citizen, who closed his eyes for the last time in the spring of 1826. I believe that Irving got the nickname 'Brom Bones' from our locality, but I know that the characters of Brom Van Brunt and Abraham Van Tassel were widely variant."[36]

    Having been born in 1841, some 15 years after his Uncle Abraham's death, Daniel Van Tassel never knew him personally, and had to have obtained the details of his life second-hand from other surviving family members, some of whom may have been less than proud of his "Brom the devil" reputation. It is possible that Daniel may not have been aware of Abraham's youthful wild streak, if it had indeed existed.

    Abraham "Bones" Van Tassel died March 15, 1826 in Sleepy Hollow. As he was a member of the Old Dutch Church, he was presumably buried in the adjacent Old Dutch Burying Ground, although his name is not listed in either the 1926 edition of *The Old Dutch Burying Ground of Sleepy Hollow* or the 1953 revision. The locations of the graves of several other Abraham Van Tassels (including his son "Indian Brom," who was buried with his wife, Sarah) may be found in these publications, but not the grave of "Brom Bones."

    The name Abraham Van Tassel is also absent from the Revolutionary Soldiers' Monument in Sleepy Hollow cemetery. As explained previously in the Abraham Boyce section of this chapter, the monument primarily listed those patriots known to have been buried in the adjacent graveyard; perhaps by 1894, almost 70 years after his death, the location of Van Tassel's final resting place had been forgotten, thus the omission of his name?

Abraham Van Alstyne

As with Ichabod Crane and Katrina Van Tassel, Kinderhook also stakes a claim to the original of Brom Bones having been one of their own, a "wild blade" named Abraham Van Alstyne.

Probably the earliest proponent of the Abraham Van Alstyne theory was, not surprisingly, Harold Van Santvoord, crediting "older residents of the village" for his information. The stories, which he said he remembered from his youth, were "amply verified by the descendants of the originals who figured in the legend."[37]

Amid his 1898 editorial debate with Edgar Mayhew Bacon in the pages of *The New York Times*, Van Santvoord referenced the same "aged lady with tenacious powers of memory" who had revealed to him the "true identity" of Katrina Van Tassel. According to Van Santvoord, this lady had also furnished "a lively account of the exploits of the redoubtable Brom Bones – one Abraham Van Alstyne, as Irving himself confessed."[38]

This was echoed by Welles and Evans, writing in 1984, who asserted that "when the author came back to visit Kinderhook, he is supposed to have told one of the residents that Abram Van Alstyne was likewise the original of Brom Bones."[39] Was this statement based on actual oral tradition, or were they more or less quoting Van Santvoord's version, embellished slightly with the "return to Kinderhook" detail?

John Ritter's July 1899 *New York Herald* article, "The Real Ichabod Crane," relied heavily on Van Santvoord's claims, adding that there were still people living in Kinderhook who "knew Abraham Van Alstyne in his later years, when he was familiarly referred to as 'Brom Bones.' "[40]

Curiously, prior to Harold Van Santvoord's 1898 editorials, no one seems to have connected Abraham Van

Alstyne (or Helen Van Alen, for that matter) to "The Legend of Sleepy Hollow." Jesse Merwin, as discussed in Chapter 5, had already been linked to Ichabod Crane as early as January 1835 in a *New York Sun* article announcing Irving's purchase of Sunnyside; then the December 1844 *Christian Advocate and Journal* contained a quote from Martin Van Buren which stated, "our friend Merwin sat for the picture of Ichabod Crane." However, neither article mentioned Van Alstyne.

A Romantic Rivalry

Mirroring the fictional feud between Brom Bones and Ichabod Crane, much of the lore regarding Abraham Van Alstyne involves a romantic rivalry with Jesse Merwin, of which there are several versions.

One version has Washington Irving observing the competition between Merwin and Van Alstyne for the affections of Helen Van Alen. However, as discussed in Chapter 6, Helen was not quite four years old in 1809, much too young to have been the "blooming lass" at the center of their conflict. Also, at the time of Irving's visit, Merwin was already married, having wed Jane Van Dyck the previous October.

Another variation has Merwin and Van Alstyne competing for the hand of Merwin's future wife, Jane. Writing in 1984, Welles and Evans said of Merwin, "while courting Jane Van Dyck he had a rival, Abram Van Alstyne, who wanted to discourage Jesse's attentions to Jane and so one night had masqueraded as the headless Hessian trooper, hoping to frighten the schoolmaster so much that he would leave Kinderhook."[41]

Since Merwin had married Jane seven months before he met Washington Irving, he would have had to have related this story to Irving after the fact. There is, however, nothing in Irving's published journals or correspondence to verify, or refute, that such a conversation ever took place.

A Halloween Party at the Van Alen's

Perhaps the most detailed version of the Van Alstyne/Merwin rivalry was provided by the current owner of Jesse Merwin's farmhouse, Mrs. Esther Leeming "Faity" Tuttle. In her 2004 book *No Rocking Chair For Me*, she wrote, "Merwin told Irving about a Halloween party he'd attended at the home of Katrina Van Alen, the girl he was in love with."[42]

Continuing Mrs. Tuttle's account, "A big burly man named Brom Van Alstyne (called Brom Bones in the story) attended the party, dressed as the ghost of a Hessian soldier, or the 'headless horseman.' Mounted on a large horse, Brom chased Merwin as he left the party, throwing a pumpkin at him as he disappeared through the covered bridge into Kinderhook."[43]

Mrs. Tuttle's detailed rendition, which she attributed to "local historians," is the first time the Halloween Party angle is introduced in the story. This has the earmarks of being a relatively recent embellishment; oral traditions have a tendency to become "improved" over time as storytellers add new details to make them more entertaining. Had the Halloween Party figured into the original story, Harold Van Santvoord undoubtedly would have included that detail in his writings in the 1890s to strengthen his case, rather than relying only on vague statements attributed to unnamed "older residents."

Another reason to question the Halloween Party story is that Halloween as we know it was not yet widely celebrated in America in the early 1800s, although autumn harvest festivals were fairly commonplace. The tradition of dressing in costumes for Halloween is believed to have been introduced in the mid-1840s, imported by Irish immigrants fleeing the potato famine. Halloween parties did not become popular until around the turn of the 20th century.

A Helter Skelter Wag

Most, if not all, post-1898 articles naming Abraham Van Alstyne as Brom Bones can be traced back to Harold Van Santvoord as the source.

However, since oral traditions and local legends often do have some basis in fact, we should not altogether discount the Abraham Van Alstyne theory. We know that Irving *did* indeed know an Abraham Van Alstyne, as evidenced by two journal entries made during his visit to Kinderhook with Martin Van Buren in September 1833; Irving's September 10 entry reads, "Brom Van Alstyne a helter skelter wag," and the following day's entry reads simply "Brom Van Alstyne."[44]

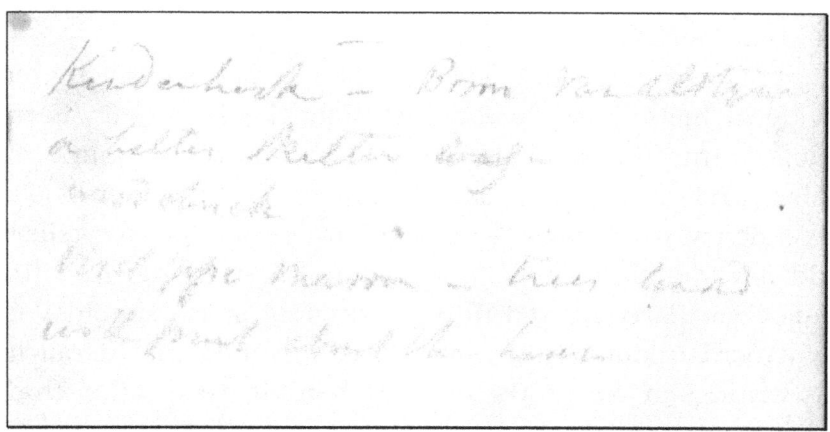

Washington Irving's September 10, 1833 Journal entry, during his visit to Kinderhook – "Brom Van Alstyne a helter skelter wag." Below that, he wrote "visit Jesse Merwin, trees loaded with fruit about the house." (Photo courtesy of The New York Public Library, Manuscripts and Archives Division; Astor, Lenox, and Tilden Foundation; Washington Irving papers)

Unfortunately, there are no additional details provided. Was Irving rekindling an old friendship from 1809? Or, was this their very first meeting? For that matter, did the two men actually converse at all? These two exceedingly brief journal entries are the only references to Abraham Van Alstyne found to date in any of Irving's published writings.

It is curious that Irving referred to Van Alstyne in his journal as a "wag" – Irving's introduction of Brom Bones in "The Legend of Sleepy Hollow" described him as having "*waggish* good humor."[45] Could Irving's use of the word "wag" when referring to Brom Van Alstyne be a clue to the identity of the original Brom Bones – something akin to "a wag in 1809 and still a wag in 1833"? (Or was Washington Irving simply using the slang of the times?)

So Who Was Abraham Van Alstyne?

Like the Van Tassels of the Sleepy Hollow region, the Van Alstynes were very prolific in Columbia County, and are still plentiful today – in fact, a prominent Van Alstyne descendant recently served as mayor of Kinderhook.

The Van Alstynes can trace their ancestry back to family patriarch Janse Martense Van Aelsteyn, who emigrated to New Netherland from Holland around 1653. Originally settling in New Amsterdam (later New York City), Janse purchased extensive properties near Albany in the 1650s, as well as Kinderhook in the mid-1660s.

By the early 1800s, the Kinderhook Van Alstynes, Van Nesses and Van Alens were all related by numerous intermarriages, so it is not unreasonable to assume that Washington Irving was probably introduced to some of the Van Alstynes during his two-month stay with the Van Ness family.

Abraham was apparently a favorite name given to Van Alstyne male offspring. Owing to that quaint Dutch custom of naming children after their grandparents, roughly every other generation of Van Alstynes seems to have contained an Abraham.[46]

Surprisingly, the 1810 Kinderhook Census lists only one Abraham Van Alstyne. This Abraham was between the ages of 26 and 44, and had one male child, aged 10-15. The entry also lists one female between the ages of 16 and 25, presumably Abraham's wife, as well as one "other free person" and five slaves, which indicates that this Abraham Van Tassel was probably fairly wealthy.

The May 1809 Kinderhook Real Estate Assessment Roll also lists only one Abraham Van Alstyne. This Abraham was moderately wealthy, with an assessed Value of Real Estate of 2,250 pounds and Value of Personal Estate of 600, for a total worth of 2,850 pounds. Was this the same Abraham as was listed in the Census?

Genealogical Records

Various genealogical sources turned up more than 20 Abraham Van Alstynes living in New York State in the early 1800s, including about a dozen in Columbia County.[47] Assuming that Washington Irving did befriend an Abraham Van Alstyne in May of 1809, which Abraham was he?

In order to narrow down the list, it was necessary to make several assumptions: (1) that the Brom Van Alstyne mentioned in Washington Irving's 1833 journal is the same person whom Irving is said to have met in 1809, thus eliminating several who were alive in 1809 but died prior to 1833; (2) that in order to have been involved in any alleged romantic rivalries, Abraham would have been an adult in 1809, about the same age as, or slightly older than, Washington Irving and Jesse Merwin, who were both in their mid-twenties; and (3) that Van Alstyne was a resident of Kinderhook, disqualifying several Abrahams from other New York locations, including a few nearby communities.

Of 23 Abraham Van Alstynes tabulated from various genealogical searches, eight were eliminated due to being from the wrong locations, and another 10 were the wrong ages or died prior to September 1833. However, five of the Abrahams warranted a closer look.

The first Abraham Van Alstyne evaluated was born on February 15, 1776, the son of Johannes Van Alstyne (1745-??) and the former Dirckje Winne (1757-??). He had a sister Gerritje (1778-??) and two brothers, Adam (1780-??) and Jacob (1782-1839). This Abraham *could* correspond to the Abraham listed in the Real Estate Assessment Roll; names corresponding to those of his father and one of his brothers appear in the Roll, and all possessed higher than average wealth. Johannes (*possibly* the father) had the greatest total wealth, 5,200 pounds, followed by Abraham (the eldest son), then Adam; Jacob, the youngest son, does not appear on the list.

This Abraham would have been 33 years old in 1809, an appropriate age to have associated with Washington Irving and Jesse Merwin, and 57 in 1833, assuming he was still alive; unfortunately, the scant genealogical records located so far do not provide the date of his death, nor do they provide any information regarding marriage or children.

A second Abraham Van Alstyne, this one baptized on December 25, 1773 in Kinderhook, might also be a possibility. This Abraham was the son of Abraham A. Van Alstyne, Jr. (1739-1815) and the former Catlyntje Van Ness (1758-??). He is probably not the Abraham listed in the 1810 census, as his first child, Abraham Fellers Van Alstyne, was not born until 1812.

He would have been 35 years old in 1809, about the right age to have been a wealthy landowner, and still only about 10 years older than Merwin and Irving. However, the genealogical records available do not provide the date of his death; was he still alive in September 1833 for Irving to have seen him and have mentioned him in his journal?

A third Abraham Van Alstyne also shows up in the genealogical records, but his information is even sketchier than the previous two. He was the son of Nicholas Van Alstyne (1745-??). His mother's name is not recorded, nor do the available records provide his birth date or the date of his death.

This Abraham's birth year may be *estimated* as approximately 1786, based on the dates of birth that are known for several of his siblings; it is also known that he was married in 1824 to Elizabeth Kelly. His *estimated* age in 1809 would have been about 23, just a few years younger than Irving. Assuming he did not experience an untimely death at a relatively young age, he would have been about 47 in 1833.

Two other Kinderhook Abraham Van Alstynes were considered briefly, but ultimately ruled out. One of them, born in 1797 to Isaac Van Alstyne (1772-1855) and the former Maria Vosburgh (1778-1851) would have been only 12 years old in May 1809, too young to have been a romantic rival of Merwin or Irving. The other, born on May 16, 1762 to Phillipus and Maritje Van Alstyne, was 47 in 1809, and would have been 71 in 1833... probably too old to be referred to as a "helter skelter wag." (He died the following year, on June 5, 1834.)

The long list of Abraham Van Alstynes has thus been whittled down to three individuals, which is still two too many, but is probably the best that can be done with the limited information available. Existing cemetery records maintained by the Columbia County Historical Society do not contain any information for these individuals; this may indicate that they were buried on private land, and the pertinent records are long lost...

Of course, it is entirely possible that the Abraham Van Alstyne we are seeking is *none of the above*. The focus of this investigation was only on those Abrahams who were residents of the village of Kinderhook, as specified by their individual genealogical records. We ignored any Abrahams who may have lived in the surrounding communities of Chatham, Hudson, Ghent, Valatie, Stuyvesant, Claverack... all a short horseback ride from Kinderhook.

The question "Which Abraham Van Alstyne?" has apparently been asked before. The Merwin Family file, housed in the Columbia County Historical Society library in Kinderhook, contains an undated information sheet composed of "Legends and Bits of History" about the Van Alstynes, which concludes that "the Columbia County Historical Society could not specify which of the many Abraham Van Alstynes or several Catharina Van Tassels were the prototypes for the story."[48]

Jesse Merwin's grandson, George Merwin, upon learning of his grandfather's relationship to the fictional Ichabod, "spent considerable time gathering lore about the other characters." Of Brom Van Alstyne, Merwin claimed to have uncovered "as many tales of prowess in the countryside as ever surrounded the fabled Brom Bones."[49]

Do any of George Merwin's notes still exist? Had he planned to write an article, or possibly even a book? Might one of his descendants still have a draft manuscript tucked away in a drawer or steamer trunk someplace?

Maybe someday someone will come across a journal among old family papers, or perhaps a 19th century letter making reference to "Brom Bones" having been one of their relatives. Until then, the identity of *the* Abraham Van Alstyne associated with the Brom Bones character will probably remain a mystery.

Assuming that Irving indeed *could have* met Van Alstyne in May of 1809, it is of course possible that some of his personality traits could have found their way into "The Legend." There has been nothing found thus far in any of Irving's published journals or notebooks to either support or refute this theory.

It is, however, equally possible that any similarities between Abraham Van Alstyne and Brom Bones are purely coincidental. As they did with Helen "Katrina" Van Alen, some Kinderhook residents may have assumed that since Jesse "Ichabod" Merwin was from Kinderhook, then *all* of the "Sleepy Hollow" characters must have been based on local individuals. Looking amongst themselves for a probable candidate, they identified a local "helter skelter wag" (who also happened to be named Brom) as being the most "Bones"-like – part braggart, part bully, and part practical joker – and concluded that their own Brom Van Alstyne *must have been* the inspiration for the fictional Brom Bones. But then again, doesn't every small town have someone who fits that description?

Fleshing Out the Character of Brom Bones

To develop the character of Brom Bones, Washington Irving appears to have also drawn from contemporary literary trends, much as he did with Ichabod Crane.

The Frontiersman

As discussed previously in Chapter 5, Irving was mindful of American tastes and attitudes while compiling *The Sketch Book*. In the early 1800s, the young nation was developing an interest in heroes of the frontier, many of whom were becoming legends through oral traditions and tall tales. The frontiersman became a popular character "type" found in American folklore, typically "lawless, ignorant, rough mannered, strong, a heavy drinker, and a ferocious fighter."[50]

In keeping with this trend, Brom Bones was introduced as "a burly, roaring, roystering blade... the hero of the country round, which rang with his feats of strength and hardihood... always ready for either a fight or a frolic."[51]

At the same time, Irving made a point of telling us that Brom had "more mischief than ill will in his composition," thereby clarifying that he was not really a bully, and keeping him somewhat likeable.

The Brom Bones character also displays the frontiersman type's penchant for bragging and concocting tall tales, usually about himself; when the unlikely story of "old Brouwer" is told at the Van Tassel's party, Brom counters with an even taller tale describing his own encounter with the Headless Horseman.[52]

Brom Bones is actually everything a hero is supposed to be – strong, good-looking, with the prettiest girl and the fastest horse... had the story been set a few decades later, he might have been a cowboy!

City Slicker vs. Frontiersman Conflict

Irving is generally credited with having been the first to create a conflict of "city vs. country," with Ichabod Crane representing the Yankee "city slicker" who is pitted against Brom Bones' frontiersman persona.

Irving did allow his Connecticut Yankee a few small victories. "Under cover of his character of singing-master," Ichabod had the perfect excuse to make "frequent visits" to the Van Tassel residence, thus edging out Brom Bones, whose horse "was no longer seen tied at the palings" outside the farmhouse.[53]

Then later in the story at the "quilting frolic," Ichabod Crane, who "prided himself upon his dancing as much as upon his vocal powers," escorted Katrina to the dance floor, while Brom Bones "sat brooding by himself in one corner" – the worldly and sophisticated city slicker knows how to dance, but the rough-and-tumble frontiersman presumably does not.[54]

Seemingly set up as the villain, or anti-hero of the story, the resourceful frontiersman Brom Bones, in the guise of a headless hessian, ultimately outsmarts the conniving Yankee, and turns out to be the *real* hero of Sleepy Hollow; and it is Brom, not Ichabod, who ultimately "conducted the blooming Katrina in triumph to the altar."[55]

Daniel Hoffman, writing in 1953, summed up the Ichabod/Brom conflict: "This first statement of the theme is among the most memorable it has ever received in our literature; it is with us yet and ever has been, in Davy Crockett outwitting peddlars, in a thousand dime novels and popular magazines in which the yokel gets the best of the city slicker."[56]

Mike Fink

Brom Bones is sometimes compared to Mike Fink (1770?-1823), the well-known frontier brawler and "king of the keelboaters." Daniel Hoffman observed, "In Brom Bones's good-natured mischief there is a tinge of Mike Fink's brutality."[57]

However, Fink did not make his first literary appearance until 1821 as a minor character in Alphonso Wetmore's *The Pedlar*, two years *after* "The Legend of Sleepy Hollow" was written. The first known appearance of Fink as the main character was not until late 1828 with the publication of *The Last of the Boatmen* by Morgan Neville.[58]

Mike Fink had certainly been the subject of a number of regional "tall tales" which circulated orally earlier than that, but probably not before 1815 when Irving left for England. Although it is unlikely that Irving would have been inspired directly by the Mike Fink character, he seems to have been influenced by the same frontiersman "type" that helped to propagate the Fink legends.

Mike Fink, the Ohio Boatman (Emerson Bennett, 1853)

Colonial Dutch Traits

In *Knickerbocker's History of New York*, Irving had caricatured the colonial Dutch as being fat, lazy and not too bright; however, in reality, the early Dutch were much more like Brom Bones. Historian Thomas A. Janvier, sharply contradicting Washington Irving's depictions of the Dutch, asserted that "they were tough and they were sturdy and they were plucky as men could be."[59]

The frontier Dutch were likewise described by author and folklorist Carl Carmer as "a hard-drinking and profane lot... rough in their play and their ideas of entertainment... they loved to gallop their horses through town at top speed in the daytime and to disturb the night by firing their guns and shouting."[60]

This brings to mind Irving's description of the antics of Brom Bones and his gang, who were often "heard dashing along past the farmhouses at midnight, with whoop and halloo, like a troop of Don Cossacks."[61]

Carmer continued, "As for humor along the Hudson in the early Dutch days, it consisted mostly of practical joking..."[62]

Brom Bones, described by Washington Irving as having "a mingled air of fun and arrogance" with "a strong dash of waggish good humor," epitomized the colonial Dutch practical jokester.[63] Suddenly threatened by Ichabod Crane's obvious interest in Katrina Van Tassel, Bones singled Crane out as the object of a number of pranks. Brom and his companions "smoked out his singing school, by stopping up the chimney" and "broke into the school-house at night... and turned every thing topsy-turvy so that the poor schoolmaster began to think all the witches in the country held their meetings there."[64]

To further humiliate Ichabod in the presence of Katrina, Brom employed "a scoundrel dog whom he taught to whine in the most ludicrous manner," successfully interrupting their singing lessons.[65]

Of course, Brom's ultimate practical joke was to exploit Ichabod's superstitious nature by (probably) masquerading as the legendary Headless Horseman, terrifying the pedagogue into (apparently) fleeing Sleepy Hollow altogether.

Pumpkin-Head Joke?

In colonial times, New Englanders, in particular those from Connecticut, were nicknamed "pumpkin-heads." This fact was known to Irving; one of his 1817 notebooks contains an explanation which he had transcribed from Thomas Anburey's 1789 book *Travels Through the Interior Parts of America*: "New Haven is remarkable for having given the epithet of pumpkinheads to the New Englanders which arose from one of the severe laws of Connecticut... enjoining every male to have his hair cut round by a cap and when caps were not readily at hand they substituted the hard shell of a pumpkin."[66]

(Anburey himself had apparently copied – or rather plagiarized? – the same passage almost verbatim from Reverend Samuel Peters' *General History of Connecticut*, published in 1781.)

The "severe laws" that Anburey (and Peters) referred to were strict religious rules known as "blue laws." They dictated, among other things, that every Saturday, every male was to have a cap (or pumpkin shell) placed on his head to be used as a guide for the hair to be cut all around it; this resulted in what we might call a "bowl cut" today.

Since Ichabod Crane hailed from Connecticut, was this the reason, at least in part, for Irving's selection of a pumpkin to serve as the false "head" wielded by the headless horseman?

Was this part of Brom's practical joke – a pumpkin head for a pumpkin-head?

Postscript – An Interesting "Confession"

Washington Irving, in his typical tongue-in-cheek fashion, appears to have deliberately left the conclusion to "The Legend of Sleepy Hollow" slightly open-ended. On the one hand, he clearly implicated Brom Bones in Ichabod's disappearance, stating that he always looked "exceedingly knowing" whenever the story was told, and would invariably "burst into a hearty laugh" when they got to the part about the pumpkin.[67]

Brom Bones selecting a pumpkin in preparation for his midnight encounter with Ichabod Crane... (Sketched by George Boughton in 1893)

Irving immediately followed this observation with a statement that "The old country wives, however, who are the best judges of these matters, maintain to this day that Ichabod was spirited away by supernatural means"... thus leaving his readers to draw their own conclusions as to what *really* happened to Ichabod.[68]

Author Donald G. Mitchell, speaking in Tarrytown at an April 3, 1883 centennial celebration of Irving's birth, recalled a visit with Irving at Sunnyside. He described how the two of them took a carriage ride through Sleepy Hollow, with Irving pointing out various landmarks mentioned in his story.

As they progressed along the Albany Post Road, Irving indicated to Mitchell, "Down this bit of road the old horse 'Gunpowder' came thundering: there away – *Brom Bones with his pumpkin* (I tell you this in confidence, he said) was in waiting; and along here they went clattering neck and neck..."[69]

So – if any question remains as to the true identity of the Headless Horseman that Ichabod encountered on his way home from the Van Tassel's, Irving's "confession" to Mitchell seems to answer it once and for all: *The "headless horseman" was indeed Brom Bones!*

Chapter 8

Conclusions

"There was one dapper little gentleman in bright-colored clothes... dipping into various books, fluttering over the leaves of manuscripts, taking a morsel out of one, a morsel out of another... here a little and there a little."
— from "The Art of Book-Making," 1820

Now that we have examined all of the evidence, what conclusions can be drawn? Was "The Legend of Sleepy Hollow" based on actual events? Were the characters of Ichabod Crane, Katrina Van Tassel and Brom Bones modeled after real people?

Before we delve too deeply into our individual analyses, let's begin with a brief discussion of Washington Irving's writing technique, which he seemingly explained in one of the other *Sketch Book* essays, "The Art of Bookmaking."

Writing from the perspective of an author "blundering upon" a secret library hidden in a museum, Irving described observing a group of modern authors "pilfering" passages from ancient books, while the original authors stared down at them from portraits lining the walls. The modern authors were busily "dipping into various books, fluttering over the leaves of manuscripts, taking a morsel out of one, a morsel out of another… here a little and there a little."[1]

These "morsels" would then be reassembled and repackaged into new manuscripts: "What was formerly a ponderous history revives in the shape of a romance – an old legend changes into a modern play…"[2]

Irving further explained – rationalized? – that authors are naturally "implanted" with a "pilfering disposition," which is "the way in which Providence has taken care that the seeds of knowledge and wisdom shall be preserved from age to age."[3]

Washington Irving has actually been criticized by some for what they perceive as a lack of originality. Biographer Stanley T. Williams likened Irving to the "predatory writers" he parodied in "The Art of Book-Making," calling him "a lawless plunderer of ancient and obsolete authors."[4] Of the essays contained in *The Sketch Book*, Williams asserted that "every one is a composite, binding together sentences from his reading, characters met in travel, and his own grief or good humor."[5]

Irving's real talent was in putting together "morsels" he gathered over the years from various sources and locales – his observations of people and scenery, along with a few obscure folktales and legends. His vivid descriptions were recorded as "thumb-sketches" in his ever-present journals and notebooks, to be drawn from at a later date and infused with new life by his masterful use of language.

So – Could Irving's "Sleepy Hollow" characters, like his stories, have been pieced together from real people in Irving's life? Certainly! Irving is known to have previously employed this technique in *Knickerbocker's History of New York*, published in 1809. In his 1851 letter to his friend Jesse Merwin, he disclosed that he had based the character Dirk Schuyler on one of their mutual acquaintances, Kinderhook resident John Moore.

It is actually common practice for authors to base fictional characters on real people. Borrowing the traits – the mannerisms, quirks, habits, appearance, theology, etc. – of living individuals makes the fictional characters more believable and easier for the reader to get to know, which in turn makes it easier to like (or dislike) them.

Many well-known literary characters have been based on real people known to their respective authors. Mark Twain admitted in his autobiography that he had based the title character from *Huckleberry Finn* on his childhood friend Tom Blankenship; Lousia May Alcott based her *Little Women* character Beth March on one of her neighbors, Elizabeth Hoar; and Sir Arthur Conan Doyle modeled his *Sherlock Holmes* title sleuth after one of his college professors, a surgeon named Dr. Joseph Bell.

More recently, J. K. Rowling, author of the *Harry Potter* series, based her Professor Snape character on her former high school chemistry teacher, John Nettleship.

However, it should be clarified that the modeling of a fictional character after a living person is usually just a starting point. The character is given some, but not necessarily *all*, of the characteristics of the original. The author will then add other qualities – sometimes drawn from other individuals, and sometimes from the author's own imagination – as needed to fit the story. It is not uncommon for a fictional character to end up as a composite of several individuals, with attributes borrowed from each to create a single, more complex character.

Likewise, while a living person may have been the *inspiration* for a character in a story, it does not necessarily mean that the person actually performed all (or for that matter, *any)* of the actions in the story. It is important to make the distinction between fact and fiction; between the real-life activities of a person and those that sprang from the author's imagination.

And – we must not lose sight of the fact that "The Legend of Sleepy Hollow" is a work of fiction.

Let's take a closer look at some of Irving's characters...

Ichabod Crane

The biggest "morsel" used in the composition of the Ichabod Crane character appears to have been Jesse Merwin of Kinderhook, New York. The similarities could not be more obvious: both men originally hailed from Connecticut; both were schoolteachers in one-room country schoolhouses; both boarded for a week at a time with the families of their students; and both were romantically involved with wealthy farmers' daughters (except Merwin succeeded where Crane failed).

However, the most compelling piece of evidence is Washington Irving's own hand-written endorsement on the reverse of a letter from Merwin: *"From Jesse Merwin, the original of Ichabod Crane."*

Even staunch Tarrytown proponent Edgar Mayhew Bacon seems to have softened his stance by 1902, when he conceded that Merwin had likely been the inspiration for Ichabod. In his book *The Hudson River*, Bacon wrote, "It has been shown by a gentleman to whom Kinderhook owes much for the presentation of matters of local interest, that there is a strong possibility at least, that the original of the immortal character of Ichabod Crane was met and studied by Irving while at the Van Ness house."[6] The "gentleman" to whom Bacon was referring was, of course, none other than his former nemesis, Harold Van Santvoord.

Washington Irving *may* also have incorporated some of Samuel Youngs' history, although to a lesser extent. Ichabod's career following his departure from Sleepy Hollow does seem to mirror that of Youngs – from schoolteacher to lawyer and politician.

(It is worth noting, however, that Jesse Merwin *also* went on to become a lawyer and local politician/judge, but this occurred several years after Irving left Kinderhook. Did Irving know about his schoolteacher friend's radical career change prior to writing "The Legend" in 1819? Did the two friends truly exchange "a great many interesting letters" through the years, as alleged by Harold Van Santvoord?)[7]

Irving did have ties to Youngs – his brother-in-law Henry Van Wart, with whom he is known to have spent much time during the period he was drafting *The Sketch Book*, was Youngs' nephew – so it is *possible* for Irving to have heard of him and appropriated parts of his history.

With a large portion of Jesse Merwin (and possibly a dash or two of Samuel Youngs) providing a base, Irving then appears to have drawn upon Connecticut Yankee and Puritan stereotypes to give a bit of flavor to the character.

Ichabod's superstitious nature was almost certainly "pilfered" from Henry Fielding's schoolmaster "Partridge," from the 1749 novel *Tom Jones* – Irving even jokingly referred to Merwin as "Partridge" in a letter written several months after their initial meeting in Kinderhook.

Irving's description of Crane's scarecrow-like appearance was clearly influenced by his recollection in November 1819 of Walter Scott's neighbor "Lauchie Long Legs," and probably imagery from Miguel de Cervantes' *Don Quixote* and Thomas Anburey's vivid description of New Englanders on horseback.

Even Irving's description of Ichabod's schoolhouse – "a rude building of logs... a wild brook running close by" – can be traced to yet another "morsel," this one recorded in an 1818 notebook containing descriptions of various scenes observed in England as well as New York state.

And finally, the name "Ichabod Crane" was almost certainly derived from Irving having met a young Army officer of that name when they were both stationed at Sackets Harbor during the War of 1812. One could not easily forget a name like Ichabod Crane...

Katrina Van Tassel

Washington Irving did not provide any clues to the identity of the prototype, assuming one existed, for his fictional Katrina Van Tassel. To date, nothing has been located in any of his published journals or correspondence that would single out anyone as the inspiration for the character.

As we have seen, most local traditions concerning Katrina's alleged "true identity" have been based purely on speculation – the individual happened to have the surname Van Tassel, was somehow linked to another character or location identified with the story, or just simply fit the profile of a wealthy farmer's daughter with whom Irving *may* have come in contact at some point.

The most prevalent tradition in Tarrytown names Eleanor "Laney" Van Tassel as the model for Katrina, apparently simply because she was the only other Van Tassel girl mentioned by Irving in any of his other writings.

At least one long-standing local tradition, the identification of Kinderhook's Helen Van Alen as the prototype of Katrina, has been effectively debunked, as Helen has been found to have been only three years old at the time of Irving's 1809 visit, much too young to have served as his muse.

With that said, however, we know better than to *totally* discount any of these "traditions," as they often do have a kernel of truth to them. In the case of Helen Van Alen and her purported romantic interest in Washington Irving, my own *theory* is that she probably did meet him, but it was during one of his *later* visits to Kinderhook, most likely in September 1833 – well after "The Legend" was written.

At the time of Irving's 1833 visit, Helen would have been 28 – a much more appropriate age to be discussing marriage! – and Irving would have been 50, still single, and wealthy, not to mention a full-blown celebrity. Helen may have indeed developed a bit of a crush on the charming older gentleman, giving rise to a Van Alen "family tradition" that was passed down over subsequent generations. But whatever her interest in Irving, he apparently didn't reciprocate, as Helen didn't rate so much as a mention in any of his known journals or correspondence...

The concept of the poor schoolmaster courting the rich farmer's daughter closely mirrors the true story of Irving's friend Jesse Merwin and his wife, Jane Van Dyck – might *she* be considered the closest thing to a prototype, by default?

Personality-wise, what did Irving really tell us about Katrina? Not a lot, actually – most of it is superficial. Katrina Van Tassel is probably the least developed character in the story. In fact, Irving devoted more than four times as many lines to his description of her father's farm than to his description of Katrina herself!

We know she was pretty; and we know she was the daughter of a rich farmer. This does little to reveal her identity, as the majority of the populace were farmers, and it stands to reason that most young women of Sleepy Hollow (or Kinderhook) would have been farmer's daughters.

An only child, Katrina was probably not so much spoiled as she was what we might call a "daddy's girl" – Baltus loved her "better even than his pipe," and "let her have her way in everything."[8]

Katrina was apparently a bit of a fashionista, her manner of dress described as "a mixture of ancient and modern fashions, as most suited to set off her charms," featuring "a provokingly short petticoat." Having caught the eye of an admirer, she was what might today be termed *high maintenance* – "universally famed, not merely for her beauty, but her vast expectations."[9]

Irving's Katrina was apparently indecisive – even *fickle* – as she vacillated between two (or more) suitors. Again, this could describe many young women, including more than a few women of modern times!

But was Katrina really being indecisive? According to Knickerbocker/Irving, "it was whispered that she did not altogether discourage" Brom's attention.[10] Perhaps she was not fickle at all, but was actually *scheming* – dare we say manipulative? – and had merely been *using* the unsuspecting schoolmaster to make Brom jealous and hurry him to the altar.

But again, the act of resorting to "coquettish tricks" to deceive one suitor and attract another does little to help with the identification of the original of Katrina. Surely legions of women – past, present and future – have, and will continue to play the jealousy card to secure the attention of their respective Broms...

It is also entirely possible that Irving did not consciously model Katrina Van Tassel after *anyone* in particular. Perhaps he was not merely being coy when he would tell inquiring women of Tarrytown that "any of them" could have been the model for Katrina. Maybe his statement could be taken literally, that his Katrina was representative of a "typical" young Dutch girl of the period... and that truly *any* of the women he had known could have served as the model for the character.

Perhaps Edgar Mayhew Bacon summed it up best: "Katrina Van Tassel is a good type of a country belle. She might exist almost anywhere. She filled her role, was pretty, an heiress, a flirt, and married the better man. Either Tarrytown or Kinderhook could find, not one, but a score, of prototypes, and so could Nyack or Danbury or Wilkesbarre, or any other place."[11]

Brom Bones

As with Katrina Van Tassel, most of the local traditions of both Tarrytown and Kinderhook concerning the "true identity" of Brom Bones are based primarily on speculation. Some Tarrytown amateur historians decided that Brom *must have been* a blacksmith, and so searched their local history for one named Brom/Abraham, ultimately focusing on the Martling family, which was rife with war heroes and at least one blacksmith.

Likewise, a few denizens of Kinderhook, aware that their own Jesse Merwin had almost certainly been the inspiration for Ichabod Crane, decided that he *must have* lived the story – he *must have been* involved in a rivalry with a local bully for the affections of a farmer's daughter. A search of their own local history for a suitable Brom turned up a Bones-like character with the surname Van Alstyne.

Taking this assumption one step further, some even concluded that "it was Irving's original intention to locate the scene of the legend in Kinderhook."[12] They theorized that Irving changed the true location of his tale, as well as the real names of the key players, so that he would not offend anyone, as he had inadvertently done with the satirical *Knickerbocker's History of New York*.

Here are the facts: Washington Irving's nephew and biographer Pierre Munroe Irving, writing in 1863, was *very clear* in describing how "The Legend" had been inspired by a conversation Irving had in the summer of 1818 with his brother-in-law Henry Van Wart. While "dwelling upon some recollections of his early years *at Tarrytown*," Van Wart had "touched upon a waggish fiction of one *Brom Bones*."[13] (Pierre presumably obtained this information first-hand from his uncle.)

Also, in his December 29, 1819 letter to Ebenezer which accompanied the "Legend" manuscript, Irving himself stated that the story had been "suggested by recollections of scenes and stories *about Tarrytown*."[14] He had no reason to conceal the "true setting" of the story in private correspondence with his own brother.

So was there really a person from the Tarrytown region nicknamed Brom Bones? *Yes, there was!* As attested to by his nephew, Tarrytown journalist and historian Daniel Van Tassel, his Uncle Abraham Van Tassel had been given the "Bones" moniker at a young age to distinguish him from several of his relatives who were also named Abraham.[15] The name "Brom Bones," along with his apparent penchant for bragging, most likely originated from Henry Van Wart's characterization of the Tarrytown individual.

How closely was Irving's Brom Bones modeled after the real Brom Bones? Daniel Van Tassel believed that any similarities between his uncle and the fictional Brom ended with their names... although Edgar Mayhew Bacon's "goin' to lick that writin' feller" anecdote would seem to suggest otherwise![16]

Although he was, at least partly, *inspired by* Abraham Van Tassel, we must not lose sight of the fact that Irving's "Brom Bones" was a fictional character, with additional personality traits and embellishments provided by the author.

For example: Was the real Abraham "Brom Bones" Van Tassel an expert horseman? We don't know. But the individual posing as the Headless Horseman in the story needed to be "as dexterous on horseback as a Tartar," so Irving gave that skill to his fictional Brom, regardless of whether or not the genuine "Bones" Van Tassel had possessed it.

As with many of Irving's characters, "Brom Bones" was probably an amalgam of several real people, along with a few imaginary ones, to give him a bit of color. Post-war Tarrytown (or Kinderhook, for that matter) had no shortage of "wild blades," including, but not limited to, the Boyces, the Martlings, the Pauldings... all of whom had performed bravely during the Revolution.

And then there were a number of other war heroes whom we have neglected to mention until now – and to do so in any detail would be far beyond the scope of this book – individuals such as Sergeant John Dean, whose heroics resulted in a Tarrytown park being named for him; John Buckhout, whose hat was shot off his head while he was being pursued by a company of Hessian dragoons; William Dutcher, who was surprised at his home and forced to flee for his life up the Albany Post Road and across the Sleepy Hollow church bridge (sound familiar?); and of course the story of Johnnie Odell and how Petticoat Lane received its name is a legend unto itself...[17]

So, in addition to regaling Irving with his tales of Brom Bones, could Henry Van Wart have also "touched upon" the exploits of one or more of these other local heroes? We can only speculate...

But regardless of how many (or how few) other individuals may have been melded to create the literary character, if Edgar Mayhew Bacon's account of the incident at See's Store can be taken at face value, Abraham "Brom Bones" Van Tassel certainly recognized his own name when he found out that Irving had used it in his story!

A Mere Whimsical Band...

So what of the storyline? Did Jesse Merwin really scheme to appropriate the inheritance of a local farmer's daughter? And was he really involved in a rivalry – good-natured or otherwise – with a local prankster who also had his eye on her?

Probably not... although there is really no way for us to ever know for certain. Nothing in Irving's published letters or journals allude to any type of rivalry between Merwin and another suitor. What the two friends discussed between themselves on their "fishing expeditions" – including any details of Jesse and Jane's courtship – was not recorded by Irving (nor by Merwin, who apparently didn't keep a journal). Details of any such conversations would be *pure speculation.*

Irving himself downplayed the story's plot, referring to it as "a mere whimsical band to connect descriptions of scenery, customs, manners &c."[18]

But what about Ichabod Crane's *(Jesse Merwin's?)* midnight encounter with a Headless Hessian? Or with someone masquerading as one?

It didn't happen.

The entire chase sequence – the initial encounter with a rider of large dimensions, his head carried before him instead of in its usual place on his shoulders; the goblin's head used as a projectile; the protagonist *tumbled headlong* to the ground; the "head" later revealed to have been a pumpkin/gourd – all was borrowed (some would say *plagiarized)* directly from Musaus' "The Fifth Legend of Rubezahl," specifically the 1791 William Beckford translation.

The narrative is rounded out with several other "morsels" pilfered from Burns' "Tam O'Shanter," most notably the protagonist's desperation to reach the safety of the opposite side of the bridge, since ghosts/witches are supposedly unable to cross running water.

The twist at the end of the story – where Brom Bones is implicated as (probably) having impersonated the legendary Headless Horseman – follows the formula of "supernatural explique," a popular method used by authors in the early 1800s to provide rational explanations for seemingly supernatural occurrences. This method was well known to Irving due to his familiarity with the works of Ann Radcliffe, Clara Reeve and Christoph Martin Wieland.

What about Kinderhook?

Were parts of *The Sketch Book* written while Irving was a guest at the Van Ness estate, now Lindenwald?

Harold Van Santvoord, among his many other assertions regarding the origins of "The Legend," declared, "Although the Sleepy Hollow romance, as Irving informed his friend Merwin, was elaborated in London, the germ of the story had its origin here," meaning Kinderhook.[19]

Van Santvoord offered as proof a letter he said he had in his possession from Frederick Saunders, librarian of the Astor Library and a close friend of Washington Irving. Saunders had apparently written that while a guest at Sunnyside, he "had a chat with [Irving] after dinner," and that Irving told him "among other things, that he wrote his 'Rip Van Winkle' and other sketches at Kinderhook." The letter, unfortunately, did not specify which "other sketches."[20]

We know that Irving adapted (OK, *translated*) much of "Rip Van Winkle" from an old German folktale, "Peter Klaus the Goatherd." This was demonstrated in 1930 by English Professor Henry Pochman with a paragraph-by-paragraph comparison of the two stories.[21]

However, Irving's study of the German language (and presumably German literature) did not commence until early 1818, as a distraction from the P. and E. Irving Company's bankruptcy proceedings – some nine years *after* his visit to Kinderhook.

Was Saunders in error? Or was he possibly confusing *The Sketch Book* with *Knickerbocker's History*, which contained similar humorous Dutch-American sketches and parodies?

Washington Irving himself provided the final word. Many years after the publication of "The Legend," Irving's publisher in England, John Murray, was involved in copyright litigations with several rival "pirate" publishers who had illegally reprinted Irving's writings; to help strengthen his case, Murray requested that Irving compile a list stating where his various works had been written. According to Irving's August 8, 1850 reply, several of his books – *Mahomet, Successors of Mahomet,* and *Abbotsford and Newstead Abbey* – had indeed been written "partly in England, partly in the United States."

Of *The Sketch Book,* however, Irving stated unequivocally, "*The Sketch Book* was written in England."[22]

In a way, Van Santvoord was correct in claiming "the germ of the story" for Kinderhook – that was, after all, where Irving found his main character, Ichabod Crane, as well as (probably) the *concept* of linking him romantically to a rich heiress. However, there is no way of knowing if, in 1809, it was Irving's intention to write about his friend someday.

It seems more likely that years later, in a moment of inspiration prompted by Van Wart's tale of Brom Bones and his race for a bowl of punch, he had the idea of making his story's protagonist a schoolteacher, and thought it would be fun to parody his old friend Merwin.

Kinderhook's pride in its association with Jesse Merwin – "the original of Ichabod Crane" – is evident. Not only is the historic one-room school on Route 9H named the Ichabod Crane Schoolhouse, but neighboring Valatie boasts an entire Ichabod Crane School District, consisting of Primary, Middle and High Schools. Known as *The Riders*, their sports teams' mascot pictures a blue silhouette of Ichabod astride Gunpowder. (Valatie is one of two villages contained in the *Town* of Kinderhook, with the other being the *Village* of Kinderhook.)

Kinderhook's annual Halloween activities feature a reading of "The Legend" at the historic James Vanderpoel House, with the billing "the Headless Horseman will again ride through the streets of Kinderhook..." (Kinderhook's Horseman apparently does not limit his appearances to just Halloween – he has been known to show up at other events throughout the year, including at least one Fourth of July parade!)

As for Washington Irving's ties to Kinderhook's Luykas Van Alen House, he almost certainly at least *visited* the residence, whether or not he found his Katrina living there. As it was situated on the main road between the Van Ness estate and Kinderhook village, he probably walked right past the house many times, and being acquainted with the Van Alens, the ever-personable Irving likely stopped to socialize from time to time.

The Horseman Rides On...

Each October, the Sleepy Hollow region welcomes thousands of visitors for the Halloween-themed festivities sponsored every weekend by Historic Hudson Valley. At "Horseman's Hollow" at Philipsburg Manor, guests explore a haunted trail where they encounter various ghouls and goblins, while across the street at the Old Dutch Church, local storyteller Jonathan Kruk performs his dramatic retelling of "The Legend of Sleepy Hollow."

Further up Route 9, the "Great Jack O' Lantern Blaze" at Van Cortlandt Manor in Croton-on-Hudson features elaborate Halloween displays created from more than 5,000 hand-carved and brightly lit jack o'lanterns; and several miles to the south, Washington Irving's Sunnyside hosts "The Legend Behind the 'Legend,'" which includes a tour of the residence and a shadow puppet production of our favorite "Sleepy Hollow" tale.

Through it all, the Headless Horseman is clearly still the "commander-in-chief of all the powers of the air" which haunt the region!

Some 200 years later, enough of Irving's Sleepy Hollow remains such that most visitors would agree that a "drowsy, dreamy influence" still persists, and one can easily imagine the "fearful shapes and shadows" that used to accompany Ichabod Crane on his long walks home in the gathering dusk.

The myriad of guests who gather annually to experience "The Legend" don't seem to care how much or how little of the story is true. The Headless Horseman will continue to ride "in nightly quest of his head," and Ichabod Crane will still be heard "chanting a melancholy psalm tune among the tranquil solitudes of Sleepy Hollow."

As Washington Irving wrote in 1819: "Faith, sir... as to that matter, I don't believe one-half of it myself."

Epilogue

"My heart dwells in that blessed little spot, and I really believe that when I die I shall haunt it..."
- Washington Irving, 1843

Does the ghost of Washington Irving still walk the halls of Sunnyside?

One of the earliest accounts of ghostly happenings at Sunnyside came from Irving himself, who suggested that the grounds were haunted by none other than the original owner of The Roost, Wolfert Acker. In his "Wolfert's Roost" essay, Irving wrote, "Wolfert Acker died and was buried, but found no quiet even in the grave: for if popular gossip be true, his ghost has occasionally been seen walking by moonlight among the old gray mossgrown trees of his apple orchard."[1]

Shortly after Irving's death, his friend Lewis Gaylord Clark, editor of *The Knickerbocker* magazine, penned a tribute to the author, in which he described an overnight visit to Sunnyside. As Clark was preparing to turn in for the night "in the bedroom over the south porch," Irving informed him, "You will not be interrupted, unless perhaps about twelve o'clock, when this particular room may be visited by the ghost of a young lady who died here of love and green apples, when the 'Roost' was owned and occupied by old Jacob Van Tassel."[2]

Irving continued, "You needn't look for her, however; for sometimes she doesn't make her appearance at all. I haven't seen her myself more than a half-dozen times, altogether!"[3]

Was Irving relating an actual ghostly encounter? Or was he, in keeping with his quirky sense of humor, simply trying to "spook" his overnight guest?

A spooky view of Sunnyside at night (from an old postcard)

Epilogue

Irving once wrote of Sunnyside, "my heart dwells in that blessed little spot, and I really believe that when I die I shall haunt it; but it will be as a good spirit, that no one need be afraid of."[4]

He may have been right – several years after his death, three people purportedly saw an apparition of Irving walk through the parlor and into his study.[5]

Reports of Irving's ghost were corroborated by his great-great-grandnephew, Washington Irving III, speaking at the October 1947 dedication of the newly restored and reopened Sunnyside. Irving claimed that his uncle's spirit had been "seen at different times by those who sleep in the front room facing the Tappan Zee." In his uncle's favor, he added, "He is said to be an extremely amiable ghost."[6]

Not only has the spectre of Washington Irving been sighted, but the doting nieces who cared for "Uncle Wash" so attentively in life are said to still linger at Sunnyside, performing their housekeeping duties just as they always did. Visitors have reported hearing their ghostly laughter, and they have been known to occasionally "tidy up" the house after the last tour group has left for the day.

The possibility of a haunted Sunnyside was one of the subjects of an episode of the 1970s TV series *In Search Of...*, hosted by Leonard Nimoy. Written by well-known paranormal investigator and author Hans Holzer, Episode 18 of Season 1, titled simply "Ghosts," took us inside Sunnyside, where Holzer interviewed one of the tour guides. She revealed that a group of them had been gathered in the basement, discussing (of all things) Washington Irving's will. They suddenly heard a loud crash from upstairs, and upon investigating, found an iron that had apparently fallen from the table – or had it been pushed? – onto the laundry room floor. (Unfortunately, Holzer did not find enough compelling evidence to label the residence haunted, and the remainder of the episode was set in a different location...)

One of the more recent sightings occurred in the summer of 2010, when a teenage girl (who wishes to remain anonymous) was visiting Sunnyside with her family. She thought she saw "something" in an upstairs window, and quickly snapped a photograph. Reviewing her pictures later on her computer, she discovered an image resembling the silhouette of an older gentleman holding an old-fashioned quill pen. Is this Irving's ghost, or just a curious reflection of the sunlight?

Irving's ghost, or glare from the sun? You decide...

And finally, in the interest of completeness, it should also be noted "for the record" that Washington Irving's ghost has occasionally been accused of pinching the bottoms of attractive female visitors to Sunnyside, although this does seem a bit out of character...

Isn't it fitting that the author of America's first (and arguably best) ghost story should become the subject of his own ghostly legend?

Endnotes

Chapter 1

1. Washington Irving, "The Author's Account of Himself" in *The Sketch Book of Geoffrey Crayon, Gent.* (London: Longmans, Green and Co. 1905), 12.

2. Andrew Burstein, *The Original Knickerbocker* (New York: Basic Books, 2007), 11.

3. Washington Irving, "Sleepy Hollow" essay, in *Wolfert's Roost and Miscellanies* (Charleston, SC: BiblioBazaar, 2007), 33-34.

4. Pierre Munroe Irving, *The Life and Letters of Washington Irving, Volume I* (London: Richard Bentley, 1864), 26.

5. P. M. Irving, *Life and Letters I*, 42.

6. Stanley T. Williams, *The Life of Washington Irving, Volume I* (New York, NY: Octagon Books, 1971), 88-89.

7. Matthew J. Bruccoli et. al., Editors, *Dictionary of Literary Biography* (Farmington Hills, MI: Thomson-Gale, 2004), 195.

8. David R. Collins, *Washington Irving: Storyteller for a New Nation* (Greensboro, NC: Morgan Reynolds, Inc., 2000), 28.

9. P. M. Irving, *Life and Letters I*, 186-87.

10. Burstein, *Original Knickerbocker*, 70.

11. P. M. Irving, *Life and Letters I*, 243.

12. P. M. Irving, *Life and Letters I*, 240.

13. P. M. Irving, *Life and Letters I,* 257-58.

14. Burstein, *Original Knickerbocker*, 100.

15. Charles Dudley Warner, *Washington Irving* (Boston: Houghton, Mifflin And Company, 1881), 74.

16. Stanley T. Williams, Editor, *Notes While Preparing the Sketch Book, 1817, by Washington Irving* (New Haven, CT: Yale University Press, 1927), 84.

17. P. M. Irving, *Life and Letters I*, 347.

18. Collins, 48.

19. Pierre Munroe Irving, *The Life and Letters of Washington Irving, Volume II* (Philadelphia: J. B. Lippincott & Company, 1870), 52.

20. Washington Irving, *Tales of a Traveler* (New York: American Book Company, 1894), 21-22.

21. Walter A. Reichart, "In England," in *A Century of Commentary on the Works of Washington Irving*, Andrew B. Myers, Editor (Tarrytown, NY: Sleepy Hollow Restorations, 1976), 305.

22. Reichart, "In England," 281.

23. Collins, 70.

24. Collins, 72.

25. William P. Trent and George S. Hellman, Editors, *The Journals of Washington Irving Volume III: Spain, Tour through the West, Esopus and Dutch Tour* (New York: Haskell House, 1970), 187-88.

26. Washington Irving, "The Legend of Sleepy Hollow" in *The Sketch Book of Geoffrey Crayon, Gent.* (London: Longmans, Green and Co. 1905), 356.

27. P. M. Irving, *Life and Letters II*, 298.

28. Washington Irving, *Wolfert's Roost and Miscellanies* (Charleston, SC: BiblioBazaar, 2007), 16.

29. Brian Jay Jones, *Washington Irving, An American Original* (New York: Arcade Publishing, 2008), 333.

30. Ralph M. Aderman et al, Editors, *Washington Irving Letters, Volume II, 1823-1838* (Boston, MA: Twayne Publishers, 1979), 939-42.

31. Burstein, *Original Knickerbocker*, 301.

Chapter 2

1. Adriaen Van der Donck, *Beschryvinge van Nieuw-Nederlant* (Amsterdam: Evert Nieuwenhof, 1656), page 8; see also the English translation by Diederik Willem Goedhuys, *Van der Donck's A Description of New Netherland*, Edited by Charles T. Gehring (Lincoln, NE: University of Nebraska, 2008), 10-11.

2. Henry Steiner, *The Place Names of Historic Sleepy Hollow and Tarrytown* (Westminster, MD: Heritage Books, 1998), 121-22.

3. Irving, "The Legend of Sleepy Hollow," 355.

4. Irving, "The Legend of Sleepy Hollow," 355.

5. Washington Irving, *Diedrich Knickerbocker's History of New York* (Norwalk, CT: The Heritage Press, 1968), 256.

6. Richard Miller (Tarrytown Village Historian), "A Brief History of Tarrytown," on the Village of Tarrytown official website, <WWW.TARRYTOWNGOV.COM>.

7. Miller, "A Brief History of Tarrytown."

8. Daniel Van Tassel, "Sleepy Hollow – Daniel Van Tassel Gives the Results of His Investigations of Many Years." Letter to the Editor, *The New York Times*, May 28, 1898, BR 357.

9. J. Thomas Scharf, *History of Westchester County, New York, Volume 2* (Philadelphia: L. E. Preston, 1886), 306; see also Steiner, *Place Names*, 130-31.

10. Ralph M. Aderman and Wayne R. Kime, *Advocate for America: The Life of James Kirke Paulding* (Selinsgrove, PA: Susquehanna University Press, 2003), pages 25-26. See also Henry Steiner's *Historically Annotated Legend of Sleepy Hollow*, 52-53.

11. Jeff Canning and Wally Buxton, *History of the Tarrytowns, Westchester County, New York, from Ancient Times to the Present* (Fleischmanns, NY: Purple Mountain Press, 1993), 145.

12. Lucille and Theodore Hutchinson, *The Centennial History of North Tarrytown* (North Tarrytown, NY: Theodore and Lucille Hutchinson, 1974), 47.

13. Hutchinson, 12.

14. "Sleepy Hollow's Legend – Among the Scenes of the Quaint Old Dutch Story," in *The New York Times*, August 13, 1882, 8.

15. Steiner, *Place Names*, 14; Hutchinson 47-48.

16. Reverend J. C. Dutcher, *The Old Home by the River* (New York: N. Tibbals and Sons, 1874), 95.

17. Dutcher, *The Old Home by the River*, 94-95.

18. Harold Van Santvoord, "Ichabod Crane Once More." Letter to the Editor of *The New York Times,* "Saturday Review of Books and Art" section, March 19, 1898, BR 190.

19. Pierre Munroe Irving, *The Life and Letters of Washington Irving, Volume III* (New York: G. P. Putnam and Son, 1869), 187-88.

20. Email correspondence with Ruth Piwonka, Kinderhook Historian, January 5, 2008.

Endnotes

21. Walter A Reichart and Lillian Schlissel, Editors, *Washington Irving Journals and Notebooks Volume II, 1807-1822* (Boston: Twayne Publishers, 1981), 257.

22. Irving, "The Legend of Sleepy Hollow," 358-59.

23. Donald G. Mitchell, *Dream Life: A Fable of the Seasons* (Charleston, SC: BiblioBazaar, 2007), in "Front Matter" section (no page number).

24. Canning and Buxton, 26.

25. Friends of the Old Dutch Burying Ground, *Tales of the Old Dutch Burying Ground* (Sleepy Hollow, NY: Friends of the Old Dutch Burying Ground, Inc., 1992), 2.

26. *Tales of the Old Dutch Burying Ground,* 1992 edition, 5.

27. *Tales of the Old Dutch Burying Ground,* 1992 edition, 6.

28. Edgar Mayhew Bacon, *Chronicles of Tarrytown and Sleepy Hollow* (New York: G.P. Putnam's Sons, 1897) 112.

29. Steiner, *Place Names,* 113.

30. Bacon, *Chronicles,* 113.

31. "A Famous Tulip Tree," in *The New York Times,* December 19, 1886; This article quotes a letter from one C. P. Carter of Kingston, who was apparently quoting an earlier article. Carter gave the tree's circumference as 29 feet at the base, a height of 111 feet, and branches extending 106 feet in diameter; see also Steiner, *Place Names,* 15-17.

32. Steiner, *Place Names,* 15.

33. "A Famous Tulip Tree," in *The New York Times,* December 19, 1886.

34. Steiner, *Place Names,* 15.

35. Steiner, *Place Names,* 14.

36. Steiner, *Place Names*, 14, 38.

37. Canning and Buxton, 66.

38. Maps referenced include: Robert Erskine's 1778 map "Survey of the Road Between Tarrytown and Croton River," in the New York Historical Society's map collection; Robert Erskine's 1779 map "Roads About White Plains," found in J. Thomas Scharf, *History of Westchester County, New York, Volume 1* (Philadelphia: L. E. Preston, 1886), page 732; William Adams' 1788 map "A Map of the Town of Mount Pleasant in Westchester County by William Adams, Surveyor," found in Scharf, Volume 2, 623; and Christopher Colles' 1789 map "From New York to Poughkeepsie," found in *A Survey of the Roads of the United States of America 1789* by Christopher Colles, published in 1961 by The Belknap Press, Cambridge, Massachusetts.

39. The 1785 John Hill map may be found in Scharf, Volume 1, Part 1, 160f; the unsigned 1725-1795 map is from the collection of the Historical Society serving Sleepy Hollow and Tarrytown.

40. Henry Steiner, Editor, *"Sleepy Hollow" and "Washington at Tarrytown"* (Sleepy Hollow, NY: Milestone Productions, 2013), 65.

41. Canning and Buxton, 76, 201; Hutchinson, 100; Scharf, Volume 2, 304; See also a Map of North Tarrytown picturing "Brombacher Lane" with a large structure at the end, presumably the Charles Brombacher residence, contained in George W. and Walter S. Bromley, *Atlas of Westchester County, New York: From Actual Surveys and Official Plans,* 1901 Edition (New York, NY: G. W. Bromley and Company, 1901) page 43.

42. Bacon, *Chronicles*, 131-32.

Endnotes

43. John Lockwood Romer, *Historical Sketches of the Romer, Van Tassel and Allied Families and Tales of the Neutral Ground* (Buffalo, NY: W. C. Gay Printing Co., 1917), 39.

44. Bacon, *Chronicles*, 133.

45. Scharf, Volume 2, 232, 266; see also Steiner, *Place Names*, 69.

46. "Sleepy Hollow's Legend" in *The New York Times*, August 13, 1882.

47. Bacon, *Chronicles*, 134.

48. Maureen McKernan, "The Van Tassel Family," in *Peekskill (NY) Evening Star*, Monday, September 10, 1951.

49. Bacon, *Chronicles*, 134.

50. Irving, "The Legend of Sleepy Hollow," 378.

51. "Sleepy Hollow's Legend" in *The New York Times*, August 13, 1882.

52. "Washington Irving," in *The Sun* (New York), January 30, 1835, 3.

53. Irving, *Wolfert's Roost and Miscellanies*, 2007 edition, 11-12.

54. Daniel Van Tassel, *Genealogy of the Van Texel – Van Tassel Family in America 1625-1900* (Privately Published, approximately 1900), 40.

55. Washington Irving, *Wolfert's Roost and Other Papers, Now First Collected*, Author's Revised Edition (New York: G. P. Putnam, 1863), 15. (Several slightly different versions of "Wolfert's Roost" exist, as Irving rewrote or edited portions each time it was republished; the 1863 version contains material not present in others.)

56. Irving, *Wolfert's Roost and Miscellanies*, 2007 edition, 24.

57. Irving, *Wolfert's Roost and Other Papers*, 1863 edition, 19-20.

58. Irving, *Wolfert's Roost and Other Papers*, 1863 edition, 22.

59. Marcius D. Raymond, Editor, *Souvenir of the Revolutionary Soldiers' Monument Dedication at Tarrytown, N. Y., October 19th, 1894* (Tarrytown, NY: Monument Committee, 1894), 119-20.

60. Raymond, *Souvenir*, 179.

61. Scharf, Volume 2, 265-66.

62. Scharf, Volume 2, 265-66.

63. *Washington Irving Letters Volume II*, 731-32.

64. Letter from Ebenezer Irving to his son William dated November 22, 1834. From a compilation of Irving Family Letters in an unpublished manuscript by Daniel Larkin Irving, titled *Dear Will*; Excerpted and edited by Catalina Hannan, Historic Hudson Valley Librarian.

65. Kathleen Eagen Johnson, *Washington Irving's Sunnyside* (Tarrytown, NY: Historic Hudson Valley Press, 1995), 5.

66. Johnson, *Irving's Sunnyside*, 5.

67. Johnson, *Irving's Sunnyside*, 5.

68. *Washington Irving Letters Volume II*, 843-44.

69. *Washington Irving Letters Volume II*, 835.

70. *Washington Irving Letters Volume II*, 875, 881.

71. Irving, *Wolfert's Roost and Miscellanies*, 2007 edition, 11.

72. Irving, *Wolfert's Roost and Miscellanies*, 2007 edition, page 28; see also Ralph M. Aderman et al, Editors, *Washington Irving Letters, Volume IV, 1846-1859* (Boston, MA: Twayne Publishers, 1982), page 564: December 11, 1855 letter to

Abiel S. Thurston thanking him for the gift of a "curious document," which was Jacob Van Tassel's pension voucher. Irving stated that he had held "a long conversation" with Van Tassel at his home, "in which I gathered some of the particulars I have since recorded" – presumably referring to his "Wolfert's Roost" essay.

73. *Washington Irving Letters Volume II,* 928-30, 940, 942.

74. Brian Jay Jones, *Washington Irving, An American Original,* 339.

75. Johnson, *Irving's Sunnyside,* 21.

76. Johnson, *Irving's Sunnyside,* 21-22.

77. Merrill Folsom, "House Where Ichabod Crane Went a-Courtin' Is Preserved" in *The New York Times,* May 30, 1967.

78. Email correspondence with Ruth Piwonka, January 5, 2008.

79. John P Ritter, "The Real Ichabod Crane – When and Where Irving Discovered Him," in *The New York Herald,* Sunday July 16, 1899, Fifth Section, 2.

80. Irving, "The Legend of Sleepy Hollow," 371, 377.

81. Hutchinson, 42.

82. Ritter, "The Real Ichabod"; see also Scharf, Volume 1, Part 1, 48.

83. Irving, *Wolfert's Roost and Miscellanies,* 2007 edition, 24.

84. Lewis Gaylord Clark, "Reminiscences of the late Washington Irving," in *The Knickerbocker* magazine, January 1860.

85. Edgar Mayhew Bacon, "Irving's Ichabod Crane Again – Kinderhook's Claim Stoutly Denied and That of Sleepy Hollow Asserted." Letter to the Editor, *The New York Times,* March 12, 1898, page SRB 162.

86. Bacon, *Chronicles*, 139-40.

87. Steiner, *Place Names*, 9, 14.

88. Romer, *Historical Sketches*, 24.

89. Aqueduct Trail information, including maps, may be obtained from the Friends of the Old Croton Aqueduct website, <WWW.AQUEDUCT.ORG>.

90. Maps consulted include: Unsigned "Manor of Philipsburgh, Tarwetown, 1725-1795" map; George Wiley's 1880 "Tarwetown One Hundred Years Ago" map; John Hill's 1785 "Plan of the Manor of Philipsburg" map, drawn for the Commission of Forfeitures; and Christopher Colles' 1789 "From New York to Poughkeepsie" map.

91. Steiner, *Place Names*, 9.

92. Bacon, *Chronicles*, 140.

93. A hand-drawn reproduction of the 1880 George Wiley map appears in *The Centennial History of North Tarrytown* by Lucille and Theodore Hutchinson, 28.

94. Cedar Hill is a 322-foot hill located between modern-day Douglas Park and Webber Avenue. Labeled Prospect Hill on some Revolutionary-era maps, it was also known for a time as Jones Hill, after Cornelius Jones, the Philipse tenant farmer who bought the 200-acre lot which included the hill from the Commission of Forfeitures in December 1785. See Arthur C. M. Kelly's *Index to Grantees and Occupants, Manor of Philipsburgh, Westchester County, N.Y., 1785-1786* (Rhinebeck, NY: Kinship, 2003), page 22; see also Steiner, *Place Names*, pages 37, 69 and 111.

95. George S. Hellman, *Letters of Henry Brevoort to Washington Irving, Part One* (New York, NY: G.P. Putnam's Sons, 1916), 123.

96. Van Tassel, "Investigations of Many Years," *The New York Times*, May 28, 1898.

97. Van Tassel, "Investigations of Many Years," *The New York Times*, May 28, 1898.

Chapter 3

1. P. M. Irving, *Life and Letters I*, 374.

2. Elihu Burritt, "Birth-Place of Rip Van Winkle," in *Packard's Monthly*, November 1869, 332-34.

3. Burritt, 332-34.

4. P. M. Irving, *Life and Letters I*, 374.

5. P. M. Irving, *Life and Letters I*, 374.

6. Burritt, 332-34.

7. Henry A. Pochman, "Irving's German Sources in The Sketch Book," in *Studies in Philology*, Number 27, July 1930, 489-94.

8. Walter A. Reichart, *Washington Irving and Germany* (Ann Arbor, MI: The University of Michigan Press, 1957), 28.

9. Irving, "The Legend of Sleepy Hollow," 379-80.

10. P. M. Irving, *Life and Letters I*, 335.

11. P. M. Irving, *Life and Letters I*, 337.

12. N. P. Willis, "Visits to Sunnyside," in *Irvingiana: A Memorial of Washington Irving* (New York: Charles B. Richardson, Publisher, 1860), 47.

13. Ralph M. Aderman et al, Editors, *Washington Irving Letters, Volume I, 1802-1823* (Boston, MA: Twayne Publishers, 1978), 542-43.

14. *Washington Irving Letters Volume I,* page 564 – September 21, 1819 letter from Irving to Henry Brevoort.

15. *Washington Irving Letters Volume I,* 564.

16. *Washington Irving Letters Volume I,* 569.

17. Irving, "The Legend of Sleepy Hollow," 358.

18. Williams, *The Life of Washington Irving, Volume I,* 156, 421.

19. *Washington Irving Letters Volume I,* 558, 577.

20. *Washington Irving Letters Volume I,* 591; In an August 15, 1820 letter to Henry Brevoort, Irving mentions "the hurry and bustle of breaking up [his] encampment... after remaining so long in one place."

Chapter 4

1. From a song written in 1934 by R. P. Weston and Bert Lee, which contains the refrain: "With her head tucked underneath her arm, she walks the Bloody Tower; With her head tucked underneath her arm, at the midnight hour."

2. Louis C. Jones, *Things That Go Bump in the Night* (Syracuse, NY: Syracuse University Press, 1983), 129.

3. Captain Johann Ewald, *Diary of the American War, A Hessian Journal,* Translated from German by Joseph P. Tustin (New Haven: Yale University Press, 1979), xxi.

4. Email correspondence with military history scholar Terry Holmes, August 29, 2008. For more information about the Hessians, see also the <WWW.FELDJAGERCORPS.ORG> website.

5. E.R. Welles III and J.P. Evans, *Legend of Sleepy Hollow, Rip Van Winkle, President Van Buren, and Brom* (Manset, ME: Learning Incorporated, 1984), 16.

6. Bacon, *Chronicles,* 115.

Endnotes

7. Mike Marinacci, *Mysterious California* (Los Angeles: Panpipes Press, 1988), 87.

8. Irving, *Wolfert's Roost and Miscellanies,* 2007 edition, 31, 37.

9. Irving, *Wolfert's Roost and Miscellanies,* 2007 edition, 33, 37.

10. Irving, *Wolfert's Roost and Miscellanies,* 2007 edition, 37.

11. Email correspondence with Dr. Elisabeth Paling Funk, April 1, 2008.

12. Sandy Schlosser's website: <HTTP://AMERICANFOLKLORE.NET/FOLKLORE/2010/07/THE_HEADLESS_HORSEMAN.HTML>.

13. Sandy Schlosser website; see also Sandy E. Schlosser, *Spooky New York* (Guilford, CT: Globe Pequot Press, 2005), 84-89.

14. Email correspondence with Sandy Schlosser, December 20, 2007.

15. Email correspondence with Sandy Schlosser, December 20, 2007.

16. William Abbatt, Editor, *Memoirs of Major-General William Heath, by Himself* (New York: William Abbatt, 1901), 73.

17. Adrian Leiby, *The Revolutionary War in the Hackensack Valley: The Jersey Dutch and the Neutral Ground, 1775-1783* (Piscataway, NJ: Rutgers University Press, 1980), 53.

18. Burstein, *Original Knickerbocker,* 145.

19. Brian Jay Jones, *Washington Irving, An American Original,* 68, 72-73.

20. *Tales of the Old Dutch Burying Ground,* 1992 edition, 14.

21. Raymond, *Souvenir,* 112.

22. Romer, *Historical Sketches*, 95.

23. Email correspondence with Jim Logan, October 7, 2009.

24. Romer, *Historical Sketches*, 27; see also pages 51 and 93.

25. "Yankee Visits Sleepy Hollow," in *YANKEE* Magazine, July 1953, 42.

26. Email correspondence with Sandy Schlosser, February 19, 2009.

27. *Washington Irving Journals and Notebooks Volume II*, 79.

28. Irving, "The Legend of Sleepy Hollow," 379.

29. Email correspondence with Dr. Elisabeth Paling Funk, April 1, 2008.

30. *Washington Irving Journals and Notebooks Volume II*, 373.

31. Prof. Susan Manning's "Legend of Sleepy Hollow" comments were included in her English Literature lecture notes, which she published online on the University of Edinburgh website, <HTTP://WWW.ED.AC.UK/>. However, Prof. Manning passed away unexpectedly in January 2013, and the material has since been removed from the site.

32. Robert Burns, "Tam O'Shanter" in *The Collected Poems of Robert Burns* (Ware, Hertfordshire, England: Wordsworth Editions Ltd, 1998) 5.

33. Irving, "The Legend of Sleepy Hollow," 382-83.

34. Burns, "Tam O'Shanter," 5.

35. Irving, "The Legend of Sleepy Hollow," 381-82.

36. Burns, "Tam O'Shanter," 5.

37. Irving, "The Legend of Sleepy Hollow," 384.

38. Burns, "Tam O'Shanter," 8.

39. Irving, "The Legend of Sleepy Hollow," 385.

40. Burns, "Tam O'Shanter," 8.

41. Irving, "The Legend of Sleepy Hollow," 385.

42. Washington Irving, "Abbotsford" in *Abbotsford and Newstead Abbey* (Charleston, SC: BiblioBazaar, 2007) 20.

43. Reichart, "In England," 285.

44. P. M. Irving, *Life and Letters I*, 329.

45. *Washington Irving Letters Volume I*, 526.

46. Pochman, "Irving's German Sources in The Sketch Book," 496-99.

47. *Washington Irving Journals and Notebooks Volume II*, 256.

48. Reichart, *Washington Irving and Germany*, 21.

49. Email correspondence with Dr. Elisabeth Paling Funk, April 1, 2008.

50. Johann Karl August Musaus, *Popular Tales of the Germans, Volume II*, translated by William Beckford (London: J. Murray, 1791), 143-151.

51. Reichart, *Washington Irving and Germany*, 31.

52. Musaus/Beckford, 143-44.

53. Irving, "The Legend of Sleepy Hollow," 362.

54. Musaus/Beckford, 145-46.

55. Irving, "The Legend of Sleepy Hollow," 381.

56. Musaus/Beckford, 146.

57. Irving, "The Legend of Sleepy Hollow," 383.

58. Musaus/Beckford, 147.

59. Irving, "The Legend of Sleepy Hollow," 383-84.

60. Musaus/Beckford, 147.

61. Irving, "The Legend of Sleepy Hollow," 384.

62. Musaus/Beckford, 149-50.

63. Irving, "The Legend of Sleepy Hollow," 384.

64. Musaus/Beckford, 151.

65. Irving, "The Legend of Sleepy Hollow," 385-86.

66. Judith Richardson, *Possessions – The History and Uses of Haunting in the Hudson Valley* (Cambridge, MA: Harvard University Press, 2003) 63.

67. Andrew Burstein, "The Politics of Sleepy Hollow," in *The New York Times*, October 30, 2005.

68. Lucas Buresch website: <HTTP://ARCHIVESLEUTH.WORDPRESS.COM/2011/03/29/CARLS-MILL/>

Chapter 5

1. *Greene County Daily World* website: <WWW.GCDAILYWORLD.COM>, July 14, 2008 Blog entry by Keith Sims.

2. David Trafton, *Jesse Merwin, the Original Ichabod Crane* (Bethesda, MD: Self-published monograph, 2006), page 1; See also *Biographical Review: The Leading Citizens of Columbia County, New York* (Boston: Biographical Review Publishing Company, 1894) 128.

3. Irving, "The Legend of Sleepy Hollow," 360.

4. "Yankee Visits Sleepy Hollow," 40.

ENDNOTES

5. Trafton, 4.

6. Trafton, 2, 4.

7. Charles Gilbert Hine, *The New York and Albany Post Road* (New York: C. G. Hine, 1905), page 90; See also Franklin Ellis, *History of Columbia County, New York* (Philadelphia: Everts & Ensign, 1878), page 222.

8. Trafton, 4-5.

9. *Cyclopedia of Biography: Containing a History of the Family and Descendants of John Collin* (Hudson, NY: M. P. Williams, Register and Gazette Office, 1872), 83.

10. Hine, 90.

11. *Washington Irving Journals and Notebooks Volume II,* xvii.

12. *Washington Irving Letters Volume I,* 263.

13. *Washington Irving Letters Volume I,* 265.

14. *Washington Irving Letters Volume I,* 280.

15. *Washington Irving Letters Volume I,* 280-81.

16. *Washington Irving Letters Volume I,* 281.

17. *Washington Irving Letters Volume I,* 482.

18. Harold Van Santvoord, "Irving's Ichabod Crane," Letter to the Editor of *The New York Times,* "Saturday Review of Books and Art" section, February 26, 1898, page BR 129.

19. *Washington Irving Letters Volume I,* 270.

20. *Washington Irving Letters Volume I,* 273.

21. P. M. Irving, *Life and Letters I,* 191-92.

22. *Washington Irving Letters Volume I,* 274.

23. *Washington Irving Letters Volume I*, 276.

24. *Washington Irving Letters Volume I*, 280-81.

25. P. M. Irving, *Life and Letters I*, 203.

26. Sue Fields Ross, *Washington Irving Journals and Notebooks Volume V, 1832-1859* (Boston: Twayne Publishers, 1986), 183.

27. Van Santvoord, "Ichabod Crane Once More."

28. P. M. Irving, *Life and Letters III*, 1869 edition, 186-88.

29. Van Santvoord, "Irving's Ichabod Crane" (February 26, 1898) and "Ichabod Crane Once More" (March 19, 1898); Bacon, "Irving's Ichabod Crane Again" (March 12, 1898).

30. Van Santvoord, "Irving's Ichabod Crane."

31. *Washington Irving Letters Volume IV,* pages 160, 198, 211, and 227 – various letters to his niece Sarah Storrow.

32. Irving, "The Legend of Sleepy Hollow," 359.

33. Van Santvoord, "Irving's Ichabod Crane."

34. "Death of Ichabod Crane," in *The New York Herald*, November 17, 1852, page 2.

35. "Washington Irving," in *The Sun* (New York), January 30, 1835, 3.

36. Bacon, "Irving's Ichabod Crane Again."

37. Harold Van Santvoord, "Irving and Kinderhook Again." Letter to the Editor, *The New York Times,* April 30, 1898.

38. Miles Merwin Association website <WWW.MERWIN.ORG>.

39. Edward A. Collier, *A History of Old Kinderhook* (New York: G. P. Putnam's Sons, 1914), 362.

ENDNOTES

40. Ritter, "The Real Ichabod."

41. Van Santvoord, "Ichabod Crane Once More."

42. Benjamin Garno, "Old New York: Five Points and Some Other Neighborhoods – Irving's Ichabod Crane," Letter to the Editor, *The New York Times,* April 23, 1898.

43. Burstein, *Original Knickerbocker,* 230.

44. P. M. Irving, *Life and Letters III,* 1869 edition, 185-86.

45. P. M. Irving, *Life and Letters III,* 1869 edition, 186.

46. "Ichabod Crane's Grandson Tells About Sleepy Hollow," *The Frederick Post,* Friday, October 23, 1925.

47. Wayne R. Kime, *Pierre M. Irving and Washington Irving: A Collaboration in Life and Letters* (Waterloo, Ontario, Canada: Wilfrid Laurier University Press, 1979), 257.

48. P. M. Irving, *Life and Letters III,* 1869 edition, pages viii and 184.

49. *Tales of the Old Dutch Burying Ground,* 1992 edition, 19.

50. Irving, "The Legend of Sleepy Hollow," 387.

51. Steiner, *Place Names,* 156-57.

52. Robert Bolton, *A History of the County of Westchester from its First Settlement to the Present Time* (New York: Alexander S. Gould, 1848), page 351; see also *Tales of the Old Dutch Burying Ground,* 1992 edition, page 21.

53. Scharf, Volume 2, 315.

54. Davis, Matthew L. Davis, *Memoirs of Aaron Burr, Volume I* (New York: Harper & Brothers, 1836), 160.

55. Davis, *Memoirs of Aaron Burr,* 164.

56. Raymond, *Souvenir,* 174.

57. Scharf, Volume 2, 732.

58. Arthur Russell Wilcox, *The Bar of Rye Township, Westchester County, New York* (New York: The Knickerbocker Press, 1918), 332.

59. Raymond, *Souvenir*, 175.

60. Irving, "The Legend of Sleepy Hollow," 387.

61. Scharf, Volume 1, 540.

62. Raymond, *Souvenir*, 174-75.

63. Scharf, Volume 1, 540.

64. Ralph M. Aderman et al, Editors, *Washington Irving Letters, Volume III, 1839-1845* (Boston, MA: Twayne Publishers, 1982), 35-36.

65. Williams, *The Life of Washington Irving, Volume I*, 429.

66. Henry Fielding, *Tom Jones* (New York, NY: W. W. Norton & Company, 1973), 325.

67. Irving, "The Legend of Sleepy Hollow," 367.

68. Fielding, *Tom Jones*, 508-10.

69. Fielding, *Tom Jones*, 354.

70. Fielding, *Tom Jones*, 657.

71. *Washington Irving Letters Volume I*, 280-81.

72. Oliver Goldsmith, *The Deserted Village* (New York: Payson and Clarke Ltd., 1927) 11-12.

73. Irving, "The Legend of Sleepy Hollow," 361.

74. Goldsmith, *The Deserted Village*, 12.

75. Irving, "The Legend of Sleepy Hollow," 361.

76. Goldsmith, *The Deserted Village*, 11-12; Irving, "The Legend of Sleepy Hollow," 361.

77. John Gibson Lockhart, *Memoirs of the Life of Sir Walter Scott, Volume 4* (Edinburgh, Scotland: Robert Cadell, 1837), page 126; *Abbotsford and Newstead Abbey,* page 39.

78. Irving, *Abbotsford and Newstead Abbey,* 39.

79. *Washington Irving Letters Volume I,* 569.

80. Irving, "The Legend of Sleepy Hollow," 358.

81. Irving, *Abbotsford and Newstead Abbey,* 39.

82. Miguel de Cervantes, *Don Quixote* (New York: Signet Classics, 2003), page 18; Irving, "The Legend of Sleepy Hollow," page 372.

83. *Washington Irving Journals and Notebooks Volume II,* 256.

84. *Washington Irving Letters Volume I,* 546.

85. Hellman, *Letters of Henry Brevoort to Washington Irving,* page 109; Brevoort's published letters include one dated October 2, 1818, followed by an 11-month gap, with his next known letter dated September 9, 1819.

86. Richard M. Dorson, "The Yankee on the Stage – A Folk Hero of American Drama," *The New England Quarterly*, Volume 13, Number 3, September 1940, page 468.

87. Daniel G. Hoffman, "Irving's Use of American Folklore in 'The Legend of Sleepy Hollow'," *PMLA*, Volume 68, Number 3, June 1953, page 425.

88. Dorson, 476.

89. Judith Richardson, *Possessions – The History and Uses of Haunting in the Hudson Valley* (Cambridge, MA: Harvard University Press, 2003) 56, 236.

90. Irving, *Knickerbocker's History of New York,* 133.

91. Donald A. Ringe, "New York and New England: Irving's Criticism of American Society," *A Century of Commentary on the Works of Washington Irving,* Andrew B. Myers, Editor (Tarrytown, NY: Sleepy Hollow Restorations, 1976), 401-02.

92. Irving, "The Legend of Sleepy Hollow," 361.

93. Irving, "The Legend of Sleepy Hollow," 366.

94. Washington Irving, "Conspiracy of the Cocked Hats," in *Wolfert's Roost and Miscellanies,* 2007 edition, 114.

95. Irving, *Knickerbocker's History of New York,* 134.

96. Irving, "The Legend of Sleepy Hollow," 361.

97. Irving, "The Legend of Sleepy Hollow," 361.

98. Irving, "The Legend of Sleepy Hollow," 359.

99. Irving, "The Legend of Sleepy Hollow," 360, 362.

100. P. M. Irving, *Life and Letters I,* 11.

101. Anya Seton, *Washington Irving* (Boston: Houghton Mifflin Company, 1960), 16.

102. Nathalia Wright, Editor, *Washington Irving Journals and Notebooks Volume I, 1803-1806* (Madison, Wisconsin: University of Wisconsin Press, 1969) 308, 313.

103. *Washington Irving Journals and Notebooks Volume II,* 164.

Chapter 6

1. Irving, *Wolfert's Roost and Miscellanies,* 2007 edition, 36.

2. Van Tassel, *Genealogy of the Van Tassel Family,* 39.

3. Scharf, Volume 2, 189.

ENDNOTES

4. Irving, *Wolfert's Roost and Other Papers,* 1863 edition, 22.

5. Irving, *Wolfert's Roost and Other Papers,* 1863 edition, 22.

6. Van Tassel, *Genealogy of the Van Tassel Family,* 75-76.

7. *Washington Irving Letters Volume IV,* 564.

8. Historical Research Society of the Tappan Zee, *The Old Dutch Burying Ground of Sleepy Hollow* (New York, NY: Montague Lee Co., Inc., 1926) 39-40.

9. Scharf, Volume 2, 266; Bacon, *Chronicles,* 134-35.

10. *Van Alen House Historic Structure Report* (Albany, NY: John G. Waite Associates, 2001) 6.

11. Van Santvoord, "Irving's Ichabod Crane."

12. Van Santvoord, "Ichabod Crane Once More."

13. Van Santvoord, "Irving's Ichabod Crane."

14. Ritter, "The Real Ichabod."

15. "Ichabod Crane's Grandson Tells About Sleepy Hollow."

16. "Yankee Visits Sleepy Hollow," 40.

17. "Yankee Visits Sleepy Hollow," 40.

18. Email correspondence with Ruth Piwonka, January 5, 2008.

19. Folsom, "House Where Ichabod Crane Went a-Courtin' Is Preserved."

20. Allan Keller, *Life Along the Hudson* (Tarrytown, NY: Sleepy Hollow Restorations, 1976), 221.

21. *Washington Irving Letters Volume I,* 740; letter to Mrs. Amelia Foster.

22. *Van Alen House Historic Structure Report,* 7-8.

23. *Van Alen House Historic Structure Report*, 7-8.

24. *Van Alen House Historic Structure Report*, 7-8.

25. *Van Alen House Historic Structure Report*, 8.

26. *Columbia County at the End of the Century*, "Published and Edited Under the Auspices of the Hudson Gazette" (Hudson, NY: The Record Printing and Publishing Company, 1900), 442.

27. Benjamin Taylor Van Alen, *Genealogical History of the Van Alen Family* (Chicago: self-published, 1902), 12-13.

28. Email correspondence with Ruth Piwonka, March 16, 2009, in which she cited *History of Cornelius Maessen Van Buren* by Harriet Peckham as her source.

29. Ritter, "The Real Ichabod."

30. Collier, *A History of Old Kinderhook*, 359-61.

31. Email correspondence with Ruth Piwonka, January 5, 2008.

32. The identification of Peter C. Van Dyck as Jane's father is corroborated by several sources in the collection of the Columbia County Historical Society, including: Arthur C. M. Kelly, *Baptism Record of Kinderhook Reformed Church, 1718-1899*, pages 133, 152 and 184; *Abstract of Wills of Columbia County, Volume 2 (1805-1814)*, page 75; and CCHS Cemetery Record Books (Book 9). Other sources, including the <WWW.ANCESTRY.COM> and <WWW.ROOTSWEB.COM> websites, tend to confuse the three Peters, along with the identities of their respective wives, and no two family trees seem to agree.

33. The Merwin Family File in the collection of the Columbia County Historical Society contains a document signed by Jesse Merwin on July 10, 1811, selling half interest in his father-in-law's *160 acre farm* to one E. P. Pumaley.

ENDNOTES

34. Arthur C. M. Kelly, *Baptism Record of Kinderhook Reformed Church, 1718-1899*, pages 133, 152 and 184; see also *Abstract of Wills of Columbia County, Volume 2 (1805-1814)*, page 75.

35. Nick Biggs, "Tales from Merwin," *Columbia County History & Heritage*, Volume 1, Number 2, Fall 2002, page 11.

36. Email correspondence with John Merwin, President of the Miles Merwin Association, September 25, 2013.

37. Email correspondence with John Merwin, President of the Miles Merwin Association, September 25, 2013. John has visited the graves of Jesse Merwin and his family in the Kinderhook Reformed Church Cemetery. He located the tombstone of Jane's mother, Maria, adjacent to the monument marking Jesse and Jane's graves. The stone was "badly weathered," but John was able to make out Maria's name and the phrase "died at 100 years." He noted that Catherine's name was also inscribed on the same stone.

38. "Ichabod Crane's Grandson Tells About Sleepy Hollow."

Chapter 7

1. Hellman, *Letters of Henry Brevoort to Washington Irving*, page 109.

2. Hellman, *Letters of Henry Brevoort to Washington Irving*, page xxiv.

3. Raymond, *Souvenir*, 38-40; also James A. Roberts, Editor, *New York in the Revolution as Colony and State* (Albany, NY: Weed-Parsons Printing Company, 1897), 224-40.

4. Raymond, *Souvenir*, 182.

5. Raymond, *Souvenir*, 38.

6. Grenville C. Mackenzie, *Families of the Colonial Town of Philipsburgh* (Westport, CT: Published by Author, 1966) 110.

7. Bolton, *A History of the County of Westchester,* 355-56.

8. Raymond, *Souvenir,* 203, 350.

9. *Washington Irving Letters Volume I,* 581.

10. *Washington Irving Letters Volume I,* 591-95.

11. Mackenzie, *Families of Philipsburg,* 460-65.

12. Mackenzie, *Families of Philipsburg,* 460.

13. Mackenzie, *Families of Philipsburg,* 460, 462-63.

14. *Tales of the Old Dutch Burying Ground,* 1992 edition, 17-18.

15. Mackenzie, *Families of Philipsburg,* 461; Bacon, *Chronicles,* 129.

16. Steiner, *Place Names,* 81; Raymond, *Souvenir,* 162.

17. James MacLean Macdonald, *The McDonald Papers* (Elmsford, NY: Westchester County Historical Society, 1927) page 849; contains Captain John Romer's statement that the Abraham Martling wounded in the galley fight had "kept Tammany Hall in New York." The owner of Martling's Tavern at Tammany Hall, located at the corner of Nassau and Spruce Streets in New York City, is identified in Mackenzie's *Families of the Colonial Town of Philipsburgh* as Abraham B. Martling (1761-1831), the son of Barent Martling (1731-??) and his second wife, Sarah Bell.

    About *The McDonald Papers*: In an effort to collect and record first-hand reminiscences of the Revolutionary War, Westchester County Judge James McLean Macdonald interviewed 241 elderly county residents between 1844 and 1851.

ENDNOTES

The result, comprised of more than 1,000 pages of wartime information obtained directly from those who had lived it, was published in two volumes in 1927 by the Westchester County Historical Society. Although the judge spelled his name "Macdonald," the collection of interviews is generally known as *The McDonald Papers*, misspelling the judge's last name.

18. Bacon, *Chronicles*, page 80; Bacon credits "the brother of that Isaac who is known as the Martyr" – which would have been *this* Abraham – as having been the leader of the raiding party.

19. *McDonald Papers*, 176-77; see also Romer, *Historical Sketches*, 96-97.

20. Mackenzie, *Families of Philipsburg*, 463.

21. Mackenzie, *Families of Philipsburg*, 463.

22. *Old Dutch Burying Ground of Sleepy Hollow*, 1926 edition, 20.

23. William Graves Perry, *The Old Dutch Burying Ground of Sleepy Hollow in North Tarrytown, New York – A Record of the Early Gravestones and their Inscriptions* (Boston, MA: The Rand Press, 1953) 17.

24. Mackenzie, *Families of Philipsburg*, 462, 464.

25. Romer, *Historical Sketches*, 96.

26. Romer, *Historical Sketches*, 96-98; *Old Dutch Burying Ground of Sleepy Hollow*, 1926 edition, 23.

27. *McDonald Papers*, 176-77.

28. *McDonald Papers*, 177.

29. Romer, *Historical Sketches*, 97.

30. Romer, *Historical Sketches*, 35.

31. Steiner, *"Sleepy Hollow" and "Washington at Tarrytown,"* 42, 62.

32. Raymond, *Souvenir*, 43-44; at the time the *Souvenir of the Monument Dedication* was published, the original handwritten Muster Roll was owned by Bashford Dean, a Professor of Zoology at Columbia University in New York City; its current whereabouts are unknown, possibly in the possession of one of Dean's descendants, or in another private collection.

33. Van Tassel, *Genealogy of the Van Tassel Family*, 54.

34. Van Tassel, "Investigations of Many Years," *The New York Times*, May 28, 1898. Note that a different Abraham Van Tassel was among several Americans captured by the British in July 1779, along with Lieutenant Jacob Van Tassel of Wolfert's Roost fame. This "other" Abraham Van Tassel, the son of Abraham and Cornelia (Delamater) Van Tassel, is sometimes confused with "Bones" Van Tassel.

35. Bacon, *Chronicles*, 117.

36. Van Tassel, "Investigations of Many Years," *The New York Times*, May 28, 1898.

37. Van Santvoord, "Ichabod Crane Once More."

38. Van Santvoord, "Ichabod Crane Once More."

39. Welles and Evans, 16-17.

40. Ritter, "The Real Ichabod."

41. Welles and Evans, 16.

42. Esther Leeming Tuttle, *No Rocking Chair For Me* (Bloomington, IN: iUniverse, 2004) 109.

43. Tuttle, 109-10.

44. *Washington Irving Journals and Notebooks Volume V,* 183-84.

45. Irving, "The Legend of Sleepy Hollow," 368.

46. Email correspondence with Ruth Piwonka, February 12, 2009.

47. The Websites <ANCESTRY.COM>, <ROOTSWEB.COM> and <FAMILYSEARCH.ORG>; Kinderhook Historian Ruth Piwonka; Glenn Fisher, conducting research on behalf of the organization Random Acts of Genealogical Kindness; Lester Van Alstine, *Van Alstyne – Van Alstine Family History, Volume 3* (Provo, UT: J. Grant Stevenson, 1981).

48. Titled "Some Legends and Bits of History Connected with the Van Alstynes and Their Relations," the undated, much-photocopied page was apparently produced on a pre-computer era typewriter, probably by Louise Hardenbrook. Ms. Hardenbrook (1881-1971) was the Columbia County Historical Society's Librarian, and was considered an authority on local lore pertaining to "The Legend."

49. "Ichabod Crane's Grandson Tells About Sleepy Hollow."

50. Walter Blair and Franklin J. Meine, *Half Horse Half Alligator, The Growth of the Mike Fink Legend* (Chicago: The University of Chicago Press, 1956) 23.

51. Irving, "The Legend of Sleepy Hollow," 367-68.

52. Irving, "The Legend of Sleepy Hollow," 379-80.

53. Irving, "The Legend of Sleepy Hollow," 369-70.

54. Irving, "The Legend of Sleepy Hollow," 377.

55. Irving, "The Legend of Sleepy Hollow," 387.

56. Daniel G. Hoffman, "Prefigurations: 'The Legend of Sleepy Hollow'," *A Century of Commentary on the Works of Washington Irving*, Andrew B. Myers, Editor (Tarrytown, NY: Sleepy Hollow Restorations, 1976) 352.

57. Hoffman, "Prefigurations," 349.

58. Blair and Meine, *Half Horse Half Alligator*, 43.

59. Thomas A. Janvier, *The Dutch Founding of New York* (New York: Harper & Brothers, 1903) 4.

60. Carl Carmer, *The Hudson* (New York: Rinehart and Company, 1939) 34-35.

61. Irving, "The Legend of Sleepy Hollow," 368.

62. Carmer, *The Hudson*, 35.

63. Irving, "The Legend of Sleepy Hollow," 367-68.

64. Irving, "The Legend of Sleepy Hollow," 370-71.

65. Irving, "The Legend of Sleepy Hollow," 371.

66. *Washington Irving Journals and Notebooks Volume II*, 212-13.

67. Irving, "The Legend of Sleepy Hollow," 387.

68. Irving, "The Legend of Sleepy Hollow," 387-88.

69. Donald G. Mitchell, "Address," *A Century of Commentary on the Works of Washington Irving*, Andrew B. Myers, Editor (Tarrytown, NY: Sleepy Hollow Restorations, 1976) 56.

Chapter 8

1. Washington Irving, "The Art of Book-Making" *The Sketch Book of Geoffrey Crayon, Gent.* (London: Longmans, Green and Co. 1905), 84-85.

2. Irving, "The Art of Book-Making," 85.

3. Irving, "The Art of Book-Making," 85.

4. Williams, *The Life of Washington Irving, Volume I,* 182.

5. Williams, *The Life of Washington Irving, Volume I,* 181.

6. Edgar Mayhew Bacon, *The Hudson River, From Ocean to Source* (New York: G.P. Putnam's Sons, 1902), 249.

7. Van Santvoord, "Ichabod Crane Once More."

8. Irving, "The Legend of Sleepy Hollow," 369.

9. Irving, "The Legend of Sleepy Hollow," 364.

10. Irving, "The Legend of Sleepy Hollow," 368.

11. Bacon, "Irving's Ichabod Crane Again."

12. Van Santvoord, "Irving's Ichabod Crane."

13. P. M. Irving, *Life and Letters I,* 374.

14. *Washington Irving Letters Volume I,* 572-73.

15. Van Tassel, *Genealogy of the Van Tassel Family,* 54.

16. Bacon, *Chronicles,* 117.

17. John Odell was a well-known Westchester Guide. The story goes that after running off several loyalists (British sympathizers) from what was known as the old McCormick House, Odell spent the night there. The following morning, he was

summoned by his commanding officer, but was unable to find his pants! The lady of the house provided him with one of her petticoats, and thus attired, he reported to his Colonel as directed. From that point on, the colonial Road to White Plains became known as Petticoat Lane... (The former McCormick House, which was at various times a private residence, stagecoach stop and tavern, may still be found on Old White Plains Road, adjacent to modern-day White Plains Road, also known as Route 119.)

18. *Washington Irving Letters Volume I,* 573.

19. Van Santvoord, "Irving and Kinderhook Again."

20. Van Santvoord, "Irving and Kinderhook Again."

21. Pochman, "Irving's German Sources in The Sketch Book," 489-94.

22. *Washington Irving Letters Volume IV,* 216.

Epilogue

1. Irving, *Wolfert's Roost and Other Papers,* 1863 edition, 15.

2. Clark, "Reminiscences of the late Washington Irving."

3. Clark, "Reminiscences of the late Washington Irving."

4. Pierre Munroe Irving, *The Life and Letters of Washington Irving, Volume III* (London: Richard Bentley, 1863), page 227; Letter from Washington Irving to his sister Catherine, written June 21, 1843, while he was living in Madrid, Spain.

5. Cheri Farnsworth, *Haunted Hudson Valley* (Mechanicsburg, PA: Stackpole Books, 2010) 99.

6. Harold Faber, "Irving Home Opens with Two Ghosts," in *The New York Times,* October 5, 1947.

Bibliography

Books and Articles:

"A Famous Tulip Tree." *The New York Times*, December 19, 1886.

Abbatt, William, Editor. *Memoirs of Major-General William Heath, by Himself.* New York: William Abbatt, 1901.

Abstract of Wills of Columbia County, New York, Volume 2 (1805-1814). Fonda, NY: Montgomery County (NY) Department of History and Archives, 1966.

Aderman, Ralph M. and Wayne R. Kime. *Advocate for America: The Life of James Kirke Paulding.* Selinsgrove, PA: Susquehanna University Press, 2003.

Aderman, Ralph M. et al, Editors. *Washington Irving Letters, Volume I, 1802-1823.* Boston, MA: Twayne Publishers, 1978.

Aderman, Ralph M. et al, Editors. *Washington Irving Letters, Volume II, 1823-1838.* Boston, MA: Twayne Publishers, 1979.

Aderman, Ralph M. et al, Editors. *Washington Irving Letters, Volume III, 1839-1845.* Boston, MA: Twayne Publishers, 1982.

Aderman, Ralph M. et al, Editors. *Washington Irving Letters, Volume IV, 1846-1859.* Boston, MA: Twayne Publishers, 1982.

Allen, Janie Couch and Elinor Griffith. *The Old Dutch Church of Sleepy Hollow.* Sleepy Hollow, NY: Friends of the Old Dutch Church and Burying Ground, 2011.

Bacon, Edgar Mayhew. *Chronicles of Tarrytown and Sleepy Hollow.* New York: G.P. Putnam's Sons, 1897.

Bacon, Edgar Mayhew. "Irving and Paulding: When They Were Boys – Tarrytown and Sleepy Hollow," *The New York Times*, October 14, 1899.

Bacon, Edgar Mayhew. "Irving's Ichabod Crane Again - Kinderhook's Claim Stoutly Denied and That of Sleepy Hollow Asserted." Letter to the Editor of *The New York Times*, March 12, 1898, Page SRB 162.

Bacon, Edgar Mayhew. *The Hudson River, From Ocean to Source.* New York: G.P. Putnam's Sons, 1902.

Benton, Jim. "The Van Alen House and the Legend of Sleepy Hollow," *Columbia County History & Heritage*, Volume 12, Number 1, Spring/Summer 2014.

Biggs, Nick. "Tales from Merwin," *Columbia County History & Heritage*, Volume 1, Number 2, Fall 2002.

Biographical Review: The Leading Citizens of Columbia County, New York. Boston: Biographical Review Publishing Company, 1894.

Blair, Walter and Franklin J. Meine. *Half Horse Half Alligator, The Growth of the Mike Fink Legend.* Chicago: The University of Chicago Press, 1956.

Bolton, Robert. *A History of the County of Westchester from its First Settlement to the Present Time.* New York: Alexander S. Gould, 1848.

Bromley, George W. and Walter S. *Atlas of Westchester County, New York: From Actual Surveys and Official Plans,* 1901 Edition. New York, NY: G. W. Bromley and Company, 1901.

Bruccoli, Matthew J. et. al., Editors. *Dictionary of Literary Biography.* Farmington Hills, MI: Thomson-Gale, 2004.

Burns, Robert. *The Collected Poems of Robert Burns.* Ware, Hertfordshire, England: Wordsworth Editions Ltd, 1998

Burritt, Elihu. "Birth-Place of Rip Van Winkle." *Packard's Monthly,* November 1869.

Burstein, Andrew. *The Original Knickerbocker.* New York: Basic Books, 2007.

Burstein, Andrew. "The Politics of Sleepy Hollow." *The New York Times,* October 30, 2005.

Canning, Jeff and Wally Buxton. *History of the Tarrytowns, Westchester County, New York, from Ancient Times to the Present.* Fleischmanns, NY: Purple Mountain Press, 1993.

Carmer, Carl. *The Hudson.* New York: Rinehart and Company, 1939.

Cervantes, Miguel de. *Don Quixote.* New York: Signet Classics, 2003.

Clark, Lewis Gaylord. "Reminiscences of the late Washington Irving." *The Knickerbocker* magazine, January 1860.

Clark, Lewis Gaylord. "Reminiscences of the late Washington Irving: Number Two." *The Knickerbocker* magazine, February 1860.

Colles, Christopher. *A Survey of the Roads of the United States of America 1789.* Cambridge, MA: The Belknap Press of Harvard University Press, 1961.

Collier, Edward A. *A History of Old Kinderhook.* New York: G. P. Putnam's Sons, 1914.

Collins, David R. *Washington Irving: Storyteller for a New Nation.* Greensboro, NC: Morgan Reynolds, Inc., 2000.

Columbia County at the End of the Century, ("Published and Edited Under the Auspices of the Hudson Gazette"). Hudson, NY: The Record Printing and Publishing Company, 1900.

Cyclopedia of Biography: Containing a History of the Family and Descendants of John Collin. Hudson, NY: M. P. Williams, Register and Gazette Office, 1872.

Davis, Matthew L. *Memoirs of Aaron Burr, Volume I.* New York: Harper & Brothers, 1836.

"Death of Ichabod Crane." *The New York Herald*, November 17, 1852, page 2.

Dorson, Richard M. "The Yankee on the Stage – A Folk Hero of American Drama." *The New England Quarterly*, Volume 13, Number 3 (September 1940).

Dutcher, Reverend J. C. *The Old Home by the River.* New York: N. Tibbals and Sons, 1874.

Ellis, Franklin. *History of Columbia County, New York.* Philadelphia: Everts & Ensign, 1878.

Ewald, Captain Johann. *Diary of the American War, A Hessian Journal*, English translation by Joseph P. Tustin. New Haven: Yale University Press, 1979.

Faber, Harold. "Irving Home Opens with Two Ghosts." *The New York Times*, October 5, 1947.

Farnsworth, Cheri. *Haunted Hudson Valley.* Mechanicsburg, PA: Stackpole Books, 2010.

Fielding, Henry. *Tom Jones.* New York, NY: W. W. Norton & Company, 1973.

Folsom, Merrill. "House Where Ichabod Crane Went a-Courtin' Is Preserved." *The New York Times*, May 30, 1967.

Friends of the Old Dutch Burying Ground. *Tales of the Old Dutch Burying Ground*. Sleepy Hollow, NY: Friends of the Old Dutch Burying Ground, Inc., 1992.

Garno, Benjamin. "Old New York: Five Points and Some Other Neighborhoods – Irving's Ichabod Crane." Letter to the Editor of *The New York Times,* April 23, 1898.

Goldsmith, Oliver. *The Deserted Village*. New York: Payson and Clarke Ltd., 1927.

Hellman, George S. *Letters of Henry Brevoort to Washington Irving. Part One.* New York, NY: G.P. Putnam's Sons, 1916.

Hine, Charles Gilbert. *The New York and Albany Post Road*. New York: C. G. Hine, 1905.

Historical Research Society of the Tappan Zee. *The Old Dutch Burying Ground of Sleepy Hollow*. New York, NY: Montague Lee Co., Inc., 1926.

Historical Society, Inc. *Images of America, Tarrytown and Sleepy Hollow*. Charleston, SC: Arcadia Publishing, 1997.

Hoffman, Daniel G. "Irving's Use of American Folklore in 'The Legend of Sleepy Hollow'." *PMLA*, Volume 68, Number 3, June 1953.

Hoffman, Daniel G. "Prefigurations: 'The Legend of Sleepy Hollow'." *A Century of Commentary on the Works of Washington Irving*. Andrew B. Myers, Editor. Tarrytown, NY: Sleepy Hollow Restorations, 1976.

Hufeland, Otto. *Westchester County during the American Revolution 1775-1783*. Privately printed, 1926.

Hutchinson, Lucille and Theodore. *The Centennial History of North Tarrytown*. North Tarrytown, NY: Theodore and Lucille Hutchinson, 1974.

"Ichabod Crane's Grandson Tells About Sleepy Hollow." *The Frederick Post*, Friday, October 23, 1925.

Irving, Pierre Munroe. *The Life and Letters of Washington Irving, Volume I*. London: Richard Bentley, 1864.

Irving, Pierre Munroe. *The Life and Letters of Washington Irving, Volume II*. Philadelphia: J. B. Lippincott & Company, 1870.

Irving, Pierre Munroe. *The Life and Letters of Washington Irving, Volume III*. New York: G. P. Putnam and Son, 1869.

Irving, Pierre Munroe. *The Life and Letters of Washington Irving, Volume III*. London: Richard Bentley, 1863.

Irving, Washington. *Abbotsford and Newstead Abbey*. Charleston, SC: BiblioBazaar, 2007.

Irving, Washington. *Bracebridge Hall, Tales of a Traveler, The Alhambra*. New York: Library of America, 1991.

Irving, Washington. *Diedrich Knickerbocker's History of New York*. Norwalk, CT: The Heritage Press, 1968.

Irving, Washington and Henry Steiner. *The Historically Annotated Legend of Sleepy Hollow*. Sleepy Hollow, NY: Milestone Productions, 2014.

Irving, Washington. *The Sketch book of Geoffrey Crayon, Gent*. London: Longmans, Green and Co. 1905.

Irving, Washington. *Tales of a Traveler*. New York: American Book Company, 1894.

Irving, Washington. *Wolfert's Roost and Miscellanies.* Charleston, SC: BiblioBazaar, 2007.

Irving, Washington. *Wolfert's Roost and Other Papers, Now First Collected.* Author's Revised Edition. New York: G. P. Putnam, 1863.

Irvingiana: A Memorial of Washington Irving. New York: Charles B. Richardson, Publisher, 1860.

Janvier, Thomas A. *The Dutch Founding of New York.* New York: Harper & Brothers, 1903.

Jarvis, Sharon. *Dark Zones.* New York, NY: Warner Books, 1992.

Jewell, Roger L. *The Sawmill River Valley War.* Fairfield, PA: Jewell Histories, 2009.

Johnson, Kathleen Eagen. *Washington Irving's Sunnyside.* Tarrytown, NY: Historic Hudson Valley Press, 1995.

Jones, Brian Jay. *Washington Irving, An American Original.* New York: Arcade Publishing, 2008.

Jones, Catherine. *Literary Memory, Scott's Waverley Novels and the Psychology of Narrative.* Lewisburg, PA: Bucknell University Press, 2003.

Jones, Louis C. *Things That Go Bump in the Night.* Syracuse, NY: Syracuse University Press, 1983.

Keller, Allan. *Life Along the Hudson.* Tarrytown, NY: Sleepy Hollow Restorations, 1976.

Kelly, Arthur C. M. *Baptism Record of Kinderhook Reformed Church, Kinderhook, New York, 1718-1899.* Rhinebeck, NY: Kinship, 1985.

Kelly, Arthur C. M. *Index to Grantees and Occupants, Manor of Philipsburgh, Westchester County, N.Y., 1785-1786*. Rhinebeck, NY: Kinship, 2003.

Kelly, Arthur C. M. *Marriage Record of Kinderhook Reformed Church, Kinderhook, New York, 1717-1899*. Rhinebeck, NY: Kinship, 1986.

Kime, Wayne R. *Pierre M. Irving and Washington Irving: A Collaboration in Life and Letters*. Waterloo, Ontario, Canada: Wilfrid Laurier University Press, 1979.

Leiby, Adrian. *The Revolutionary War in the Hackensack Valley: The Jersey Dutch and the Neutral Ground, 1775-1783*. Piscataway, NJ: Rutgers University Press, 1980.

Lockhart, John Gibson. *Memoirs of the Life of Sir Walter Scott, Volume 4*. Edinburgh: Robert Cadell, 1837.

Lossing, Benson J. *The Hudson From the Wilderness to the Sea*. Troy, NY: H.B. Nims & Co., 1866.

Lossing, Benson J. *The Pictorial Field-Book of the Revolution*. New York, NY: Harper & Brothers, 1852.

Macdonald, James MacLean. *The MacDonald Papers*. Elmsford, NY: Westchester County Historical Society, 1927.

Mackenzie, Grenville C. *Families of the Colonial Town of Philipsburgh*. Westport, CT: Published by Author, 1966.

Marinacci, Mike. *Mysterious California*. Los Angeles: Panpipes Press, 1988.

McKernan, Maureen. "The Van Tassel Family." *The Peekskill (NY) Evening Star*, Monday, September 10, 1951.

BIBLIOGRAPHY

Miles Merwin Association. *The Merwin Family in North America*, published in Four Volumes. Hartford, CT: Connecticut Historical Society, 1978-2003.

Miller, Harry Edward. "In The Sleepy Hollow Country." *New England Magazine*, Volume 23, September 1900 – February 1901 bound issues. Boston: Warren F. Kellog, Publisher, 1900.

Miller, Richard. "A Brief History of Tarrytown." Official Village of Tarrytown website: <WWW.TARRYTOWNGOV.COM>.

Mitchell, Donald G. "Address." *A Century of Commentary on the Works of Washington Irving*. Andrew B. Myers, Editor. Tarrytown, NY: Sleepy Hollow Restorations, 1976.

Mitchell, Donald G. *Dream Life: A Fable of the Seasons*. Charleston, SC: BiblioBazaar, 2007.

Musaus, Johann Karl August. *Popular Tales of the Germans, Volume II*, English translation by William Beckford. London: J. Murray, 1791.

Myers, Andrew B., Editor. *A Century of Commentary on the Works of Washington Irving*. Tarrytown, NY: Sleepy Hollow Restorations, 1976.

Myers, Andrew B. "Washington Irving." *Dictionary of Literary Biography: Antebellum Writers in New York and the South, Volume 3*. Detroit, MI: Gale, 1979.

Neider, Charles, Editor. *The Complete Tales of Washington Irving*. Cambridge, MA: Da Capo Press, 1998.

Perry, William Graves. *The Old Dutch Burying Ground of Sleepy Hollow in North Tarrytown, New York – A Record of the Early Gravestones and their Inscriptions*. Boston, MA: The Rand Press, 1953.

Pochman, Henry A. "Irving's German Sources in The Sketch Book." *Studies in Philology*, Number 27, July 1930.

Raymond, Marcus D., Editor. *Souvenir of the Revolutionary Soldiers' Monument Dedication at Tarrytown, N. Y., October 19th, 1894.* Tarrytown, NY: Monument Committee, 1894.

Reichart, Walter A. "In England." *A Century of Commentary on the Works of Washington Irving.* Andrew B. Myers, Editor. Tarrytown, NY: Sleepy Hollow Restorations, 1976.

Reichart, Walter A. *Washington Irving and Germany.* Ann Arbor, MI: The University of Michigan Press, 1957.

Reichart, Walter A. "Washington Irving's Interest in German Folklore." *New York Folklore Quarterly*, Autumn 1957, pages 181-192.

Reichart, Walter A. and Lillian Schlissel, Editors. *Washington Irving Journals and Notebooks Volume II, 1807-1822.* Boston: Twayne Publishers, 1981.

Reichart, Walter A., Editor. *Washington Irving Journals and Notebooks Volume III, 1819-1827.* Madison, WI: The University of Wisconsin Press, 1970.

Richardson, Judith. *Possessions – The History and Uses of Haunting in the Hudson Valley.* Cambridge, MA: Harvard University Press, 2003.

Ringe, Donald A. "New York and New England: Irving's Criticism of American Society." *A Century of Commentary on the Works of Washington Irving.* Andrew B. Myers, Editor. Tarrytown, NY: Sleepy Hollow Restorations, 1976.

Ritter, John P. "The Real Ichabod Crane – When and Where Irving Discovered Him." *The New York Herald*, Sunday July 16, 1899, Fifth Section, page 2.

Roberts, James A., Editor. *New York in the Revolution as Colony and State*. Albany, NY: Weed-Parsons Printing Company, 1897.

Rodes, Sara Puryear. "Washington Irving's Use of Traditional Folklore." *New York Folklore Quarterly*, Spring 1957 pages 3-15.

Romer, John Lockwood. *Historical Sketches of the Romer, Van Tassel and Allied Families and Tales of the Neutral Ground*. Buffalo, NY: W. C. Gay Printing Co., 1917.

Ross, Sue Fields, Editor. *Washington Irving Journals and Notebooks Volume V, 1832-1859*. Boston: Twayne Publishers, 1986.

Scharf, J. Thomas. *History of Westchester County, New York, Volumes 1 and 2*. Philadelphia: L. E. Preston, 1886.

Schlosser, Sandy E. *Spooky New York*. Guilford, CT: Globe Pequot Press, 2005.

Schlosser, Sandy E. "The Headless Horseman – A New York Ghost Story." Published on her American Folklore website: <HTTP://AMERICANFOLKLORE.NET/FOLKLORE/2010/07/THE_HEADLESS_HORSEMAN.HTML>.

Seton, Anya. *Washington Irving*. Boston: Houghton Mifflin Company, 1960.

"Sleepy Hollow's Legend – Among the Scenes of the Quaint Old Dutch Story." *The New York Times*, August 13, 1882, page 8.

Steiner, Henry, Editor. *"Sleepy Hollow" and "Washington at Tarrytown."* Sleepy Hollow, NY: Milestone Productions, 2013.

Steiner, Henry. *The Place Names of Historic Sleepy Hollow and Tarrytown*. Westminster, MD: Heritage Books, 1998.

Trafton, David. *Jesse Merwin, the Original Ichabod Crane*. Bethesda, MD: Self-published monograph, 2006.

Trent, William P. and George S. Hellman, Editors. *The Journals of Washington Irving Volume III: Spain, Tour through the West, Esopus and Dutch Tour.* New York: Haskell House, 1970.

Tuttle, Esther Leeming. *No Rocking Chair For Me.* Bloomington, IN: iUniverse, 2004.

Van Alen, Benjamin Taylor. *Genealogical History of the Van Alen Family.* Chicago: self-published, 1902.

Van Alen House Historic Structure Report. Albany, NY: John G. Waite Associates, 2001.

Van Alstine, Lester. *Van Alstyne - Van Alstine Family History, Volume 3.* Provo, UT: J. Grant Stevenson, 1981.

Van der Donck, Adriaen. *A Description of New Netherland.* English translation by Diederik Willem Goedhuys; Edited by Charles T. Gehring. Lincoln, NE: University of Nebraska, 2008.

Van der Donck, Adriaen. *Beschryvinge van Nieuw-Nederlant.* Aemsteldam (Amsterdam): Evert Nieuwenhof, 1656.

Van Santvoord, Harold. "Ichabod Crane Once More." Letter to the Editor of *The New York Times,* "Saturday Review of Books and Art" section, March 19, 1898, page BR 190.

Van Santvoord, Harold. "Irving and Kinderhook Again." Letter to the Editor of *The New York Times,* April 30, 1898.

Van Santvoord, Harold. "Irving's Ichabod Crane." Letter to the Editor of *The New York Times,* "Saturday Review of Books and Art" section, February 26, 1898, page BR 129.

Van Tassel, Daniel. *Genealogy of the Van Texel – Van Tassel Family in America 1625-1900.* Tarrytown, NY: Privately Published, circa 1900.

Van Tassel, Daniel. "Sleepy Hollow - Daniel Van Tassel Gives the Results of His Investigations of Many Years." Letter to the Editor of *The New York Times*, May 28, 1898, Page BR 357.

Warner, Charles Dudley. *Washington Irving*. Boston: Houghton, Mifflin And Company, 1881.

"Washington Irving." *The Sun* (New York), January 30, 1835.

Welles, E.R. III and J.P. Evans. *Legend of Sleepy Hollow, Rip Van Winkle, President Van Buren, and Brom*. Manset, ME: Learning Incorporated, 1984.

Wess, Robert C. "The Use of Hudson-Valley Folk Traditions in Washington Irving's Knickerbocker History of New York." *New York Folklore Quarterly*, Volume 30, Number 3 (September 1974).

Wilcox, Arthur Russell. *The Bar of Rye Township, Westchester County, New York*. New York: The Knickerbocker Press, 1918.

Williams, Stanley T., Editor. *Notes While Preparing the Sketch Book, 1817, by Washington Irving*. New Haven, CT: Yale University Press, 1927.

Williams, Stanley T. *The Life of Washington Irving, Volume I*. New York, NY: Octagon Books, 1971.

Williams, Stanley T., Editor. *Tour in Scotland 1817 and Other Manuscript Notes by Washington Irving*. New Haven, CT: Yale University Press, 1927.

Willis, N. P. "Visits to Sunnyside" *Irvingiana: A Memorial of Washington Irving*. New York: Charles B. Richardson, Publisher, 1860, pp. 47-50.

Wright, Nathalia, Editor. *Washington Irving Journals and Notebooks Volume I, 1803-1806*. Madison, Wisconsin: University of Wisconsin Press, 1969.

"Yankee Visits Sleepy Hollow." *YANKEE* Magazine, July 1953, pp. 32-42.

Maps:

Adams, William. "A Map of the Town of Mount Pleasant in Westchester County," dated 1788, found in Scharf, *History of Westchester County, New York*, Volume 2, page 623.

Bromley, George W. and Walter S. Map of North Tarrytown found in *Atlas of Westchester County, New York: From Actual Surveys and Official Plans,* 1901 Edition, page 43.

Colles, Christopher. "From New York to Poughkeepsie," dated 1789, found in Colles, *A Survey of the Roads of the United States of America*, page 129.

Erskine, Robert. "No. 59 Roads About White Plains," dated 1779, found in Scharf, *History of Westchester County, New York*, Volume 1 Part 2, page 732.

Erskine, Robert. "Survey of the Road Between Tarrytown and Croton River," circa 1778, New York Historical Society map collection.

Hill, John, "Plan of the Manor of Philipsburg in the County of Westchester," dated 1785, drawn for the Commission of Forfeitures; found in Scharf, *History of Westchester County, New York*, Volume 1 Part 1, page 160f.

Hutchinson, Theodore. Hand-drawn copy of George Wiley's 1880 map; found in Hutchinson, *The Centennial History of North Tarrytown*, page 28.

"Manor of Philipsburgh, Tarwetown, 1725-1795." Unsigned map in collection of Historical Society Serving Sleepy Hollow and Tarrytown.

Wiley, George L. "Tarwe-town in the Manor of Phillipsburgh, Westchester Co, N.Y., One Hundred Years Ago," dated September 23, 1880, in collection of Historical Society Serving Sleepy Hollow and Tarrytown.

Index

Abbotsford (estate), 8, 63, 90, 111, 155
Abbotsford and Newstead Abbey, 244, 265, 271
"Abbotsford" essay, 110, 265
Acker, Abraham and Catherine (Van Tassel), 60
Acker, Wolfert, 59-60, 64, 166, 247
Adams, William, 50, 256
Adventures of Ichabod and Mr. Toad, ii
Albany Post Road, 18, 26, 28-30, 32, 43-44, 47, 51, 53, 55, 67, 70-71, 73-79, 198, 230, 241, 267, 287
Alcott, Louisa May, 233
Alf Tales, ii
Allston, Washington, 87
Analectic Magazine, 7, 110-111
Anburey, Thomas, 157, 227, 235
Andre, Major John, 18, 42-44, 58, 84
Andre's Brook, 33, 44-46, 75-76
Andre's Tree, 33, 42-44, 58, 70, 74, 109
Arnold, Benedict, 43
"Art of Book-Making," 231-232, 281
Asbury Methodist Cemetery, Staten Island, 126-127
Astor, John Jacob, 138
Austin, Mr., 56

"Author's Account of Himself," 2, 9, 251

Bacon, Edgar Mayhew, 25, 31, 54-55, 57, 73-74, 77, 97, 138, 140, 172-173, 210-211, 213, 234, 238-241, 255-257, 259-260, 268, 277, 281
Baltus Van Tassel, 54, 58, 67-70, 72, 158, 171-172, 185, 237
Battle Hill, 47, 202
Beach, L., 158
Beckford, William, 115, 118-119, 242, 265-266
Bedford Road, 27, 29, 76-79
Beekman Avenue, 26, 76
Beekman, Gerard G., 25
Begley Jr., Ed, ii
Beharie, Nicole, iii
Bell, Dr. Joseph, 233
Beth March, 233
Blackwood's Edinburgh Magazine, 108, 111
Blankenship, Tom, 233
Blauvelt, John P., 101
Boleyn, Anne, 94
Bolton, Robert, 55, 194-196, 269, 276
Bontempi, Marcel, iv
Boyce, Abraham (1745?-1780), 192-193, 197
Boyce, Abraham (1760?-1839), 193-197

299

Boyce, Abraham (1766-??), 194
Boyce, Jacob, 193
Boyce, Thomas, 192-193
Bracebridge Hall, 12, 107
Brando, iv
Brevoort, Abraham, 192, 196-197
Brevoort, Henry, 11-12, 79, 89, 111, 131-133, 158, 192, 196, 260, 262, 271, 275
Bridge, Headless Horseman, 46-54, 73
Bridge, Washington Irving Memorial, 48, 51, 73
Broadway, 26, 30, 35, 43-45, 47-48, 54, 73-75, 77, 80, 209
Brom Bones
  appearance, 191, 223
  as the Headless Horseman, 114-115, 226, 229-230, 242
  blacksmith, 197-198, 207-208, 239
  braggart, 86, 222-223, 240
  bully, i, 222-223, 239
  city vs. country, 159, 223-224
  frontiersman, 222-224
  hero, i, 223-224
  horsemanship, 197, 207-208, 226, 240
  jealous, i, 161, 224, 238
  likeability, 223, 226
  occupation, 197, 207-208, 239
  practical joker, 210, 222, 226-227, 229, 241
  sense of humor, 217, 224, 226
  strength, 197, 207-208, 223
Brombacher, Charles, 54, 256
Brouwer, Jane, 107
Buckhout, John, 241
Bucktails, The, 158
Buresch, Lucas, 40, 121-122, 266
Burger, Gottfried August, 108, 112-113
Burns, Robert, 108, 110, 242, 264-265
Burr, Aaron, 4, 34, 101-102, 147, 269
Burritt, Elihu, 82, 85, 261,
Burstein, Andrew, 2, 101, 251, 253, 266, 269
Burton, Tim, iii
Busching, Johann Gustav, 86
Butkus, Dick, ii
Buxton, Wally, 29, 254-256
Byce, Brom, 192, 196-197

Cabell, Joseph C., 66
Campbell, Mrs. Archibald, 132
Canning, Jeff, 29, 254-256
Carae, William L., 29-30
Carl's Mill, 98-99, 101-102, 121-122, 210
Carmer, Carl, 226, 280
Carver, Brent, iii

INDEX

"Castle Von Tromp," 82-83
Cedar Hill, 77-78, 80, 260
Cervantes, Miguel de, 156-157, 235, 271, 285
Christian Advocate and Journal, 141, 214
Clark, Lewis Gaylord, 72, 248, 259
Close, Glenn, iii
Cockspur Lane, 91
Coleman, William, 118
Colles, Christopher, 50, 256, 260
Collier, Edward, 183, 268, 274
Columbia County Historical Society, 70, 220-221, 274, 279
Commission of Forfeitures, 25, 51-52, 56, 60, 260
Companions of Columbus, 12
Conquest of Granada, 12
"Conspiracy of the Cocked Hats," 160, 272
Continental Road, 26, 29, 76-78
Crane, Col. Ichabod Bennett, 8, 123-127, 152, 236
Crosby, Bing, ii
Croton Aqueduct, 29, 75-78, 96, 260
Currier and Ives, 50
Cutler, Joseph, 56

Dale Cemetery, Ossining, 150
D'Angelo, Beverly, ii
De Lancey, Gen. Oliver, 201-202, 204
Dean, Sgt. John, 241
Decatur, Capt. Stephen, 124
Dell Street, 52-54, 80
Depp, Johnny, iii
Deserted Village, The, 152, 154-155, 270-271
Diedrich Knickerbocker, 6, 12, 26, 59, 64, 81, 96, 98-99, 238, 253
Dirk Schuyler, 136, 233
Disney, Walt, ii
Don Quixote, 156-157, 235, 271, 285
Doyle, Sir Arthur Conan, 233
Dullahan, 94
Dund, 93
Dutcher, Rev. Jacob Conkling, 30-31, 254
Dutcher, William, 241

Ecker, Wolfert, *see Acker*
Edward Street, 91-92
Emmerick, Maj. Andreas, 102, 201
Erskine, Robert, 50, 75, 256
Evans, J. P., 213-214, 262, 278

Ferris, Benson, 61-62
Ferris, Oliver, 61
Fielding, Henry, 132, 152-154, 235
"Fifth Legend of Rubezahl," 114-119, 242
Fink, Mike, 224-225, 279
Foreign Quarterly Review, 111
Foster, Meg, ii

Frederick Post, 175, 269
Funk, Elisabeth Paling, 99, 107, 114, 263-265

Galley Fight, 200-201, 276
Gargoyle Sox, iv
Geoffrey Crayon, ii, 9-10, 12, 64, 72, 251-252, 281
Gleason's Pictorial, 30, 98, 121
"Gnome King," 118
Goldblum, Jeff, ii
Goldsmith, Oliver, 154-155, 270-271
Gratz, Rebecca, 133
Grimm, Brothers, 94

"Haddon Hall Notebook," 107-108
Halloween, v, 215-216, 244-246
Hardenbrook, Louise, 279
Harry Potter, 233
Harvey, George, 14, 62
Headless Havoc, iv
Headless Horseman Legends, 93-97, 99-100, 105-108, 119
Heath, Gen. William, 101, 263
Hellman, George S., 132, 252, 260, 271, 275
Herrick, Maria Van Alen, 175-178, 183
Hessians, 95-96, 100-105, 108, 119, 168, 241, 262
Highland Turnpike, 47, 74-75, 79

Hill, John, 51-53, 76, 256, 260
Historic Hudson Valley, 5, 10, 39-40, 66, 245, 258, 289
Historical Society Serving Sleepy Hollow and Tarrytown, 51, 58, 76-79, 211, 256
History of Old Kinderhook, 183, 268, 274
Hoar, Elizabeth, 233
Hoffman, Daniel, 224, 271, 280
Hoffman, Josiah Ogden, 3-4, 80, 133,
Hoffman, Matilda, 4-6, 131, 177-178
Hoffman, Mrs., 131, 134
Holloway, Mrs., 91
Holzer, Hans, 249
"Horseman's Ride," 47, 53, 80
Howe, Gen. William, 100
Huckleberry Finn, 233
Hudson Bee, 179
Hutchinson, Lucille and Theodore, 29, 254, 256, 259-260

Ichabod Crane School District (Valatie, NY), 244
Ichabod Crane
  appearance, i, 90, 124, 156-158, 235
  city slicker, 159, 224
  city vs. country, 159

302

Connecticut Yankee, 158-160, 224, 234-235
   educated, 148, 155, 159
   gossip, 160
   greedy, 160
   puritanical attitudes, 154, 161-162, 235
   scheming, 153, 160, 189
   schoolmaster, i, 27-31, 33, 35, 124, 127-128, 138-139, 141, 147-148, 154-155, 234-235
   self-serving, 152-153
   singing teacher, 31, 161, 223, 226
   superstitious, 153-154, 161, 226, 235
   worldy/sophisticated, 156, 160, 224
Ichabod!, iii
In Search Of..., 249
Irving, Alexander Duer, 66
Irving, Ann (sister), 3
Irving, Catherine (niece), 65-66
Irving, Charlotte (niece), 65
Irving, Ebenezer, 4, 8-10, 15-16, 65-66, 81, 89-90, 107, 240, 258
Irving, Julia (niece), 65
Irving, Louis, 66
Irving, Mary (niece), 65
Irving, Oscar (nephew), 14, 61-62
Irving, Peter (brother), 4, 6, 8, 14, 63, 92, 101, 106, 144
Irving, Pierre Munroe, 17, 66, 82-83, 85-87, 89, 134, 145-146, 239, 251-252, 254, 269, 282
Irving, Sarah (mother), 2
Irving, Sarah (niece), 65-66
Irving, Washington
   biographer/historian, 12, 16-17, 138
   biographies, 1-2, 82, 146
   celebrity, 11-13, 237
   childhood, 2-3, 30, 43, 56, 61, 69, 71, 87, 97-99, 119, 167, 170, 172
   death, 18-19
   diplomat, 12-13, 15, 63, 66, 142, 144
   discovers Catskill Mountains, 3
   discovers Hudson River, 3
   discovers Sleepy Hollow, 2-3, 43, 48, 56, 61, 80, 85, 97-99, 167, 172
   education, 2-4, 111
   family business, 8-9, 82-83, 111, 243
   family, 2-6, 8-9, 14-16, 64-66, 81-83, 107, 239-240, 249
   ghost, 247, 249-250
   health issues, 4, 17, 136, 138
   High School, Tarrytown, 58
   in England, 8-13, 34, 81-85, 87, 89, 91-92, 106, 111, 118, 132, 142, 144, 152, 158, 163, 180, 243-244
   influence on future writers, 11

journals and notebooks, 33-35, 70, 80, 86, 89, 106-107, 113, 130-131, 134, 138, 157, 162-163, 178, 215-218, 220, 222, 227, 232, 236-237, 241-242

legal career, 3-4, 8

letters/correspondence, 4, 9, 11-12, 14, 16, 31-32, 61-64, 66, 87, 89-92, 111, 129-139, 144-146, 151, 154, 156, 158, 162, 180, 189, 196, 233, 235-237, 240, 258, 262, 273, 282

military career, 7-8, 125

postage stamp, iv, v

religion, 161-162

returns to America, 12-13

travels, 2-4, 8, 12-13, 16, 92, 106

visits to Kinderhook, 6-7, 13, 16-17, 105-106, 132-138, 143-144, 177-178, 180-181, 213, 216, 237, 243-245

writing influences, 108-118, 242

writing method, 11, 35, 231-236, 240, 242

Irving, Washington III, 249

Irving, William (brother), 2, 4-5

Irving, William (father), 2, 161-162

Jackson, Andrew, 144

Janvier, Thomas A., 225-226, 280

"John Bull," 81, 90

Jonathan Oldstyle, 4, 101

Jones, Brian Jay, 2, 253, 259, 263

Jones, Louis, 95, 262

Kalem Company, ii

Kalm, Peter, 34

Katrina Van Tassel
  appearance, i, 165, 170, 176, 237-238
  farmer's daughter, i, 153, 188, 234, 237, 241
  fickle/indecisive, 188, 238
  flirt, 188, 238
  heiress, i, 153, 160, 188-189, 238, 241, 244
  rich, 160, 188, 237
  scheming/manipulative, 238
  typical Dutch girl, 238-239

Keller, Allen, 177, 273, 289

Kemble, Gouverneur, 64, 151

Kime, Wayne R., 145, 254, 269

Kinderhook, 6-7, 13, 16, 31-33, 66-71, 105-106, 128-144, 152, 154, 173-189, 191, 213-222, 233-240, 243-245, 254, 259, 268, 274-275, 279, 282

King's Highway, *see Albany Post Road*

Kip, Elizabeth, 107

Kleinrood, 6, 129

Knickerbocker magazine, 14, 16, 59, 63-64, 72, 96-97, 99, 160, 171, 248, 259
Knickerbocker's History of New York, 6-8, 11, 64, 133, 136, 138, 159-160, 225, 233, 239, 243, 253, 272
Kruk, Jonathan, 245

Lady in White, 41-42, 99
Lamouroux, Andrew, 56
Landmark Condominiums, 58, 73
Last of the Boatmen, 224
"Lauchie Long Legs," 90, 155-156, 235
Law, Stephen D., 28
Lefevre, Rachelle, iii
Lent, Bill, 197-198
Life and Voyages of Columbus, 12
Life of George Washington, 16-17
Lindenwald, 6, 16-17, 181, 187, 243
Lindsley, A. B., 158
Little Women, 233
Lockhart, John G., 91, 271
Logan, Jim, 104, 264
Lorey, Capt. Friedrich Heinrich, 96
Lossing, Benson, 48-50, 65

Macdonald, James MacLean, 200, 276-277
Mahomet, 16, 244
Mahomet's Successors, 16, 244

Manning, Prof. Susan, 108, 264
Marinacci, Mike, 97, 263
"Marlin, Brom," 204
Martlenghs, Abraham (1693-1761), 54-55, 198-199, 201
Martling, Abraham (1719-1786), 200-202, 204, 208
Martling, Abraham (1742-1830), 203-204, 208
Martling, Abraham (1761-??), 200-201
Martling, Abraham (1763-1841), 202, 204-207, 209
Martling, Abraham, 197-198, 239
Martling, Daniel, 200
Martling, Isaac "the Martyr," 199, 202, 204, 277
Martling's Landing, 26, 200
Masterson, Henry, 3
Mather, Cotton, 161-162
Merwin, Daniel, 130
Merwin, David, 134, 139-140, 187
Merwin, George, 145, 175, 188, 221
Merwin, Jesse, 6-7, 13, 31-33, 123, 128-146, 152, 175, 177-178, 180, 186-189, 214-222, 233-235, 237, 239, 241-244, 266, 274-275
Merwin, Peter, 130, 187
Merwin, Washington Irving, 130, 137, 187
Milton, John, 87
Mison, Tom, iii

305

Mitchell, Donald G., 35, 230, 255, 280
Moore, John, 136, 233
Morning Chronicle, 4, 101-102
Mott House, 54-58, 70-73, 171-173, 199
Mott, Jacob (junior), 54, 56-58, 171-173, 199
Mott, Jacob Lawrence (senior), 56-57
Mott, Sarah (Fowler), 57, 171-173
Murray, John, 243-244
Musaus, Johann Karl August, 94, 114-119, 242, 265-266
Mystery Legends - Sleepy Hollow, iv

Nachtigal, Johann Karl Christoph, 113
Nettleship, John, 233
Neville, Morgan, 224
New York Herald, 175, 213, 259, 268, 286
New York Mirror, 58
New York Sun, 58, 139, 146, 214, 257, 268
New York Times, 27, 29, 31, 132, 174, 177, 181, 210, 213, 253-255, 257, 259, 261, 266-269, 278, 282
Newton, Gilbert Stuart, 10
Nimoy, Leonard, 249
North Tarrytown, 25

Odell, Johnnie, 241, 281-282

Odell, Jonathan, 56
Old Brouwer, 107, 223
Old Croton Aqueduct, 29, 75-78, 96, 260
Old Dutch Burying Ground, 33, 37-38, 80, 99, 102-105, 110, 150-151, 166, 169-170, 199, 202-203, 208-209, 212, 255, 263, 269, 273, 276-277
Old Dutch Church, 18, 23, 33, 35-40, 46-48, 50-51, 53, 55, 60, 71, 73, 77, 79-80, 96, 103-104, 110, 170, 193, 197, 199, 202-203, 210-212, 241, 245
Onderdonk, Abraham, 101-102
Otmar, 86, 113

P. and E. Irving company, 8-9, 83, 243
Paris, Catherine Irving (sister), 3, 15-16, 61, 65
Paris, Sarah (niece), 64
Partridge, 131-132, 152-154, 235
Paulding, James Kirke, 2, 5, 28, 158, 254
Paulding, John, 43-44, 75
Paulding, Julia, 2
Pedlar, The, 224
Pegazus, iv
"Peter Klaus," 86, 111, 243
Peters, Rev. Samuel, 227
Petticoat Lane, 241, 281-282
Philip, Mrs. Van Ness, 105-106

INDEX

Philipsburg Manor, 24, 36-37, 39-40, 51, 59, 71, 95, 245, 260
Philipse, Frederick I, 24, 26, 35-37, 39, 59-60
Philipse, Frederick III, 24-25, 55-56, 69, 260
Pierson School, 58
Pocantico River, 3, 22-24, 39, 46-47, 50-54, 78, 98, 121
Pochman, Henry, 85-86, 115, 243, 261, 265, 282
Portfolio magazine, 110
Praetorius, Johannes, 114
"Pride of the Village," 81, 90
Professor Snape, 233
Prospect Hill, 77-78, 260
Putnam, G. P., 16, 66, 138
Putnam, Gen. Israel, 101

Queen's Highway, *see Albany Post Road*

Radcliffe, Ann, 114, 242
Raup, Gertrude, 129
Raven Rock, 40-42, 99
Raymond, Marcius D., 53-54, 258, 263, 269-270, 275-276, 278
Real Ghostbusters, The, ii
Real Legend of Sleepy Hollow, iv
Reeve, Clara, 113-114, 242
Reichart, Walter, 11, 86, 113, 252, 255, 261, 265
Requa's Dock, 26, 200
Reviere, Abraham, 209

Revolutionary Soldiers Monument, 47, 148, 193, 202-203, 209, 212, 258
Ricci, Christina, iii
Ringe, Donald, 160
Rip Van Winkle, 9, 85-86, 111, 243, 261-262
Ritter, John P., 175, 182, 213, 259, 269, 273-274, 278
Robinson, J., 158
Rockefeller, John D. Jr., 41-42, 66
Rockefeller, William, 48
Rockwell, George G., 49-50
Rogers, Will, ii
Romer, Captain John, 102-105, 200-201, 204-206, 276
Romer, John Lockwood, 75, 77, 103-105, 257, 260, 264, 277-278
Roosevelt, Eleanor, 33
"Roscoe," 9
Route 9, *see Broadway*
Rowling, J. K., 233
Rubezahl, 108, 114-119, 242
"Rural Funerals," 90

Sackets Harbor, 8, 125, 236
Salmagundi, 5, 11,
Saunders, Frederick, 243
Scharf, J. Thomas, 52, 55, 61, 148, 168, 173, 254, 256-259, 269-270, 272-273
Schlosser, Sandy, 99-100, 106, 263-264
Scooby-Doo, ii

Scott, Sir Walter, 8-9, 63, 90-91, 110-111, 113, 155-156, 235, 271
See, Eliza Ann, 27-29
See's Store, 210-211, 241
Select Reviews magazine, 7
Sharpney, William, 29-30
Sherlock Holmes, 233
"Sir Gawain and the Green Knight," 94
Skandhahata, 93
Sketch Book of Geoffrey Crayon, Gent., ii, 2, 9-12, 81, 89, 108, 115, 138, 157-158, 172, 192, 196, 222, 231-232, 235, 243-244, 251-252, 261, 265, 281-282
Slapershaven, 21-22
Sleepy Hollow High School, 76
Sleepy Hollow movie, iii
Sleepy Hollow TV series, iii
"Sleepy Hollow" essay, 3, 21, 59, 97-98, 167, 251
Sleepy Hollow, village/region, iii, 2-3, 14, 21-29, 31, 33, 35, 37-38, 42-43, 50, 56, 66, 71, 76-77, 79-80, 85, 96, 99-102, 106-107, 140, 146-148, 152, 159, 165, 167, 173, 191, 197, 202, 209-210, 212, 217, 224, 226, 230, 235, 237, 245-246, 253-255, 257, 264, 266, 269
Smurfs, The, ii

Steiner, Henry, 23, 25, 44, 48, 75, 77, 253-260, 269, 276, 278
Stewart, Charisse, iii
Story, Tim, iii
Sunnyside, 5, 13-16, 18, 30, 57-59, 62-63, 65-66, 70-73, 86-87, 114-115, 135, 138-139, 171, 214, 230, 243, 245, 247-250, 258-259, 261
"supernatural explique," 114, 242

Talavera, 105
Tales of a Traveler, 11-12, 252
Tales of the Alhambra, 12
"Tam O'Shanter," 108-110, 119, 242, 264-265
Tarrytown Argus, 27, 53, 209
Tarrytown, 2, 7, 18, 24-31, 33, 42-43, 45, 47-48, 50-51, 53-54, 58, 61, 66, 69, 71, 73-75, 78-84, 87, 96, 100, 103, 140, 146-147, 162, 167, 172, 194, 197-198, 200, 202-204, 208-211, 230, 234, 236, 238-241, 252-256, 258, 260, 272-273, 277-278, 280
Temple, Shirley, ii
Tom Jones, 132, 152-154, 235, 270
Tompkins, Gov. Daniel D., 7, 125
Tour on the Prairies, 13, 144
Tremain, Augustus, 179

INDEX

Troiani, Don, 95
Tuttle, Esther Leeming "Faity," 215, 279
Twain, Mark, 233
Tyler, Royall, 158

Upper Mills, 24-25

Van Aelsteyn, Janse Martense, 217
Van Alen Evert, 181-182
Van Alen House, 33, 67, 69-71, 173-176, 179-183, 245
Van Alen, Adam, 183
Van Alen, Benjamin Taylor, 181, 274
Van Alen, Catherine (Van Alstyne), 183-184
Van Alen, Catherine, 181-182, 188
Van Alen, Congressman James Isaac, 136, 180-181
Van Alen, David, 68, 173, 179
Van Alen, Dirck, 181-182
Van Alen, Elizabeth, 176
Van Alen, Helen, 68, 173-183, 188, 214, 222, 236-237
Van Alen, Helena, 176
Van Alen, Johannes, 182
Van Alen, John D., 176
Van Alen, Katrina, 175, 181-182, 215
Van Alen, Laurens, 68, 179, 182
Van Alen, Laurentius, 173, 183

Van Alen, Luykas, 33, 67-68, 70, 173-176, 179-180, 182-183, 245
Van Alen, Maria, 68, 173, 179
Van Alen, Peter, 68, 176
Van Alstyne, Abraham (1762-1834), 220
Van Alstyne, Abraham (1773-??), 219-220
Van Alstyne, Abraham (1776-??), 219
Van Alstyne, Abraham (1786?-??), 220
Van Alstyne, Abraham (1797-??), 220
Van Alstyne, Abraham A. (1739-1815), 219
Van Alstyne, Abraham Fellers (1812-??), 219
Van Alstyne, Abraham, 188, 213-222, 239
Van Buren, Martin, 6, 13, 16-17, 134, 141-144, 186-187, 214, 216
Van Cortlandt Manor, 71, 245
Van der Donck, Adriaen, 22-23, 253
Van Dyck, Catherine, 185, 187, 275
Van Dyck, Dr. Cornelius, 184
Van Dyck, Hendrick Thomasse, 184
Van Dyck, Hendrick, 184
Van Dyck, Jane, 129-130, 177, 184-189, 214, 237, 242, 274-275

Van Dyck, Maria (Schuyler), 184
Van Dyck, Maria (Volandt), 185-187, 275
Van Dyck, Peter C., 185-186, 274
Van Houter, Roelof (Ralph), 56
Van Ness, Dominie, 135
Van Ness, William P., 6-7, 69, 105, 129, 131-133, 135, 142-143
Van Ness, William W., 105
Van Nutt, Robert, iii
Van Santvoord, Harold, 31-33, 132-134, 138-140, 174, 181, 189, 213, 215-216, 234-235, 243-244, 254, 267-269, 273, 278, 281-282
Van Tassel Tavern, 55-56, 171-172, 198-199, 209
Van Tassel, Abraham "Bones," 209-212, 240-241, 278
Van Tassel, Abraham "Indian Brom," 210, 212
Van Tassel, Catharine, 56, 73, 171-173
Van Tassel, Catriena Ecker, 166-167, 170, 172
Van Tassel, Cornelius and Elizabeth, 55, 102-105, 167, 206
Van Tassel, Daniel, 27, 55, 79-80, 209-212, 240, 253, 257
Van Tassel, Eleanor "Laney," 167-172, 236
Van Tassel, Elizabeth, 55-56
Van Tassel, Jacob, 60-61, 64, 72, 168, 171, 205, 248, 259, 278
Van Tassel, John (Johannes), 55-56, 73, 172, 209-210
Van Tassel, Leah, 102-104, 200
Van Wart, Abraham, 151
Van Wart, Henry, 8, 48, 80, 82-86, 151-152, 163, 171, 197, 235, 239-241, 244
Van Wart, Isaac, 43, 84
Van Wart, Sarah (Irving), 8, 82, 151-152
Van Winkle, Cornelius, 10
"Voyage, The," 9

Wakeman, Thomas, 83
Walpole, Horace, 113-114
Warner, Charles Dudley, 1, 252
Washington, George, 16-17, 100
Water Guard, 60, 204-205
Weber, P. A., 50
Welles, E. R. III, 213-214, 262, 278
West, Kanye, iv
Westchester County Historical Society, 276-277
Westchester County Militia, 43, 47, 55, 60, 147, 192-194, 196, 200, 203, 209-210

Westchester Guides, 147, 194, 281
Westchester Herald, 58, 139-140
Westminster Bridge, 87, 92, 118
Wetmore, Alphonso, 224
White Plains Battle, 100-102, 104
Wieland, Christoph Martin, 113-115, 242
"Wife, The," 9
"Wild Huntsman of Hacklenburg," 113
"Wild Huntsman," 108, 112-113
Wildey, Caleb, 45-46
Wiley's Swamp, 44-46, 75, 109
Williams, David, 43
Williams, Stanley T., 1, 152, 154, 232, 251-252

Willis, N. P., 87, 89, 261
Winter, Katia, iii
Wishbone, ii
Wolfert's Roost (house), 59-62, 64, 71-72, 166, 168, 170, 205, 247-248, 278
Wolfert's Roost (book), 16, 64, 99, 251, 253, 257-259, 263, 272-273, 282
"Wolfert's Roost" essay, 59, 64, 166, 168-169, 171, 247, 257, 259

YANKEE magazine, 105-106, 175-176, 264, 266, 273
Yankee stereotype, 158-161, 223-224, 235, 271
Youngs, Joseph and Susannah, 103, 147, 151, 195
Youngs, Mary, 147, 151
Youngs, Samuel, 123, 146-152, 235

About the Author

Gary Denis grew up in Tupper Lake, a small town in the Adirondack Mountains of New York, some 280 miles north of Sleepy Hollow.

His fascination with "The Legend" began at a very early age after seeing one of the many cartoon versions on TV during the Halloween season. Always a history buff, a question long persisted in the back of his mind: *Is "The Legend of Sleepy Hollow" a true story?*

An avid stamp collector and exhibitor (specializing in the 1940 Washington Irving and 1974 "Legend of Sleepy Hollow" stamps), Gary has authored numerous articles and columns in the philatelic press.

A life-long history and trivia enthusiast, Gary prides himself on being a walking encyclopedia of useless information. He also enjoys cooking and experimenting with new recipes, watches way too much television, and has been at various times a musician and songwriter. Gary is an electrical engineer in real life.

Gary currently lives in Maryland with his wife Sharon, a chihuahua named Lucy, and a thriving herd of cats.

Made in the USA
Monee, IL
11 September 2022